PENGUIN BOOKS

LEARNING FROM THE COLD WAR

Jonathan Stevenson is a professor of strategic studies at the U.S. Naval War College. He spent most of the 1990s in sub-Saharan Africa and Northern Ireland, and his previous books include "*We Wrecked the Place*": *Contemplating an End to the Northern Irish Troubles* and *Losing Mogadishu*. He has published articles in *Foreign Affairs, Foreign Policy,* and *The National Interest,* as well as *The New York Times, The Boston Globe, The Wall Street Journal,* and *The New Republic.* He lives in Mystic, Connecticut.

Learning from the Cold War

*Rebuilding America's Strategic
Vision in the 21st Century*

JONATHAN STEVENSON

PENGUIN BOOKS

Previously published as
Thinking Beyond the Unthinkable

PENGUIN BOOKS

Published by the Penguin Group

Penguin Group (USA) Inc., 375 Hudson Street, New York, New York 10014, U.S.A.

Penguin Group (Canada), 90 Eglinton Avenue East, Suite 700, Toronto, Ontario,
Canada M4P 2Y3 (a division of Pearson Penguin Canada Inc.)

Penguin Books Ltd, 80 Strand, London WC2R 0RL, England

Penguin Ireland, 25 St Stephen's Green, Dublin 2, Ireland (a division of Penguin Books Ltd)

Penguin Group (Australia), 250 Camberwell Road, Camberwell,
Victoria 3124, Australia (a division of Pearson Australia Group Pty Ltd)

Penguin Books India Pvt Ltd, 11 Community Centre, Panchsheel Park, New Delhi – 110 017, India

Penguin Group (NZ), 67 Apollo Drive, Rosedale, North Shore 0632,
New Zealand (a division of Pearson New Zealand Ltd)

Penguin Books (South Africa) (Pty) Ltd, 24 Sturdee Avenue,
Rosebank, Johannesburg 2196, South Africa

Penguin Books Ltd, Registered Offices:
80 Strand, London WC2R 0RL, England

First published in the United States of America as *Thinking Beyond the Unthinkable* by
Viking Penguin, a member of Penguin Group (USA) Inc. 2008
Published in Penguin Books 2009

10   9   8   7   6   5   4   3   2   1

THE LIBRARY OF CONGRESS HAS CATALOGED THE HARDCOVER EDITION AS FOLLOWS:
Stevenson, Jonathan, 1956–
Thinking beyond the unthinkable : harnessing doom from the Cold War
to the War on Terror / Jonathan Stevenson.
p.   cm.
Includes bibliographical references and index.
ISBN 978-0-670-01901-4 (hc.)
ISBN 978-0-14-311574-8 (pbk.)
1. Nuclear weapons—Government policy—United States—History.
2. Deterrence (Strategy)   3. Cold War.   4. War on Terrorism, 2001–   I. Title.
UA23.S695 2007
355.02'170973—dc22   2007043554

Printed in the United States of America
Designed by Carla Bolte · Set in Celeste

For Sharon

Contents

Our ideas held no water but we used them like a dam.

—Isaac Brock, *Modest Mouse*

Learning from
the Cold War

1

Harnessing Doom

This book seeks to answer a very simple set of questions: What was it about the strategic thinking of the Cold War era that *worked?* How did we manage not to incinerate ourselves with nuclear weapons? How much of our salvation was due to the intellectual fertility of the think tanks? How much was about military strategy or diplomacy? What complexes of people and ideas deserve the bulk of the credit—the think tanks, the Pentagon, or the State Department? Why does our intellectual infrastructure appear less adept at dealing with new threats? And how can the intellectual dynamics that worked so well during the Cold War be replicated to meet the challenges that the September 11 attacks—and the policies of President George W. Bush—have made all the stiffer?

The short and somewhat familiar answer is that both the abject horror of nuclear war and the diametric ideological opposition of the two superpowers were universally apprehended, so that the devotion of the best strategic thinkers to fine-tuning nuclear deterrence was sharp and nearly exclusive. The prospect of nuclear devastation made its avoidance the undisputed top priority for both Washington and Moscow, while the rank unacceptability of Soviet communism to Americans and American democratic capitalism to Soviets made each side view the other as the consuming foe that dwarfed all others and had to be repelled. Yet, while these outsized features clarified the strategic landscape, they also distorted it. Exhaustive simulations of nuclear crisis and war gave the superpowers a full understanding of what would be in store for the world if they lost control and unleashed nuclear bombs, and the resulting fear of direct military confrontation moved the United States and the Soviet Union to use proxies. But the resulting conflicts had unintended consequences—in particular, the empowerment of radical Islam—that strategists and officials had spent virtually no time trying to understand or to learn to manage. Because the adversaries that thus arose aimed not merely to threaten apocalyptic violence but to perpetrate it, strategists did not enjoy the Cold War–era luxuries of mutual dread and the time to think that comes with it. And geopolitical bipolarity had conditioned them to think in terms of politically implacable, monolithic enemies toward which pragmatic flexibility and accommodation would be unavailing. They were not ready for the messy nuance of the post–Cold War world.

The full answer, though, is a story. It starts with the dawning of the nuclear age.

The Shock of the New

Heedless of the march of civilization, in derogation of rising technological sophistication, minimizing the lethality of war has been a dare untaken. Genghis Khan's conquest of northern China in 1211–18 may have cost eighteen million Chinese lives. Two or three million soldiers, and at least twice that many civilians, probably perished in the Thirty Years War (1618–48). Between twenty and forty million were killed in the Taiping Rebellion in

China (1850–64). Some five to six million died in the Napoleonic Wars. Over the next fifty years, advances in rifling and artillery allowed the more adaptable generals in the American Civil War to use entrenchments and field fortifications to avoid the senseless slaughter endured by those who stuck to the Napoleonic-era tactic of massing infantry and artillery together. Long artillery barrages followed by frontal assault became the standard for ground attack, but after trench warfare proved so ghastly and costly in World War I—in which fourteen million died—it yielded to shorter artillery bombardment and more artful infiltration by infantry.

During the remainder of the twentieth century, technological advances cascaded at an unprecedented pace. Between 1917 and 1939, internal combustion engines, improved aircraft design, and innovations in radio and radar facilitated the blitzkrieg, carrier-based naval aviation, and strategic aerial bombardment. The Second World War netted almost sixty million dead, nearly a 300 percent increase over the First World War. By VE Day—May 8, 1945—fatalities had far exceeded those of any previous war. Yet to end the war, the United States would, at the very least, have to attack Japan's sovereign territory with more than conventional air power. Influential people—most important, Secretary of State James Byrnes and Secretary of War Henry Stimson—convinced President Harry S. Truman that to persuade a great power like Japan to surrender unconditionally (as dictated by U.S. policy) via conventional means would have required the United States to mount a massive amphibious assault on the Japanese home islands that might have cost the lives of American servicemen in the hundreds of thousands and entailed over a million Japanese dead.*

---

*The military necessity of dropping the atomic bombs on Hiroshima and Nagasaki remains a sharply debated issue. Skeptics now appear to hold the upper hand, arguing that the depleted state of Japanese industry, the isolation of the

Instead, that August atomic bombs were used on Hiroshima and Nagasaki, immediately killing over one hundred thousand and condemning many more to disfigurement, radiation sickness, and agonizing death. It was not just the numbers that dealt the shock to civilization. It was the efficiency of the weapons. Two air strikes, one hundred thousand–plus dead. Even at a distance of five thousand feet—almost a mile—from the center of damage, directly under the airburst explosion of the bomb, mortality was 50 percent. On the basis of such single-stroke economy, atomic fission bombs raised the possibility of true Armageddon, the end of days. Nearly eight thousand years on, civilization had scarcely gotten past the barbarity of Genghis Khan. By 1952, the worst case got worse with the advent of thermonuclear fusion weapons.

It was in fact transcendentally bad. In the Great War, the losses were largely human, and consisted almost entirely of combatants. The machinery of the Second World War obliterated the physical infrastructure of much of civilian life, and the lion's share of its direct victims were civilians. In a nuclear exchange, swathes of geography would be rendered uninhabitable, entire nations of people dead or diseased. Yet conventional war had never actually been "pure" in casualties. Margaret Macmillan encapsulates France's evisceration in World War I:

A quarter of French men between eighteen and thirty had died in the war, over 1.3 million altogether out of a prewar population of 40 million. France lost a higher proportion of its population than any other of the belligerents. Twice as many again of

---

bulk of the Japanese army in northern China, and the willingness of the Soviet Union to enter the Pacific war strongly suggest that Japan could have been induced to surrender with a little inventive and flexible diplomacy on the part of the United States. See, for example, Gar Alperovitz, *The Decision to Use the Atomic Bomb* (New York: Vintage, 1996).

its soldiers had been wounded. In the north, great stretches of land were pitted with shell holes, scarred by deep trenches, marked with row upon row of crosses. Around the fortress of Verdun, site of the worst French battle, not a living thing grew, not a bird sang. The coalmines on which the French economy depended for its power were flooded; the factories they would have supplied had been razed or carted away into Germany. Six thousand square miles of France, which before the war had produced 20 percent of its crops, 90 percent of its iron ore and 65 percent of its steel, were utterly ruined.[1]

The collateral damage just grew. Details of operations like the British fire-bombing of Hamburg in 1943 (Operation Gomorrah) make for even more grisly conceptions of war: it resulted in a fireball two kilometers high that imploded the oxygen in the air and raised windstorms strong enough to uproot trees; household sugar boiled, glass melted, and bubbling asphalt sucked people into the streets; in one night forty-five thousand civilians were killed.[2] These tableaux reflected unalloyed military devastation by any material standard. But what set anticipated nuclear destruction apart was its blink-of-an-eye suddenness, the effortlessness of rendering it almost literally by just pressing a button, and the soul-destroying prospect that the radioactive contamination of masses of people and large areas could, as Herman Kahn would muse, make the survivors envy the dead.

"The drift of modern history," wrote Paul Fussell in 1975, "domesticates the fantastic and normalizes the unspeakable."[3] The inhumanity and mass slaughter that led up to the nuclear age— the world wars, the Armenian genocide, the Spanish Civil War, the Stalinist pogroms—could all be sublimated or deflected at least to a certain extent by those who wanted to look on the bright side. Stalin remarked that "a single death is a tragedy; a million deaths are a statistic." Hitler asked rhetorically, "Who still talks in our day of the extermination of the Armenians?"[4] Gulag survivors and the grandchildren of Armenian refugees would ruefully attest to some truth in these ugly utterances. The Spanish Civil War could be rendered lyrical by Hemingway in *For Whom the Bell Tolls* and by Picasso in *Guernica.* But like the Nazis' substantial extermination of European Jewry, nuclear war was resistant to this kind of cultural inoculation. The Hiroshima and Nagasaki bombs may have been wryly called "Little Boy" and "Fat Man," but after they were dropped, their horror was lost on nobody. Kenneth Bainbridge, director of the inaugural Trinity test of the atom bomb on July 16, 1945, said to J. Robert Oppenheimer, supervising scientist for the Manhattan Project, "Now we are all sons of bitches." Oppenheimer's more grandiose, but nonetheless genuine, reaction became the keynote for pacifist scientists and nuclear abolitionists who were to be estimable political counterweights to Cold Warriors. "I am become death," he famously said, quoting from the Bhagavad Gita (Hindu scriptures), "the destroyer of worlds."[5] Less histrionically and more reflectively, he wrote in 1946: "It did not take atomic weapons to make man want peace. But the atomic bomb was the turn of the screw. It has made the prospect of war unendurable."[6]

Before the nuclear age, strategy focused more on winning than avoiding wars. This approach may have reflected the default assumption of rationality and civility that intellectuals, particularly after the Enlightenment, tended to make. Even as far back as the fifth century B.C., Sun Tzu wrote that "in the practical art of war, the best thing of all is to take the enemy's country whole and intact" and counseled that "supreme excellence consists in breaking the enemy's resistance without fighting."[7] These exhortations were an awkward fit with hydrogen bombs, which as war-fighting tools seemingly precluded the first objective, but as instruments of deterrence stood to fulfill the second one as no weapon had before. More broadly, Sun Tzu's preoccupation with guile, maneuver, and tactics—a reminder of which was an important antidote to the operational clumsiness of the American Civil War and the First World War—seemed altogether inapposite to nuclear war in its transcendent, all-trumping destructiveness.

Likewise, Carl von Clausewitz, the Prussian general generally regarded as the greatest modern military strategist, had a markedly reasonable attitude about the choice to undertake war and its conduct in his three-volume treatise *On War*. In the early nineteenth century, when he resolutely characterized war as an extension of politics by other means, no one had yet borne witness to the cynical, idiotic carnage in the trenches in the First World War, or the concept of "total war" as practiced in the Second World War, when all major participants targeted civilians from the air. Instead, the Napoleonic Wars from 1803 to 1815—which, to be sure, yielded casualties at very high rates and in alarming volume—were the "cautionary examples of destructive power" that provided his theory with "tone and character."[8] In his strategic world, the military extremes to which any state could go were also constrained by how much the people could be fiscally taxed and motivationally driven. Absent a charismatic dictatorship like Napoleon's, this state of affairs produced a kind of minimum deterrence: "Safe from the threat of extremes, it was no longer necessary to go to extremes."[9] Thus, Clausewitz tended to envisage a fairly orderly, deliberate, and—as a means to achieving a victory sufficiently merciful to allow for a peace that was valuable to the victor—sensible escalation from diplomacy to the controlled use of force.

Nuclear weapons' "bigger bang for the buck" overcame the limitations of military economics and weakened the assumption of rationality and control as applied to political-military decision-making. The bomb's sheer destructiveness meant that large and expensive armies did not have to be logistically and operationally mobilized to wage total war. That, in turn, meant that the general population need not be politically on board for nuclear weapons to be used to conclusive effect. These revolutionary developments did not inspire confidence among professional soldiers and strategists. To the contrary, coupled with their dearth of experience in observing the consequences of nuclear war and the knowledge nonetheless that it would involve a new kind and degree of devastation, the ease of initiating nuclear war instead made them dread any confrontation that might call for an all-out military effort. New technology and its consequences, then, prompted a shift in the paradigm of war. It was no longer merely a viable, if extreme, political option undertaken to advance historically comprehensible political objectives—as, indeed, Germany's initial aggression in both world wars had been. Instead, war had become terrorism on a massive scale.

For all the blood they spilled, the two world wars of the twentieth century were not intellectually comparable to the imagined nuclear war that so consumed nations and peoples for the ensuing fifty years. The appalling losses produced by the attritional trench warfare of the Great War turned mainly on an anachronistic mismatch between tactics and technology—that is, the singular inappropriateness of massed infantry assault against artillery with greater range than small arms. At bottom, the talismanic newness of airpower dictated massive civilian destruction of the Second World War: girded by the specter of a militarily strong and ideologically implacable Nazi Germany and imperial Japan, airpower operationally bedazzled the military so as to overwhelm ethical instincts toward restraint. The first impulse, that is, was to use the new technology to kill people more abundantly and efficiently. So it was with atomic weapons.

Initial Relief

Hiroshima and Nagasaki were stunningly terrible. But the very gravity of the shock of the new gave rise to the paradoxical instinct to deny the revolutionary nature of atomic warfare. Among the scientists at Los Alamos who designed, produced, and tested the first bombs, a kind of cognitive dissonance took hold. Intellectually, of course, they always understood that they were trying to produce a weapon of unprecedented destructive power. At the same time, the psychological compulsion of Oppenheimer and his team was to leaven this weightier, darker understanding with the grand view that they were inventing a "gadget" that would end the war and save countless lives that would otherwise be spent in ground combat action.[10] Only after the bomb had been tested did Oppenheimer and others seem fully to appreciate the greater and more insidious danger—that they had created an omnipresent shadow of mass doom.[11]

Precisely because the A-bomb had indeed been used, albeit hideously, on Hiroshima and Nagasaki and putatively forestalled a bloody Allied land invasion of Japan, from a psychological point of view atomic war could not easily be characterized as morally out-of-bounds or "unthinkable." Indeed, the reaction of most of the men who would become leading nuclear strategists was profound relief. Sergeant Herman Kahn was then a communications NCO in Burma. The man who would become notorious for thinking (and talking) about the unthinkable had no interest in being stranded there.[12] At least some of those who would later be the most articulate nuclear abolitionists, like physicist Freeman

Dyson, then in the operational research section of the Royal Air Force's Bomber Command, unabashedly report the same feeling. About Hiroshima, he recalls, "Oh, I thought it was great. I'd been fighting the real war, and we [the RAF] were doing just as awful things. We killed as many people as died in Hiroshima and Nagasaki combined. And we'd have gone on killing them. We were just about to fly out to Okinawa to join [the Americans] in the strategic bombing of Japan. In fact, I myself was all set to fly to Okinawa, even though I was a civilian. So for me it was a fantastic relief that the killing was going to *stop*."[13]

The bomb, then, was seen as decisively ending the war in the Pacific and precluding an invasion that would have cost both a weary West and a besieged Japan more casualties than those that resulted from Little Boy and Fat Man. The fact that the destructiveness of those bombs, however spectacular, still fell well short of the aggregate explosive tonnage of conventional Allied bombs dropped on Germany and Japan also blunted (though it hardly extinguished) the sense that warfare had undergone a profound and historic qualitative change. Thomas C. Schelling, who would become one of the great strategists of the Cold War, was working in Washington for the Bureau of the Budget at Pennsylvania Avenue and Seventeenth Street when he read the news in the Washington *Daily News,* a tabloid. "I was stunned," he recalls. "I think for most people it took a while to sink in what it had been for Japan, what it would likely do to war in the future, and if we could do it who else could do it. I was preoccupied with what the postwar economy was going to look like."[14] Albert Wohlstetter, who would rank alongside Schelling, registered the bomb's "enormous import" but also "somehow . . . that it had been very wrong to drop it on populations."[15]

The popular perception was that man had assumed greater

command of the physical universe. Dyson remembers that the headline of his local newspaper in England, the *News Chronicle,* read "New Force of Nature Harnessed," and that "it was something much bigger than winning the war."[16] But the main preoccupation among strategists right after the war was not any stark paradigm shift but rather operational considerations and technical comparisons—to wit, whether the atomic option made strategic bombardment a less than optimal ongoing strategy for the West. Especially with the advent of radar and jet fighters, wartime experience accorded the advantage to air defenses, in that they forced offensive bombers to fly higher and bomb with a degree of inaccuracy that made the net effect of conventional munitions strategically nondecisive. The sheer lethality of the atom bomb gave a slight edge back to the offense. But British strategist P. M. S. Blackett was quick to point out that it would still take four hundred Little Boys to match the damage from aerial bombardment that Germany suffered in World War II.[17] Vannevar Bush, the civilian coordinator of the Manhattan Project, noted that large fleets of bombers would still be required to penetrate air defenses sufficiently to strike a conclusive strategic blow, and that accordingly the A-bomb was "a very important but by no means absolute weapon."[18] While there was an appreciation for its singular firepower, and more vaguely for the deterrent force of guaranteed retaliation in kind, no one was yet imagining that the fact and fear of the bomb would keep more from falling. In fact, as of 1948, there prevailed a grim resignation that nuclear weapons would be used again. What made the situation even more harrowing was that, as the RAND Corporation's James Digby reflected at the Cold War's end, whereas conventional strategy offered well-defined thresholds of war such as territorial invasion, "there was no useful strategic framework" for controlling the risks of nuclear war.[19]

The first book on nuclear strategy as such, published in 1946 and edited by Bernard Brodie, was titled *The Absolute Weapon*. That title was intended to be ironic in a certain sense. It was straightforward in denoting the distinct advantage that a bomb of such preemptive power afforded to whoever successfully struck first, in indexing the demonstrated vulnerability of densely populated cities to atom bombs, and in highlighting the diminished capacity of defense to limit damage and deter surprise attack. But with the tide of intellectual reluctance to concede a revolution in military affairs to the emergence of the atom bomb, Brodie and Jacob Viner, among others, expressed skepticism that the A-bomb would afford a surprise attacker an insuperable strategic advantage as long as the adversary retained the capacity to retaliate in kind. William Bader, a Yale colleague of Brodie's, simultaneously wrote *There Will Be No Time*, arguing, against Brodie, that the atomic bomb's greatest value was as a first-strike "counterforce" weapon that could cripple an adversary's warfighting capacity so thoroughly as to leave it "no time" to recover before being conquered. Over the years, what Lawrence Freedman calls the four "basic axioms of the nuclear age" crystallized: "the impossibility of defence; the hopeless vulnerability of the world's major cities; the attraction of sudden attack; and the necessity of a capability of retaliation."[20]

In the event, of course, the atom bomb did not turn out to be the absolute weapon. Hydrogen bombs, employing thermonuclear fusion, won that distinction after the first one was tested in 1952. What the atom bomb did do, however, was to make the strategic preoccupation with technological military means so intense that political objectives became obscured through subordination.

As Freedman has put it: "Specific conflicts, with added complications supplied by geography and the weight of past military traditions, were not revisited with the new technology. There were some nightmarish speculations on the subject of how Hitler might have acted if he had been in possession of a nuclear arsenal, but there seemed no new conflict so immediate or so dangerous that it could provide an occasion for nuclear attacks."[21] Very early on, then, the strategic environment began to ossify around the idea of avoiding a nuclear war. The resulting intellectual stasis stifled any serious contemplation of the use of nuclear weapons by anyone—like, say, a terrorist—except a state.

This shortsightedness exemplified what Wohlstetter would label the fallacy of "lesser included cases." Military power was seen as linear, cumulative, transitive. If it could deter an ultimate outcome, it could deter all less momentous ones. In this first iteration, such imperfect logic led to the narrow view that as long as the Anglo-American monopoly on nuclear weapons could be maintained the world was sufficiently controllable. From the 1960s forward, similar reasoning would cast nonproliferation—in essence, denial of access—as the answer to any inclination of terrorists or insurgents to use WMD (weapons of mass destruction), and condition a general resistance to probing the ideological and religious bases for insurgency and terrorism. Yet the rub was not that ideology was irrelevant to strategy—quite to the contrary, by 1947 a notionally titanic struggle between Western capitalism and Soviet communism became the defining constant of world affairs. This prospective struggle was so dominant, however, that it crowded most other ideological tensions out of major-power calculations. Not only other countries but also other nations and cultures were either with us or against us. This magisterial (if simplistic) political dispensation rendered any further ideological hand-wringing ancillary to international politics, and enabled the technological imperatives of war in the nuclear age to preoccupy strategists for two generations. It also laid the groundwork for the unfortunate dualism of the Bush administration's post-9/11 foreign policy.

Nuclear War-fighting

President Truman—having assumed the burden of inaugurating nuclear warfare—viscerally resisted regarding the atom bomb as merely an especially devastating weapon that was not qualitatively distinct from conventional explosives. The horror of Hiroshima and Nagasaki had demonstrated to him that it should be a weapon only of last resort, and he decreed as much. But the president's view did not hold sway. The Berlin Crisis of 1948–49, in which a massive American airlift sustained for almost a year thwarted the Soviet Union's attempt to prevent the creation of a separate West German state and eliminate a Western outpost in eastern Germany through a blockade of Berlin, laid bare certain discomfiting realities about even a nonnuclear Soviet Union's military power. Russia had conventional military advantages: a huge army, a proven tolerance for heavy casualties, and strategic depth by virtue of its physical immensity. From a strictly military point of view, the U.S.-British corner on the atom bomb merely diminished these advantages; it did not eliminate them.

These considerations—coupled with rising economic efficiency in the use of fissionable materials and the availability of long-range B-36 bombers that would decrease the United States' need for overseas bases—impelled the U.S. Air Force to integrate early nuclear use into its war plans by the end of 1948. Interservice rivalry only increased the salience of nuclear weapons as war-fighting tools. At a meeting at the Naval War College in Newport, Rhode Island, in August 1948, the secretary of defense and the Joint Chiefs of Staff decided that while the Air Force would retain primary authority over emergency war plans involving nuclear weapons, the other services would have access to them.

Thus, from the beginning of the Manhattan Project until the first hydrogen bomb test in October 1952, the U.S. defense establishment—led by the interservice Armed Forces Special Weapons Project (AFSWP)—was dominated by military as opposed to civilian leadership and consumed with testing and assembling atomic weapons and gaming out the use of atomic bombs, and not with nuclear doctrine.[22] For the time being, the notion that atomic weapons were only those of last resort had been shelved, and an "atomic blitz" became a key offensive option. Although the Army and Navy eventually registered their unease with such a plan, and incorporated the more modest conventional and defensive goal of retarding Soviet advances into Europe, a nuclear offensive was envisioned to a high degree of specificity: a thirty-day series of primary nuclear attacks against seventy target areas encompassing twenty-eight million people of whom 10 percent would be killed and 15 percent wounded.[23]

In the late 1940s, notwithstanding the president's post-Hiroshima reservations, nuclear war simply was not considered unthinkable or apocalyptic. Despite a general horror of the attacks on the Japanese islands, the Western inclination to view the exploitation of scientific advance as a hallmark of civilization muted moral qualms about atomic weapons. Further obscuring such worries was the fact that the Western monopoly made for an especially strong deterrent: even though A-bombs were awful, after the "demonstration effect" of Hiroshima and Nagasaki, no nonnuclear aggressor would be likely to push the West to the brink of major war. And compared to the large standing armies that would be needed to defeat the Soviet Union conventionally, nukes were cheap. To be sure, atom bombs were initially conceived as an "adjunct" to a conventional strategic bombing campaign, a strategic "last resort."[24] But it evolved that a declaratory policy of possible first use made sense from the standpoint of global stability and economic efficiency—two major priorities of a world traumatized by world war and depression.

First use, however, had credibility problems. Even before the Soviet Union acquired the bomb, Stalin had made it clear through his enunciation of the five "Permanently Operating Factors"—a set of military imperatives drawn from World War II—that he would not be intimidated by the West. As long as the "rear" (which meant essentially the political and economic integrity of the state and the readiness of its citizenry) was kept stable, morale was maintained, the quantity and quality of divisions remained high, the army was well armed, and officers maintained command authority, the Soviet Union would prevail. Permanent mobilization and an arch refusal to concede any Western military edge obtained both before and after the Soviet Union went nuclear, and resonated well beyond Stalin's death in 1953. It was Russian *policy* to portray the nuclear devastation that the Western Everyman would consider unthinkable and apocalyptic as merely a possible incident—albeit a historic one— of Marxist-Leninist destiny. Stalin's notorious remark that a million dead were but a statistic suggested a degree of credibility to this position, as did the Soviet Union's grim endurance of tens of millions of casualties in the two world wars. But the moral economies of scale never took hold in the West, where the individual was sacrosanct and even one death momentous. So Western brinkmanship always had an overlay of self-preservative palsy and "mirror-imaging"—that is, the assumption that the Soviet leadership regarded matters of nuclear war with pretty much the same consternation as their U.S. counterparts—in the very notion that adversaries would be deterred by threats to bring on Armageddon. True Soviet attitudes about nuclear war were a matter of speculative inference, and would not be known with an appreciable degree of certainty until the Cold War was over. In the 1950s, mirror-imaging was an intellectual bias that cast serious doubt on the integrity of first-use deterrence.*

The fifties, then, was a terrifying decade for the United States. Michael Wheeler, a retired Air Force officer and former director of operations of a Minuteman III wing in the mid-1960s as well as a scholar of post–Cold War history and strategic policy, reflects: "It was probably as frightening for us then as it would have been for the British in the fall of 1940. We had very poor intelligence on the Russians in terms of what their strategic

---

*Herman Kahn, in particular, would question this psychological parochialism, and point up the relevance of differences in the Soviet worldview to the effectiveness of deterrence. Others, such as Herbert Dinerstein, criticized the ethnocentricity of American strategic analysis but construed Soviet military doctrine as essentially defensive, while the hawkish Harvard historian Richard Pipes loathed such "Sovietology" and believed that Soviet leaders considered nuclear war winnable. H. S. Dinerstein, *War and the Soviet Union: Nuclear Weapons and the Revolution in Soviet Military and Political Thinking* (New York: Praeger, 1959); Richard Pipes, "Why the Soviet Union Thinks It Can Win a Nuclear War," *Commentary*, July 1977, pp. 21–34. George Quester characterizes the group of thinkers exemplified by Pipes as "a cottage industry who studied Soviet nuclear strategy and said, 'The Russians are different, the Russians are different'—and claimed that to mirror-image was misleading, that the Russians don't even have a word for deterrence." There were another group of people who said the Chinese were different. Then there were antidotes in each case. Raymond Garthoff, a Sovietologist nemesis of Pipes's, contended that the Soviets really didn't think so differently from the Americans. See, for example, Raymond L. Garthoff, *The Great Transition: American-Soviet Relations and the End of the Cold War* (Washington, DC: The Brookings Institution, 1994). Post–Cold War studies based on previously undisclosed Soviet documents and interviews with former Soviet officers indicated that Stalin believed that atomic weapons would indeed be used, though his successors blanched at his bloody-mindedness and did move toward the morally reluctant American approach. See, for example, David Holloway, *Stalin and the Bomb: The Soviet Union and Atomic Energy, 1939–1956* (New Haven: Yale University Press, 1994), pp. 224–72, 320–45.

intentions really were. We were relieved that Stalin was dead, but very uncertain about what now was the struggle going on there, and Khrushchev didn't help with all the blustering that he did. It was a disorganized period, there was a big arms race going on, the services were in competition with one another, ballistic missile programs were in competition with one another."[25]

After the Soviet Union developed the atomic bomb in 1949, the hydrogen bomb was seen mainly as a means of retrumping Soviet offensive threats. Led by Oppenheimer, some senior Manhattan Project scientists in a late 1949 report to the Atomic Energy Commission (AEC) discouraged the development of "the Super," which the then-notional H-bomb was called, characterizing it as a militarily useless "weapon of genocide." But the consensus among American officials—officially enshrined National Security Council Paper 68 (NSC-68) in April 1950—was that the Soviets were implacably aggressive, would themselves inevitably pursue the H-bomb, and would be impossible to control unless the West had it, too. Development proceeded. Thus, the first H-bomb test on Eniwetok Atoll in the Pacific in 1952 produced a ten-megaton explosion, a thousand times Little Boy's yield and more powerful than all of the conventional bombs dropped in World War II combined. The horrific possibilities suggested by H-bomb calculations prompted a more pronounced and urgent intellectual crisis than the arrival of the atom bomb had in New Mexico and Japan in 1945. Thus, it was in 1952, not 1945, that the notion of strategic or military apocalypse—of the unthinkable— took deep root in the Western psyche.

On the surface, Truman did more than anyone else to make the use of nuclear weapons credible simply by, in fact, dropping them on Hiroshima and Nagasaki at the end of World War II. In another, deeper way, though, Hiroshima and Nagasaki sharpened the stigma associated with those weapons and established a kind of reflexive moral deterrent—later called "self-deterrence"—that disfavored their use. The H-bomb tests critically intensified that stigma, and the unthinkable had operational consequences early in the Cold War. While most of the senators who voted for the North Atlantic Treaty believed that nuclear weapons made the American guarantee of Western Europe's security a cheap proposition requiring few boots on the ground overseas, Truman did not. To the contrary, he felt that conventional U.S. deployments in Western Europe were essential to credibly deterring a Soviet invasion. Notes Harry Rowen—a RAND economist who became its president and later served as chairman of the National Intelligence Council—"the political as well as the technical aspects of the early Cold War were fraught with uncertainty. What was going to happen to Europe? In hindsight it all seems so certain—the Europeans were not going to become communists, they weren't going to be taken over, the Russians were too cautious, they weren't going to invade, blah, blah, blah. Looking ahead, it didn't seem so certain."[26]

Thus, NATO adopted a "forward strategy" that included substantial conventional ground forces in Europe and the rearmament of West Germany. That general strategy was based in part on the inevitability of a comparably robust Soviet thermonuclear capability, and an assumption that nukes were too destructive to allow for precisely calibrated deterrence based on feasible military exchanges. And the willingness of the United States to tolerate—indeed, encourage—the military reempowerment of West Germany, the prime culprit in two crippling and recent world wars, may reflect in part the lessons of Versailles about the perverse effects of the humiliation of the vanquished. But these features of the strategic landscape circa 1950 also indicate just how frightened world leaders still were of normalizing nuclear use—threatened or actual—in strategic doctrine. At that point, says Lawrence Freedman, "everybody was basically an amateur."

Nuclear strategy "inevitably wasn't really anybody's profession" because nuclear weapons were so new.[27]

The early fifties, then, was an especially dangerous interregnum in the Cold War. The central question remained: whether nuclear weapons would be part of American war-fighting doctrine or retained merely as an insurance policy against an adversary's first use. The initial post-fusion impulse was, counterintuitively, toward a policy of use—that is, toward the notion of less destructive nuclear war via battlefield or "tactical" nuclear weapons designed to hit military targets as opposed to civilian populations. The integration of war-fighting and second-strike "insurance" into a single "deadly logic" whereby a plan for war that contemplated nuclear use increased the likelihood that an enemy would be deterred from using nuclear weapons for fear of retaliation was as yet inchoate. Thus, the immediate doctrinal impact of the advent of the H-bomb was not to make nuclear weapons less usable but rather to render the strategic threat to the Soviet population more essential to deterrence. With the stockpile of bomb material small in the early 1950s, at least until conventional Western capabilities were enhanced to reach parity with the Soviet Union's, tactical nukes had to be relegated to the status of optional supplements to the bomber-based strategic nuclear force. That force functioned as a protective shield for European countries under NATO (which came into being in April 1949) as well as the United States itself. But the involvement of hundreds of thousands of Chinese infantrymen in the Korean War amplified the potential utility of tactical nukes, and their use was not unthinkable to either Truman (despite his disenchantment with nuclear weapons) or General Douglas MacArthur, who was commander of the U.S.-led United Nations forces in Korea until relieved in 1951. Both men mooted the possibility. In the event, the political shock and the prospect of collateral damage to friendly troops from tactical nuclear bombs were insuperable hurdles. So the Korean War—as the first major conventional conflict of the nuclear age—showed that when push came to shove, the nuclear option was both technically and morally unattractive.

The Civilian Vision: Economical Intimidation

If Truman's team was reluctant to institutionalize thinking about the unthinkable so soon after Hiroshima and Nagasaki, the succeeding Eisenhower administration was not. Indeed, the Eisenhower contingent faulted Truman for foreclosing nuclear options, manifested in forbearance from pursuing the North Korean and Chinese troops across the Yalu River, believing that it had led to an unduly timid and expensive prosecution of the Korean War that allowed the other side to dictate military terms. But this critique had less to do with greater confidence in the military practicality of nuclear weapons or superior moral courage than with the severe resource constraints—set out in a National Security Council paper on "Basic National Security Policy" (NSC-162/2) in October 1953— imposed by simultaneously having to contain the Soviet Union and maintain the integrity of the U.S. economy and federal system.

NSC-162/2 marked the U.S. civilian leadership's first major assertion of authority over nuclear strategy. The document emphasized not only strong U.S. nuclear and conventional forces, but also the indispensability of allies. In contrast to NSC-68, it also contemplated an eventual nuclear stalemate that would diminish the chance that either side would initiate general war. In the short term, though, the defense economics of the nuclear age had enabled "tactical" as well as "strategic" nuclear weapons to be efficiently produced in large quantities. They provided a "bigger bang for a buck," which appealed to fiscally conservative Eisenhower Republicans, and at least the possibility of feasible nuclear use on the battlefield in direct support of ground action as well as the strategic bombing of industrial and population centers.

In this epoch of nuclear adolescence, Secretary of State John Foster Dulles provided a faith-based overlay to the mundane technocratic realities in his philosophical interpretation of the U.S.-Soviet confrontation. The push to develop the H-bomb derived considerable momentum from moral and religious assumptions about the Soviet leadership. AEC chairman Lewis Strauss had set the tone with his comment, in arguing for the development of a fusion weapon, that communist atheists were not likely to be put off producing the hydrogen bomb on moral grounds.[28] In enunciating the doctrine of "massive retaliation" as the centerpiece of the "new look" of U.S. foreign policy in a speech at the Council on Foreign Relations in New York in January 1954, Dulles also enlisted American righteousness as an element of nuclear strategy. In what became a catchphrase, he announced that "the way to deter aggression is for the free community to be willing and able to respond vigorously [to Soviet aggression] at places and with means of its own choosing."[29]

Son of a Presbyterian minister, Dulles was a deeply religious man, and he injected American piety into nuclear strategy. Fred Kaplan, for instance, has noted that "Dulles' position on the atomic bomb and its use took on an almost religious quality."[30] Initially, he seemed to tilt toward the Marxist historical interpretation of the rise of Soviet power as a product of capitalist selfishness and oppression. By 1946, however, Dulles had discarded any such sympathies. That year he published two articles in *Life* magazine characterizing the Cold War as a Manichean struggle between two universalist creeds—Christianity and communism—in which "the most important demonstration that can be made is at the religious level."[31] What he had in mind then was that "men are created as the children of God, in His image," and that "the human personality is thus sacred and the State must not trample upon it."[32] By 1952, he had become more directly accusatory toward the Soviets, proclaiming that "a moral and natural law" had been "trampled by the Soviet rulers, and for that violation they can and should be made to pay."[33] Thirty years later, Ronald Reagan would echo this sort of strident, confrontational idealism in a way that—whether by luck or by design—helped the United States win the Cold War. Twenty years after that, George W. Bush renewed Dulles and Reagan's tone in throwing down the gauntlet to Islamist terrorists and rogue states with no real thought as to how it would be received in a more complicated world.

In the CFR speech, Dulles explained the massive retaliation doctrine in essentially dispassionate, lawyerly terms as a means of reinforcing local conventional defenses by the threat of nuclear reprisals. The operational effect was to reverse Truman's emphasis: to center American leverage on airpower—that is, the Strategic Air Command (SAC)—and lift some of the strategic burden from forward-deployed ground forces. Dulles's follow-up April 1954 article in *Foreign Affairs,* "Policy for Security and Peace," was similarly sanitized of religious language and qualified any impression given by the CFR speech earlier that year that the threat of nuclear annihilation could check all Soviet temptations to encroach on the West. Nevertheless, the sonorous and sanctimonious tone of Dulles's pronouncements and their salient if implicit religious provenance had the effect of blessing thoughts about (and threatening) the unthinkable by invoking godliness and moral superiority as comfort. Backed by confidence that the good would win out, "massive retaliation" came to signify an indiscriminate nuclear first strike as the United States' ace in the hole; America's fundamentally unilateral and potentially capricious prerogative to determine how, when, and where to respond to Soviet depredations; and the routinization of loudly and publicly declared warnings to the Kremlin about Washington's resolve. The popular term for this set of factors was "brinkmanship," and its gloss was as a kind of noble recklessness.

The irony was that, at least in technical terms, the critics sold massive retaliation short as a strategic doctrine. As Freedman recounts:

> Up to the early fifties, there were not that many people around who had a lot of intellectual and conceptual innovation. Then there was a burgeoning of strategic studies as we came to know it—basically following the massive retaliation speech. It was provocative, it was caricatured, and it wasn't meant for the sophisticate. It was meant to signal that the Americans weren't going to try and match Soviet conventional forces because they didn't think they could afford it or needed to. Nuclear deterrence was probably working because [the Americans] were in it for the long haul and the Soviets understood that. So I think Dulles was signaling things that were actually in many respects perfectly okay.

But people seized on the "dogmatic terms" in which Dulles presented the case.[34]

Contrary to prevailing caricatures, neither NSC-162/2 nor Dulles himself actually said that a primary U.S. strategic dependency on nuclear weapons would dictate a massive nuclear strike in response to communist provocations anywhere. In the *Foreign Affairs* piece, Dulles noted that "massive atomic and thermonuclear reaction is not the kind of power which could usefully be evoked under all circumstances."[35] Furthermore, he was explicit that the United States "need[ed] allies and collective security" and that the doctrine was intended to make them more effective and efficient. To the approval of the Eisenhower administration, Britain (now under Churchill again) signed up to the primacy of nuclear deterrence for both the defense of Europe and the larger ideological confrontation in early 1953. And the vigorous declaratory policy was intended to minimize the possibility of Soviet "miscalculations"—that is, underestimations—about Western toughness and ultimately to avoid potentially nuclear confrontations and lower the risks of war. But there remained a palpable tension between the unthinkable horror of nuclear war and, for precisely that reason, the undeniable appeal of threatening it to keep communism at bay. A strategy pegged to nuclear deterrence was virtually inevitable.

Deterrence in Earnest

Until the massive retaliation doctrine was established, whether the West's containment strategy would be, at bottom, a *nuclear* strategy had been unsettled. Massive retaliation, however inadequate from an analytic point of view, copper-fastened nuclear deterrence in Western grand strategy—particularly that of NATO, for which ground troops were not sufficient to repel a Soviet offensive but rather served as a tripwire for a possible U.S. nuclear strike. At the same time, it tantalized the best minds of the nation and the wider strategic studies community. Reflects Freedman: "Once you clearly have two nuclear powers, how do you extract political benefit when the other guy can blow you up as well? I think that question started to attract interesting minds like Wohlstetter and Schelling."[36] But the doctrine remained a dangerously flawed and incomplete way of thinking about the unthinkable. In particular, Dulles drew an unfortunate analogy between a national law-enforcement system, under which substantial order and compliance is reasonably assured, and a U.S.-dominated international security system, under which, by Dulles's own terms, enforcement would be a matter of speculation—"at a time and place of our choosing." Dulles's brand of deterrence enshrined ambiguity about specific Western responses as the key to ensuring Soviet uncertainty and, therefore, restraint. But by the same token, if the Soviets or their clients deemed possible American responses as lacking in credibility—as it might with respect to massive retaliation to a limited regional provocation—they might well deem the risk acceptable, call America's bluff, and elude punishment.

If deterrence was a risky proposition under Dulles's massive retaliation doctrine, subsequent Cold War strategic thinking nonetheless privileged nuclear deterrence. And that thinking was undeniably rich and, in both its genesis and its structure, perhaps uniquely American. After Dulles's enunciation of the massive-retaliation doctrine, William Kaufmann, then at the RAND Corporation, wrote an essay arguing that the United States may in fact have to face a number of crises for which atomic bombs aren't going to be the appropriate weapons, and that to be able to "put up" rather than "shut up," the country needed an army that was equipped to fight a conventional war and capable of being dispatched overseas when necessary.[37] The U.S. Army made thousands of copies of the piece and distributed it to officers: Kaufmann had provided the Army, which had felt overwhelmed by the Air Force and SAC, with its raison d'être. Thus the notion of "flexible response" was planted. This episode highlighted the central importance that civilian analysts assumed in the formulation of nuclear strategy, and in particular the critical role they played in supporting their government "customers" in their struggle to maintain organizational power against their bureaucratic competitors.*

While the specter of instant annihilation was still new and singularly terrible in the late 1950s and early 1960s, calmer analytic minds in the United States and Europe had reached an impressive consensus, agreeing that offensive strategic (i.e., nuclear) bombing was the most cost-effective way of both waging and deterring war; that a nuclear stalemate was developing; that the USSR was by nature aggressive and expansionist; and that the West enjoyed nuclear superiority that trumped the East's numerically greater conventional forces. The bulk of intellectual attention came to be focused on ensuring that this nuclear edge became sufficiently refined not only to constitute a credible deterrent of a Soviet attempt at outright military victory—the only scenario under which massive retaliation was a convincing threat—but also to deter and possibly repel lesser forms of Soviet aggression designed to eat away at Western ideological influence. Although George F. Kennan argued that his seminal strategy of containment was more political and less militaristic than this mind-set (and history) might reflect, the prevailing view was that the virtues of capitalist democracy had to be backed by the robust threat of force. Skepticism about meaningfully limiting nuclear war began to fade.

In the political zeitgeist of the decade that witnessed

---

*"The most important role of an analyst," notes Schelling, "is to decide what policy he favors, identify who else favors or should favor it, and provide them with the ammunition [to have it implemented]. Kaufmann on his own wouldn't have been able to denigrate John Foster Dulles's strategy. But by providing the Army with something they could use over and over again with congressional committees and so forth, explaining why the atom bomb is not the solution to every little outbreak, he could do it." Author interview with Thomas C. Schelling, Bethesda, Maryland, December 1, 2003.

McCarthyism, what became as unthinkable as the use of nuclear weapons was the possibility of American capitulation in the absence of the moral courage to use them. Writing in 1947, the eminent British military historian Basil Liddell Hart had provided an important bridge to the Cold War from Clausewitz's notion of war as part of the normal cycle of international relations and the *total war* concept that reigned in World War II. He pointed out that total war was suicidally nonsensical in the nuclear age, and from that it followed that the sheer destructiveness of nuclear weapons made the normalization of war untenable. His prescription was limited conventional war, subject to more rules and qualifications than generals and statesmen had previously observed. These could function as side constraints on Soviet strategic escalation by demonstrating Western resolve without resort to risky brinkmanship. But the common sense of this view was tempered by the general perception of the Soviets as an implacably determined adversary, the struggle as Manichean and at least figuratively to the death, and the reality of Soviet conventional superiority. The natural compromise was a concept of limited war that contemplated the circumscribed use of nuclear as well as conventional weapons. This notion had found its way into U.S. doctrine very early in the Cold War, but receded with the dawning of the H-bomb. What revived it was Henry Kissinger's *Nuclear Weapons and Foreign Policy,* published in 1957, which squarely confronted the reality that due to nuclear proliferation it was "no longer possible to impose unconditional surrender at an acceptable cost" or to "combine a deterrent based on a threat of maximum destructiveness with a strategy of minimum risk." Thus, Kissinger contemplated a policy of limited war in order "to reintroduce the political element into our concept of warfare and to discard the notion that policy ends when war begins or that war can have goals distinct from those of national policy."[38]

Realism thus emerged in the nuclear age. The West, for the sake of efficiency and closure, would have preferred a direct and conclusive military confrontation with the Soviet Union to limited war, and vice versa. But the prospect of apocalypse did not permit it. And if limited war was analytically the core of a stable and credible deterrent, limited objectives constituted its political-military correlative. The dynamic problem was that limited objectives did not causally guarantee limited war, as both world wars attested. Even though Korea roughly, and fortunately, followed the favorable pattern, the risk of escalation to the nuclear level was patent and more momentous when the stakes were essentially ideological rather than merely territorial. Soviet conventional strength also kept rearing its ugly head. The West would mainly be defending territory against Soviet expansion. Kissinger developed the theory that a small, highly accurate, and mobile Western battlefield nuclear capability would discourage Soviet aggrandizement by presenting the Soviets with a functionally conventional nuclear deterrent. Concerns about the vulnerability of such a capability to conventional attack, the credibility of damage limitation with respect to *any* nuclear weapon, and the jarring psychological effect that crossing the nuclear threshold would have on both the initiating and the target leadership cast severe doubts on the viability of this theory. And the Soviets wouldn't play ball: they rarely countenanced even the notion of "tactical" nukes in their strategic literature, generally characterized them as triggers for broader nuclear use, and manifested every intention of continuing to press their conventional advantage in a war of attrition even *after* a nuclear exchange.

The Soviets seemed to understand that the intellectual

machinations prompted by nuclear weaponry had distorted the classical (Clausewitzean) meanings of "strategic" and "tactical"—that all war was strategic in that it aimed to achieve political ends, and all weapons tactical in that they were applied to realize military objectives that were subsidiary to strategy. This implicit fundamentalism on the part of the Soviets stimulated an important advance in the theory of deterrence. In 1959, Glenn Snyder introduced a distinction between deterrence by punishment or threatened punishment—the kind theretofore usually under consideration—and deterrence by denial.[39] Whereas the former affected the enemy's calculation of the net costs of aggression, the latter affected his assessment of the chances of accomplishing his objective through that aggression. A ready corollary of this conceptual disaggregation was that even if the Soviets were willing to incur catastrophic losses in advancing a given territorial objective, rendering the realization of that objective improbable would make such losses less acceptable. In that case, the punishment required to deter action would have to be tailored closely to the tactical objective in question. Threatening Russian cities in the event of battlefield advances would not directly implicate the tactical objective, and therefore should be dismissed in favor of threatening only the forces used for those advances absent wider Soviet aggression. Harry Rowen generalized this point in rejecting the notion of "minimum deterrence," whereby the United States would maintain a nuclear force that threatened only Soviet cities. In executing this threat, he asked, "What U.S. national objective would be advanced? It might serve as a lesson to future aggressors or provide a horrible example to shock the world into total disarmament. But the chance of this hardly seems enough to warrant the sacrificing of much of the United States and possibly all of it. The dilemma of a policy of large-scale retaliation against enemy cities is that what it makes sense to threaten is not necessarily the best policy actually to execute."[40]

This chain of reasoning formed the basis for "graduated deterrence," developed mainly by British analysts against the skepticism of both compatriots and Americans, under which the limited and general spheres of warfare were bounded by distinct and contiguous deterrence scenarios. In theory, the distinction between limited and general nuclear war—and between tactical and strategic nuclear weapons—thus became more concrete, reinforcing the proposition that tactical nuclear weapons favored the defense. Graduated deterrence ultimately entrenched in strategic thinking the idea that, especially in the nuclear context, the *smaller* the threatened punishment, the more credible the deterrent. At the end of the day, though, it was a flawed concept. It seemed to recommend early use of tactical nuclear weapons as long as the other side didn't possess them, which implicitly downplayed the symbolic significance of the nuclear taboo. Neither corollary squared with laws of war that decried disproportionality in the use of military force and the psychological sense that nuclear weapons were inexorably a breed apart. Graduated deterrence was not appreciably more credible than massive retaliation because the idea of limited nuclear war still seemed a contradiction in terms. But the debate itself had its uses. Snyder's distinction remained one of the most durable and recursive constructs of deterrence theory. More immediately, the colloquium on graduated deterrence laid to rest any illusion that nuclear weapons could be seamlessly insinuated into a traditional nineteenth-century land war—any illusion that a nuke was just another weapon.

In spite of the intense anxiety over nuclear use, in the fifties and sixties those near the center of the debate were not ready to consign the notion of winning a nuclear war to absurdity.

The U.S. government seriously entertained the notion of preemption—that is, launching a first strike on Soviet population centers on the pretext of an imminent Soviet attack—from the early to mid-1950s until the Cuban Missile Crisis in 1962, during which time the United States maintained clear nuclear superiority. Over time, though, positioning threatened genocide at the heart of U.S. security policy became increasingly distasteful. Targeting populations also had obvious diminishing tactical returns, as it progressively contracted the incentives for surrender and increased those for vengeance. But discriminately targeting military assets—dubbed *counterforce*—had both ethical and operational legs provided it could neutralize the enemy's capacity to visit destruction on the attacker before the attacker's society had been debilitated. This formula did not necessitate a preemptive first strike: as long as the United States' nuclear capability could substantially survive a Soviet first strike, counterforce worked as a second-strike strategy. Retaliating against military installations would still give the Soviets reason to give up to save their populations from nuclear strikes implicitly threatened.

So the Air Force—which controlled the strategic bombers of the Strategic Air Command, the United States' primary nuclear capability in the 1950s—considered a truly limited nuclear war impossible, and regarded counterforce as a means of making total nuclear war winnable and thus strengthening the American deterrent. The idea, as Lawrence Freedman has put it, was that "the most effective deterrent . . . would be based on power that could actually be used with confidence."[41] As long as the United States maintained nuclear superiority, this stabilized the "balance of terror" that had been so tenuous in the context of massive retaliation. But as the Soviet Union's nuclear capability moved toward parity with that of the United States, counterforce lost appeal as a second-strike option, stability was again imperiled, and the notion of limiting nuclear war regained currency. A ruminative pattern in U.S. strategic thinking, in which nuclear war bounded and subjugated other considerations and was itself sent through a repeating intellectual cycle, was firmly established.

2

American Ways of Thinking

The United States was at once in awe of its own military power and terrified of the potential consequences of its exertion. For nuclear war was not merely about the mechanization of war and what it can do to flesh and blood. It was also about the decimation of mankind and the ruination of the earth. Those who chose to think about how to avoid it—and, beyond that, how to deal with its consequences should it occur anyway—could not merely pick up where Clausewitz left off. Clausewitz himself concluded his historical survey of the Napoleonic Wars with the observation that "the events of every age must be judged in the light of its own peculiarities. One cannot, therefore, understand and appreciate the commanders of the past until one has placed oneself in the situation of their times, not so much by a painstaking study of all its details as by an accurate appreciation of its major determining features." But, he exhorted, "war, though conditioned by the particular characteristics of states and their armed forces, must contain some more general—indeed, a universal—element with which every theorist ought above all to be concerned."[1] Strategists of some kind were still needed.

The pioneers of nuclear strategy were Albert Wohlstetter,

Thomas C. Schelling, Herman Kahn, Bernard Brodie, William Kaufmann, and Henry Kissinger. It is significant that all of them were civilians. During World War II, the military had been focused on fighting rather than thinking. It was already in a monumental war, so avoiding one was past consideration. Thus, it had been the professional warfighters, the generals and admirals, who reigned supreme in strategy. During the Cold War, the ranking priority was to avoid general war because it could become nuclear, and the consequences of nuclear war were potentially catastrophic for mankind. If the provisional remedy for the First World War was political (treaties arrived at during the six-month Paris Peace Conference in 1919), and for the next one economic (the Marshall Plan), fixing the damage from nuclear war strained the imagination. It was natural enough, then, that the Cold War evolved into a painstaking and elaborate intellectual effort on the part of the West to avoid nuclear war. This dispensation by itself constituted a departure. The premium was now on thinking rather than fighting. Such a priority was at odds with the military mind-set. Civilian intellectuals were therefore ascendant. They dared to "think about the unthinkable"— about what would happen if there were a nuclear war—precisely in order to craft better ways to deter it.

Systematic thinking about the unthinkable started in earnest at the RAND Corporation. During World War II, with the Manhattan Project, university professors readily became veritable intellectual soldiers in a cause behind which there was broad intellectual and popular consensus. Spurred by the recognition that America's intellectuals were national-security assets, Project RAND (an acronymic term for "research and development") began in 1946 as part of the Douglas Aircraft Company—at the prompting of U.S. Air Force general H. H. "Hap" Arnold and other U.S. officials—to facilitate teamwork among the military, civilian government agencies, industry, and the academic community through research, and to continue the Army Air Corps' wartime operations research efforts as a federally funded element of Douglas Aircraft Corporation to address strategic and operational issues facing the Air Force (made a separate service at the end of 1945) in particular. Army and Navy operations research capabilities underwent similar transformations, and the naval counterpart to RAND—the Center for Naval Analyses—survives to this day.

Project RAND was initially housed in a private company on the basis of the Air Force's assessment that no university would welcome classified work, few scientists would enlist in an enterprise directly run by the military, and an insufficient number of highly talented people would accept the compensation packages and employment practices to which the civil service was limited. Within the Defense Department and private industry, the consensus soon developed that such a cozy relationship between the government and one particular company could engender a conflict of interest, and RAND was reconstituted in 1948, with seed money of $10 million from the Ford Foundation, as a new not-for-profit corporation.[2] It was thus insulated from day-to-day military oversight and political influence. Quite deliberately, RAND was located in Santa Monica, California, so that its work would not be disturbed by daily queries from the Washington defense bureaucracy. The Project RAND contract with the Air Force, however, remained a principal source of funding throughout the Cold War. Since its inception, RAND has been statutorily distinct from strictly independent think tanks (e.g., the Center for Strategic and International Studies, The Brookings Institution, the American Enterprise Institute) in that it has had a long-term sponsoring agreement with the federal government and most employees have been cleared for and given regular access to highly sensitive classified information.* Yet, to encourage objective analysis, such institutions are, by explicit design, managerially and intellectually independent. "The Air Force," remembers Schelling, "essentially decided in 1946 that its own people couldn't understand the new strategic situation, and they had to invent an institution where people would have freedom to, and were in fact encouraged to, exercise their own imaginations. They deliberately located it in Santa Monica so that it would not be at the beck and call of the Air Force, because the Air Force said, 'We don't even know what questions to ask—we want them to ask the questions.' RAND had a $10 million budget and an advisory group of Air Force officers, but the Air Force rarely approved an overall RAND project. There was a lot of money for RAND to use any way RAND wanted to."[3]

RAND recruiters were as lucky as they were good. For example, when Yale president A. Whitney Griswold took office in 1950, he decided to end the university's funding for—hence abolish—the Yale Institute for International Studies, which had been established in 1935. The institute was populated by interventionist realists, or "new nationalists," who—following Kennan—considered the Soviets a singular threat and believed that only decisive action by the United States could maintain the balance of power. Though apparently sympathetic with this view, Griswold considered policy research on international affairs unsuited to Yale's liberal arts tradition. Bernard Brodie and William Kaufmann were untenured members of the institute. Feeling unloved, they went elsewhere, and both eventually wound up at RAND.[4] Had Griswold not pulled the plug on the institute, RAND would have had a far harder time hiring top-flight talent. John

---

*In 1961, Congress designated such organizations "federal contract research centers" and in 1967 renamed them "federally funded research and development centers," or, familiarly, FFRDCs.

Williams, a mathematician, had done the initial staffing in 1946. RAND's first hirees were mathematicians, engineers, statisticians, and physicists. By 1947, it became clear that RAND needed to be a broader church, and political scientists, historians, sociologists, psychologists, and economists were brought on. Nevertheless, Andrew Marshall, who spent over twenty years at RAND before working for Henry Kissinger at the National Security Council and then heading the Pentagon's Office of Net Assessment, reflects: "apart from a handful of people to set the general tone of the place, other people who came in and carried forward what they'd started were not established experts. The average age of the professional staff at RAND for the first decade was about 27. The only person who had any kind of an established reputation was Brodie."[5] (Kaufmann, who decamped to Princeton from Yale, would join him there as a staff member in 1956.) Indeed, Brodie had published *A Layman's Guide to Naval Strategy* in 1942, and the U.S. Navy was so impressed that it had the word *Layman's* deleted from the title, bought ten thousand copies, and distributed them to everyone above the rank of lieutenant. He was virtually the only preeminent nuclear strategist professionally engaged in postwar military strategy who had been professionally so engaged before the war.

As the Cold War dawned, however, the sociological fortuity of "the greatest generation" made the talent pool very rich. "We were favored," says Marshall, "by the fact that this problem [of nuclear deterrence] arose so soon after the end of World War II. My view tends to be that people who went through the thirties and the war and reached the middle of their careers were serious in a way that in many respects has vanished from American society. I think one big lesson they'd learned was that you don't kick problems down the road in the hope that they will go away or get better; you really must address problems and try to do something about them."[6] Early in the Cold War, RAND had no real private-sector competition because think tanks were new and nuclear strategy was almost virgin territory. Competition from military institutions was also thin: since experience with nuclear weapons was so sparse, military strategists enjoyed no comparative advantage over civilian ones. RAND researcher Alain Enthoven's exquisitely supercilious, and oft quoted, remark to a military officer while at the Pentagon—"General, I have fought just as many nuclear wars as you have"—was neither factually wrong nor merely legend.[7] Likewise, Herman Kahn, responding to a Pentagon official's indignation over his claim that he and his colleagues were ranking world experts on ending nuclear war, snarled: "I put two junior people on it for a couple of days last week. We've thought more about it than the entire Defense Department has."[8] This, too, was probably true.

Back in the day, RAND was far bigger than its mandate. It was the well-spring of the burgeoning relationship among government, academia, and independent research institutions. In March and April 1952, a team of RAND analysts assisted physicist Edward Teller—the so-called father of the hydrogen bomb—in composing and presenting a series of highly technical briefings to officials from the State Department, the Defense Department, and the Joint Chiefs of Staff on the effects of thermonuclear bombs and the Soviet Union's determination and capability to build the weapon. These presentations critically increased bureaucratic momentum behind the creation of a new government weapons laboratory to complement the existing Los Alamos National Laboratory and accelerate American research, and, in September 1952, Lawrence Livermore National Laboratory (initially known as Project Whitney) officially opened.[9] RAND's main customer may have been the Air Force, and its next most important one the Defense Department. During the fifties and early sixties, though, its leading lights became not only influential voices within these organizations, but also, though to a limited extent, public intellectuals who used the growing mystique of the think tank to deepen and amplify their public voices. This dual status marked them as men with both access to secrets and strategic vision that captured the imagination of the common man, which in turn increased their credibility within the Air Force and the Pentagon, and extended it to the White House and the State Department.

Wohlstetter's Pragmatics

Albert Wohlstetter, who died in 1997, for twenty-five years influenced government policy more than anyone else at RAND. His gravitas had not a little to do with his personal style and bearing. He loved good food and fine wine, quoted Shakespeare, and had studied quite seriously with Charles Weidman, one of the founders of American modern dance. His mother wanted him to be an opera singer. He spoke with a kind of swagger, and in his later years he wore an Achesonian mustache that set him apart and emphasized his magisterial cast, from a commanding-heights perch. As Fred Kaplan has written, "his tone, style and manner . . . seemed cultivated to convey the image of a man on top of *everything*."[10] His background in logic and native inquisitiveness also afforded him a searching method that seemed to pervade his life. Wohlstetter's daughter, Joan Wohlstetter Hall, remembered that when she was immersed in the study of math in school, the first sentence out of her father's mouth at the dinner table would begin "Now, you take X . . . ."[11] The fact that he didn't even broach strategic studies until he got to RAND, when he was almost forty, after an early manhood of intellectual itinerancy across the capitalist landscape, only added to his legend.

Born in Manhattan in 1913, Wohlstetter was of Austrian lineage. His father sold record players (Rex Talking Machines) but was driven out of business in World War I—in considerable part for having a Germanic name—and died young, when Albert was four.[12] To the exasperation of his older brothers—who, during the Depression, wanted him to make some real money—Albert embraced the Depression as a kind of opportunity by default. The Depression "was curious," he recalled in 1985. "In some ways it reinforced a natural tendency that I had not to really be thinking very much about money. In this case it was in part because you couldn't get jobs anyway. So you were really a kind of free spirit during the Depression."[13] He had a series of offbeat jobs and attended the City College of New York, then, after a one-year fellowship at Columbia Law School that he found "dull," trained as a mathematical logician at Columbia. Albert was an exceptional student but remained intellectually and culturally promiscuous. He frequented the Metropolitan Opera; sat in on courses like, in his recollection, Romanesque Monumental Stone Sculpture and French Illuminated Manuscripts, given by art historian Meyer Schapiro; and explored economics from Marx to Keynes and Alfred Marshall.[14] A pragmatist in the making, Wohlstetter found the abstraction of formal logic insufficiently practical, and felt compelled to undertake work that involved "handling data." He took a fellowship at the National Bureau of Economic Research (NBER), where he studied randomness in time series, the measurement of cyclical behavior, and the axiomatization of utility.[15] The latter, especially, presaged his work as a strategist.

After the NBER, during World War II, Wohlstetter worked as an industrial quality control expert for a company called Atlas

Aircraft Products that made electrical generators and motors used for communications. "It was sort of like a cold bath because I was now in a factory in which the people I would normally have thought of as plumbers—engineers—were now the theoreticians and I was looking at the stuff that was coming out of the machine shop and the assembly line and trying to compare it with the designs, and then going back to argue with them about how they ought to really design it."[16] He and his RAND collaborators would later have an analogous relationship of constructive antagonism with the Air Force and, as he acknowledged, his work in the factory was "the sort of thing that made it possible for me to work with the engineers and physicists and so forth at RAND."[17] Wohlstetter's interests soon surpassed his duties at Atlas. To keep him on board as he contemplated a return to academia, management persuaded him to devote half his time to research and development for an affiliated company, General Panel Corporation, on a process of manufacturing modular housing units based on the visions and concepts of the iconoclastic architects Konrad Wachsmann and Walter Gropius. Then, for a year, he worked in Washington, as director of programs for the National Housing Agency, on remedying the housing shortage for demobilizing veterans. In 1947, he returned to General Panel, which had established a manufacturing arm in California and had taken a loan from the federal government to produce several thousand prefabricated houses. Wohlstetter became president of the company, but the enterprise turned out to be technically and economically unrealistic, which soon made him available, as a consultant, to RAND. He signed on in 1951.

Wohlstetter first worked in RAND's mathematics department on mathematical methodological issues related to logistics, and he was still there when RAND president Charles Hitch proposed that he spearhead what appeared to be the "rather dull logistics problem" of how the SAC's bases would be most cost-effectively positioned.[18] Wohlstetter led a team of RAND researchers in conducting a study of SAC's basing strategy (familiarly known as "R-266," its designation under RAND's internal classification system). What began as essentially a cost-efficiency exercise ended up demonstrating that the offensive military advantage afforded the SAC in basing its long-range bombers forward, close to their targets, was not worth their high vulnerability to Soviet surprise attack.[19] Although basing the strategic bomber force farther away from the Soviet Union would reduce the swiftness of a first strike, it would decrease their susceptibility to preemptive attack so as to facilitate an effective second strike at much lower cost. The practical result was the substantial redeployment of the SAC to the U.S. interior. Thus, a "dull logistics problem" resulted in the first detailed operational articulation of arguably the most fundamental distinction in nuclear strategy: that between first-strike and second-strike deterrence.

For all the thought and verbiage that was ultimately invested in the refinement of nuclear deterrence, it was fundamentally the notion of retaliatory capability, or second-strike deterrence— transported by Brodie and others from the conventional to the nuclear sphere, operationalized by Wohlstetter and his team at RAND—that deserved most of the credit for staving off general nuclear war during the early years of the Cold War and, beyond that, laying a durable foundation for nuclear deterrence. The force of that notion owes much to its simple, intuitive, and powerful logic. George Quester, a droll, lanky political scientist now at the University of Maryland and a quiet but steady influence on U.S. nuclear strategy for decades as an analyst and consultant, notes how, upon hearing the news that the Soviets had exploded an atomic bomb, he felt "a certain kind of angst about 'what if somebody used the bomb against us, wouldn't that be terrible,' and slowly the logic of deterrence sinking in."[20] Deterrence was not some revelation of the nuclear age; it had been around a lot longer. Its elementary logic—that they can do it to us no matter what we do first, that they can hit us back with a second strike—nested pretty early in the nuclear age, with Brodie's work. But the premise of Quester's doctoral dissertation was that planners and airpower advocates who thought the conventional strategic bombing of World War II was equivalent to the atomic bomb were wrong; atomic weapons could concentrate far greater destructiveness. The fact that the atomic bomb was much more of an "unignorable" second-strike threat than any of the bombing in World War II elevated the notion's importance.[21]

"The Delicate Balance of Terror," which first appeared for wide consumption in the January 1959 issue of *Foreign Affairs,* was arguably the seminal open-source document of the "first" (i.e., pre-détente) Cold War. In those twenty-odd pages, Wohlstetter distilled his team's disturbing technical findings into a sobering set of strategic observations. The article was cast against the backdrop of the Soviets' October 1957 launch of *Sputnik I,* the first man-made satellite. That event had revealed a technological capacity to produce intercontinental ballistic missiles—a public shock that scared the hell out of the United States by eviscerating Americans' assumptions about their security and exploding convenient American myths of Soviet intellectual decadence. The United States now had a scientific equal as an enemy, and the Cold War seemed instantly up for grabs. A consensus of scientists and security specialists believed that technological breakthroughs would yield transitory strategic advantages to the West that would give way to new advantages to the Soviets, which in turn would succumb to Western innovations, and so on, with the escalatory cycle repeating itself indefinitely. The 1957 report of the Gaither Committee (composed by Eisenhower of leading science, business, and military experts) counseled a higher airborne alert status for the SAC (to guard against surprise attack) and a new emphasis on defensive measures, including early-warning systems, antiballistic missiles, and a national fallout shelter program. But this mind-set registered as lugubrious and potentially expensive, and Eisenhower rejected most of the Gaither Report's recommendations. Notwithstanding *Sputnik* and Wohlstetter's exposure of the vulnerabilities of the American deterrent, Eisenhower was at heart a military man, and uncomfortable with the hortatory leeriness of the civilian strategists. He fundamentally believed that the American nuclear arsenal was decisively superior to that of the Soviets, which gave him sufficient cover to keep taxes and the national debt low by restraining the growth of the military budget. By the late fifties, however, in both the United States and the Soviet Union, interest was rejuvenated in a less defeatist alternative: a capacity for preemptive attack. The push-button quickness with which ICBMs could be launched and the absence of effective air defenses now complicated the picture, however. Both sides acutely feared surprise attack and the accidents that could ensue from inadequate operational control over military assets, which the civilian strategists regarded as two of the principal potential causes of conflicts.

Noting that stable deterrence depended more on second-strike than first-strike capability, Wohlstetter said that the United States' second-strike capability was not secure, and deterrence therefore not stable, for a whole basket of reasons: the uncertainty of sufficient forces' surviving a first strike, the difficulty of imparting a decision to retaliate to SAC pilots, the underrated effectiveness of Soviet air defenses and challenge of penetrating them, the totalitarian advantage of secrecy about war-fighting doctrine, and the new wild card of post-*Sputnik* Soviet offensive missile capabilities.[22] Wohlstetter's piece analytically and technically encapsulated the psychological trauma that the American policy elite and public alike felt over *Sputnik*. U.S. policy makers—including the Air Force—quickly postulated a prospective "missile gap," and with it a Soviet intention to seek nuclear superiority so as to make nuclear war winnable.

Thanks to Wohlstetter, bolstering deterrence became the paramount objective of U.S. nuclear policy. And since deterrence by its nature enshrined a nuclear stalemate, the United States became a status quo power on the nuclear issue. But the conditions for maintaining the stalemate became more fastidious. Wohlstetter and Herman Kahn, who had been at RAND since 1948, shared the concern that the Soviets' tolerance for casualties—manifested by their twenty million dead in the Second World War with nary a hint of capitulation—was far higher than the Americans' and inferred a lower degree of Soviet deterrability. Although British commentators decried what they saw as a paranoid American imputation of irrational aggression to Moscow, the Soviets had fueled this worry after Stalin's death in 1954 with more fulsome discussions of the role of the bomb in Soviet strategy—notably, discarding the assumptions among his "Permanently Operating Factors" that socialism would always have greater political staying power than capitalism and that the advantage of military surprise was inherently fleeting. The advent of ICBM technology tended to support this rejection. Although second-strike deterrence had replaced first-strike deterrence as the more stable theoretical option, persistent worries about surprise attack in the early sixties prompted each side to build up its preemptive counterforce capability sufficiently to neutralize the other's ability to strike back (which meant deploying more missiles) and to improve its second-strike capability (which meant decreasing vulnerability through mobile launchers and hardened missile silos and submarine deployment). This dynamic guaranteed a technological arms race, but this was not inherently a bad thing. As it turned out, the relative invulnerability of ICBMs as standoff weapons and their inaccuracy as first-strike weapons compared to strategic bombers came to favor the defense. The stalemate and nuclear stability were ultimately reinforced.

Reflecting years later on the stark revelations of RAND's seminal basing study, Wohlstetter himself said:

> Here's something which I think people never understand. I didn't say, "Ah ha! What would happen if he attacked us?" or something like that. I was coming without the background of what people thought the problem was, so I was thinking what were the elements of the problem myself, and what attracted me to it was that there were forces working in opposing directions. There were some forces that would make you want to be up close, so that you could have close access to targets, be able to act quickly, get in many sorties, use shorter range weapons and so on. And on the other hand, there were some things that made you want to be back because if you were close to him, why, there was just as good a chance he would also be close to you. So he would be getting in a lot of whacks. He would get in the first whacks since it is obviously ridiculous, though people pretended it isn't, that we would attack him without provocation. So that made you want to be far away. But then you could see that this meant you would need a larger aircraft or you would have to refuel a lot of times, and so on. And it struck me that in the *abstract* there was no way of resolving this.

Location, he noted, would affect penetration ability, delivery costs, and bomber attrition in different ways, and it was impossible to know how in an operationally precise way without considering specific geography. He decided that it would be very interesting to "try to bring some simple order into this complexity" by designing systems that would respectively offer the greatest advantages for each parameter and then comparing them.[23]

Reaching back to his NBER work on the axiomatization of utility, Wohlstetter noted that one axiom of utility

> says that given any two alternatives, you either prefer one or you are indifferent. And for a variety of reasons I think that that axiom of connectedness, that you *can* make that judgment about any two alternatives, is very implausible and wrong. If you think about preferences as not simple sensuous [*sic*] pleasures like preferring vanilla to chocolate, but complex alternatives, in many cases you just don't know how to compare them at all. You don't *know* whether you are indifferent or prefer one or the other, and when you think about how you make decisions, that part of your job is that you construct an order as you find out about things, so that you are always in the process of constructing your preferences.[24]

Constructing an order as you find out about things and *you are always in the process of constructing your preferences* enshrine the importance of the ongoing input of empirical information into practical decision-making. They also define Wohlstetter's— and RAND's—analytical method about as well as any two phrases could.

The phrases are also conspicuously compatible with the philosophy of pragmatism. Pragmatism operated across a much narrower intellectual spectrum during the Cold War than it had in the late nineteenth and early twentieth centuries, when it was the dominant strain of American thought. But pragmatism did not completely disappear. The SAC basing study, led by Wohlstetter, involved constructing an order precisely as Wohlstetter described. The study—which comprises nearly four hundred pages of charts, graphs, and calculations as well as narrative exposition—is an exemplar of the kind of sequential empirical rigor that propelled deterrence from slogan to principle. One of Wohlstetter's bugbears was the widespread perception that the base study very *un*pragmatically enshrined SAC offensive targeting plans. Questioned on this point for posterity in 1985, he snarkily responded: "No, no. You see, this goes back to my origins in the logic of science." He mentioned two famous essays by Charles Sanders Peirce, one titled "The Fixation of Belief," the other "How to Make Our Ideas Clear."

> The first looks at how we arrive at, "fix" our beliefs, and it's an attack on Descartes to begin with. Descartes [with his "systematic doubt" methodology] says he is questioning everything. This is a fake. You can only question something on the basis of some things which you are *not* questioning. If you are saying, well, that's five feet long, you have to believe that your measuring rod isn't shrinking and expanding in random ways. So there are some things which you don't question. Now, that doesn't mean they are unquestionable. It means that you are holding them provisionally, and *most* of your beliefs are unquestioned at any given time. You can only question some on the basis of what you hold. Now, I didn't believe for a second that all those targeting objectives were optimal. But I *was* going to say, let's assume that this is what you want to do. . . . I was not trying to pick targets, I was trying to pick basing systems.[25]

In "How to Make Our Ideas Clear"—which first appeared in *Popular Science Monthly,* a serious scholarly publication despite its title—Peirce wrote that "the opinion which is fated to be ultimately agreed to by all who investigate, is what we mean by truth, and the object represented in this opinion is the real."[26]

Peirce's pragmatism is basically a Popperian logic of science, whereby the validity of ideas turn on their very susceptibility to being tested—and, by implication, refuted or falsified.* Certainly that is what Wohlstetter drew from Peirce. If Wohlstetter had an overarching professional axiom, it was that truth springs from rigorous investigation. His purposeful interpretation and application of pragmatism had planted in RAND a form of investigator-initiated research, in which the researcher was not narrowly confined to someone else's notion of what the right questions might be. His work was always marked by his penchant for reformulating the customer's original terms of reference. The plumbing of all relevant facts and circumstances that were available was especially important given that the business of nuclear strategy was to fight a theoretical war. Wohlstetter's primary concern sprung from the fact that steep increases in the destructive power of nuclear weapons had made controlling the effects of a nuclear second strike more and more difficult. He asked the question: How likely is it that we would in fact respond if we would rain unavoidable catastrophe on civilian populations? "The only thing that made any prudential or moral sense," he said, "was to attack military forces." Since "we don't want to make a threat that we wouldn't be willing to execute, the proper thing is to aim at military forces." Doing so "was a *deterrent* measure, but it was a *better* deterrent if you had a response which

---

*William James, considered a founder of pragmatism as such, characterized it as follows: "*True ideas are those that we can assimilate, validate, corroborate and verify. False ideas are those that we cannot.* That is the practical difference it makes to us to have true ideas; that, therefore, is the meaning of truth, for it is all that truth is known as.... The truth of an idea is not a stagnant property inherent in it. Truth *happens* to an idea." William James, "Pragmatism's Conception of Truth," from *Pragmatism* (1907), reprinted in Louis Menand, ed., *Pragmatism: A Reader* (New York: Vintage Books, 1997), p. 114 (emphasis in original).

was not just inviting chaos, but which tried to keep things under gross control."²⁷ This mode of thinking yielded a city-avoidance concept that prevailed in U.S. nuclear strategy from the early sixties until the end of the Cold War.

Yet Wohlstetter's employment of pragmatism was highly selective. Basic ideas and beliefs about America's imperatives were off-limits. These were fixed constants that his team decidedly was "*not* questioning." He and his colleagues cast themselves as strategic realists first, and philosophical pragmatists only a strictly subordinate second.* They did not challenge, in particular, the fundamental validity of containment, which they assumed was necessary for protecting American interests, but only how best to execute the policy. They were concerned not about ends, which were taken as givens, nor about history or political nuance, which nuclear weapons were regarded as having vitiated, but about the repleteness and efficiency of intellectual processes, which they believed would yield the right result if properly framed, calibrated, and orchestrated. In that overarching sense, while RAND thinkers like Wohlstetter may have admired the

---

* *Realism,* of course, was in the eye of the beholder. The most influential Cold War realist was George Kennan, who crafted the containment policy as the prudent alternative to any dangerous outright attempt to vanquish the Soviet Union in the nuclear age, and regarded Wilsonian idealism as impracticable on a broad scale. But Kennan considered the Soviets aggressively evil and never doubted that the American system was superior or that it would ultimately prevail. Other prominent realists—Hans Morgenthau, in particular—disdained such "American exceptionalism" and the crusading, self-righteous opposition to communism that it had spawned. To him, foreign policy was purely a matter of prosecuting national interests without morally judging the ethical or political predilections of adversaries. Hans Morgenthau, *Scientific Man vs. Power Politics* (Chicago: University of Chicago Press, 1946); *Politics Among Nations* (New York: Alfred A. Knopf, 1948); *In Defense of the National Interest* (New York: Alfred A. Knopf, 1951). For political as well as intellectual reasons, the species of realism that came to prevail among civilian strategists internalized Soviet malevolence as a determinant of policy—which smacked incongruously of Wilsonian idealism—and never reached Morgenthau's level of purity. Bruce Kuklick, *Blind Oracles: Intellectuals and War from Kennan to Kissinger* (Princeton and Oxford: Princeton University Press, 2006), p. 78.

methodological agility of pragmatism, they were philosophically more consistent with logical positivism, which originated in Europe with the Vienna Circle in the 1920s. Positivism differed crucially from pragmatism in its convictions (a) that science was value-free and operated inside strict "boundary conditions," (b) that facts and values were distinct, and (c) that scientists and ethicists ought to operate in mutually exclusive spheres.* That kind of rigidity fit well with an age in which national goals and values were threatened and did not seem to need further justification, and the overriding concern was how scientifically to fulfill and consolidate them. Indeed, positivism, led in part by Germans, like Carl Hempel, who had emigrated to the United States after Hitler came to power in the 1930s, had overtaken pragmatism as the dominant philosophy in America following World War II.[28] Wohlstetter and his colleagues at RAND, then, were in line with prevailing intellectual trends, and thus well positioned to enhance their influence.

Intellectual Hegemony

Nobody had ever fought a nuclear war. On a more intuitive level, the immense destructiveness of nuclear weapons and the near-instantaneous nature of their effects devalued the individualistic qualities of leadership and heroism that had given warriors ownership of war. A nuclear war, if it were fought, would involve no infantrymen storming the beach, and few dogfights or pitched naval battles. If, as preferred, it were not fought, it would be be-

*Indeed, Wohlstetter was notorious for his antagonism toward physical scientists who presumed to insinuate their moral judgments into the domain of strategy. Strategy, he said, should be assigned to a new discipline and set of experts who applied "the method of science" but did not rely on "the authority of science." Albert Wohlstetter, "Scientists, Seers, and Strategy," *Foreign Affairs*, vol. 41, no. 32 (Spring 1963) 2 p. 468.

cause the United States' force structure had a clear answer for the full range of Soviet threats that deterred Moscow from making good on them. Thus, civilian strategists had a voice during the Cold War that they never had before. This had to do not only with the serendipitous confluence of brainpower at RAND, but also with the unique character of nuclear war. Once the strategic infeasibility of a first-strike counterforce strategy became clear, the links to traditional war-fighting doctrine became terminally loose. In terms of intellectual capital, then, the military had no comparative advantage over civilians. RAND's arch pronouncement in 1960 that all military problems were, in essence, "economic problems in the efficient allocation of resources" was received by the generals with more resignation than incredulity.[29] Underpinning this shibboleth was the normative conviction—stemming from the view that a hydrogen bomb was not just another weapon—that using a nuclear bomb was at bottom a futile military act but an act that could nevertheless materialize from unstable political circumstances.

The strategists' core objective became how to determine how resources would best be directed to stabilize the global political environment in order to minimize the probability of nuclear use. Attaining that goal involved an array of activities in a number of different, though overlapping, areas. Intelligence agencies ascertained enemy capabilities, and informed both diplomacy and defense policy by illuminating the discrepancy between stated and actual capabilities. Diplomats negotiated arms control agreements in order to establish communications routines about nuclear threats to diminish the risk of surprise or misunderstanding, and in order to make the strategic environment more static and the technological parameters of deterrence more durable. And they firmed up alliances and special relationships to implement the nonmilitary side of the containment policy. The Pentagon and the military services ensured that force structure (for example, the nuclear triad*) was consistent with prevailing strategic doctrine (for instance, second-strike counterforce), and fought those conventional "proxy" wars, like Korea and Vietnam, whose prosecution was considered to yield political advantages in containing the Soviet Union or China and consolidate spheres of influence without posing undue risk of nuclear escalation. Think tanks like RAND and academics like Schelling sussed out and articulated the connections among the activities in these different realms.

The strongest methodological influence at RAND was operations research, a fundamentally empirical enterprise that had customarily involved accumulating and quantifying data from past military operations, analyzing it, and inferring lessons for future operations. But of course, there was virtually no experience with nuclear warfare. What emerged was a species of systems analysis that Wohlstetter called "conflict systems," under which the strategists would extrapolate policy recommendations mainly from data concerning the effects of nuclear bombs and the operating characteristics of the vehicles that would be used to deliver them under different scenarios. The strength of this approach lay in its capacity to determine the optimal exploitation of the capabilities of defense technologies based on the assumption of a rational adversary. But the subtlety and precision of the technical analysis occurred in an oversimplified political framework based on sometimes glib and ahistorical assumptions about the strategic choices that leaders and soldiers would make and the psychological characteristics of their behavior during crisis. For example, while U.S. and NATO nuclear superiority was regarded as a neat answer to Soviet conventional superiority, the moral and

*That is, strategic bombers, ICBMs, and submarine-launched ballistic missiles.

psychological difficulty of breaking the nuclear threshold was underplayed.

The conflict-systems methodology embodied a species of pragmatism, but of an eclectic sort that was self-limiting and, at least in effect, tendentious. In his exegesis on conflict systems, Wohlstetter accepted the positivistic view, developed by organizational behavior theorists, that rationality was relative to goals, so that means could be deemed "rational" only with reference to such goals. He was primarily interested in how pathways to different goals interacted. With a nod to pragmatic philosopher John Dewey's disdain for sterile distinctions between scientific facts and social or political values, he argued that the viability of goals depended on whether they were attainable through various possible means and compatible with other goals.[30] That determination would be made through rigorous analysis. Yet what was centrally important for Wohlstetter was not so much the absolute validity of ultimate goals, but whether a given subsidiary goal could be harmonized with other goals of comparable weight; to the extent that it could be, the overarching goals had value. Whereas the pragmatist philosophers would have argued that experience and investigation could lead to a change in ultimate (in the Cold War context, strategic) objectives, the inquiries of Wohlstetter and the civilian nuclear strategists ring-fenced the goals of containment and deterrence as sacrosanct and practically untouchable.

The peculiar nature of the Soviet threat catered to this insular sort of approach. Now in his eighties and still at the Pentagon, Andrew Marshall believes that the Soviets constituted "a very cautious, elite government" that, as RAND's Nathan Leites argued in 1951 in *The Operational Code of the Politburo*, was, in a certain way, extremely rational. The task of refining deterrence, he suggests, "was helped by the fact that the Soviets were hyper-rational both because of the Bolshevik views and, as we found out later, because they had made notions of making war into a science. So we may have been very fortunate in having them as an opponent." That is, the Soviet Union constituted a massive amount of destructive power commanded by a relatively small elite guided by a rigidly doctrinaire set of principles. Consequently, it made an extraordinarily well-defined target that, by virtue of its singularity, allowed its adversaries to minimize historical and other secondary considerations in considering how best to thwart it. But Marshall also observes that after the initial assumption of Bolshevik rationality was made, it went relatively unexplored, so that nuances were not spun out. "One of the things that was under-developed back then was trying to understand in more detail the calculations of the Soviet military and the idiosyncrasies of the Soviets."[31]

Despite this substantial methodological shortcoming, the conflict-systems approach was remarkably effective both diagnostically and prescriptively, helping Wohlstetter to become first among equals at RAND by the early sixties. His wife, Roberta—a historian who published in 1962 the definitive study on the Japanese surprise attack on Pearl Harbor—was a consultant there as well. Leavening his haughtiness, Albert also had great charm and, remembered George Quester, who spent a summer at RAND in 1962, considerable "panache." These qualities enabled him to exert a considerable pull on a great many protégés. Quester "got invited out to his house to meet the great man. Roberta Wohlstetter was charming without ever rumpling anybody. He was charming but crossed swords with people."[32]

Sir Michael Howard—who had known Albert when he and Roberta spent a year at the London-based Institute for Strategic Studies (ISS)* writing a study of the Cuban Missile Crisis—refers

* Presently known as the International Institute for Strategic Studies, or IISS.

to Wohlstetter as a "dangerous person."[33] The staying power of this impression, though possibly fueled by a degree of misunderstanding, had much to do with Wohlstetter's forensic aggressiveness. "He could be merciless," admits Schelling.[34] Howard, then a professor at King's College in London, where he founded the War Studies Department, was one of Wohlstetter's interlocutors in London. He was subsequently a professor of history at Oxford and Yale, and with Peter Paret translated and edited the foremost modern edition of Clausewitz's *On War*. Howard was also a decorated World War II veteran, having earned the Military Cross (equivalent to the U.S. Silver Star for gallantry) in the Italian campaign, during the breakout from Salerno into the mountains, for leading a successful assault on a German machine-gun emplacement. Now he is Sir Michael and over eighty, but still sharp and courtly. He describes the engagement as "an old-fashioned bayonet charge, basically. The first thing that happened was that everything went wrong. Everybody got lost. We lost touch with the artillery barrage, and it looked as if the whole thing was going to collapse. And I had one of those military furores which one could have when one was young, and played the part of the gallant young officer and rallied the troops. We did charge uphill, and everybody was so delighted that they gave me a medal. Never again was I going to do anything quite so absurd."[35]

Howard, like many of his contemporaries, was about to ship out to the Far East when the Hiroshima and Nagasaki bombs were dropped. Having already had at least one near-death combat experience, he, too, was "delighted," feeling "a sheer sense of joy that providentially this thing had happened. I'm afraid I couldn't have cared less about the fact that 70,000 people were annihilated in a single moment. My approach was entirely self-centered, as indeed was that of everybody I knew at the time." But he soon got involved in a group at the Royal Institute for

International Affairs* whose purpose it was to discuss the moral aspects of nuclear war. This activity led to the Brighton Conference, the creation of the ISS in 1958, and, through its quarterly journal *Survival,* the development of a Europe-based body of knowledge on nuclear deterrence. He concluded that neither side "really wanted a war anyhow, and it's not all that easy to start a war when neither side wants it. With all other wars that I can think of, one side basically was prepared if necessary to fight a war to get its way even if it was to avoid surrender. In the Cold War, both sides regarded a nuclear war as the worst possible outcome. There was an element of self-deterrence." But his wartime experience, and his immersion in Clausewitz and understanding of Clausewitzean "friction," planted in Howard "a considerable skepticism about neatly laid plans and long-range forecasts of any kind."[36]

Paramount for Howard was an appreciation of the human factor in war of whatever kind. In his view, of the two preeminent nuclear strategists of the 1950s, Brodie took account of this ingredient in nuclear war and Wohlstetter did not. "In his great conflict with Albert Wohlstetter, I was firmly on Bernard's side," Howard proclaims. As far as he was concerned, one of the major sources of uncertainty as to the integrity of nuclear deterrence was Wohlstetter himself. "The one thing which one did really get very scared about was when one would meet Americans who were seriously prepared to think through what they called *prevailing.*" Wohlstetter "tended to want to quantify everything, which made it less real. Especially in the case of nuclear strategy, Europeans found this frightening." For Howard and other European strategists, RAND in general underestimated the "unquantifiable complexity of the strategic world."[37] Howard explains that while Wohlstetter

---

*Informally known as Chatham House.

was "severely logical in his thinking, politics has its own logic—or rather does not have the same kind of logic. He started with the assumption of a total enemy in a zero-sum game—that the Russians were an adversary who could be relied upon to do the worst thing that you could conceive. He worked on the assumption (a) that they were diabolically clever, and (b) that they're going to follow through their logic and destroy us. You then have to assume the worst, and you then get set on an unbreakable escalatory chain of expenditure and hostility."[38]

Unlike Wohlstetter, says Howard, Brodie "did realize that war cannot be detached from its context, that it is heavily involved with politics, and that nuclear war cannot be thought about separately from the people who were fighting it and from what it was all about." Brodie, like Howard, started with the "messy reality of international politics." There was still some continuity between classical and nuclear strategy. Although Howard remained a hard-nosed realist, resigned to the perpetual salience of force in international relations and equally to the necessity of controlling it, he argued that the nuclear bomb was not just another weapon because it substantially eliminated the crucial element of *duration* from war. "The thing is that *if* you can devise a nuclear device that is just another weapon, it fits into the Clausewitzean framework extremely well," muses Howard.

> But he did say something to the effect that if you can conceive of a war which is fought by weapons which are so destructive that in a single instant all the complicating factors of the war are combined in such a way that the war is finished at once, then nothing of what I'm going to write about in the next 5,000 pages is going to be of any validity, but war is not like *that*. One of the major features that complicates war is *duration*. It takes place over quite a long period in which all the factors will gradually

change. It's nice if everything can be made neat after one single great battle—and he then tells you how to fight that great battle; he gets fascinated by it—but he says, it is not like that. Understanding war is really understanding all its complexities, and you don't know what is going to be around the next corner. So if a nuclear weapon is something which can be simply fitted into a normal kind of war, with duration and extent, then it is no more than another kind of bomb. But if [its destructiveness] is on such a huge scale that the duration and extent are abolished, then this is not a war. In order to make nuclear war thinkable at all, there's got to be duration. And those unfortunate people who have to think about a real war with nuclear weapons came up against the problem of what happens after the first nuclear exchange."[39]

Along with Brodie, Howard believed that even with the advent of nuclear weapons, strategic thought was evolutionary and had to be closely informed and determined by history and the path of international affairs. What Clausewitz had said was that "war does not consist of a single short blow," and that "the very nature of war impedes the *simultaneous concentration of all forces*."[40] This reality of restraint in combat left room for restoring "equilibrium"—that is, for bargaining. "Anything omitted out of weakness by one side," he explained, "becomes a real, *objective* reason for the other to reduce its efforts, and the tendency toward extremes is once again reduced by this interaction."[41] Insofar as one thermonuclear salvo could theoretically concentrate enough of a nation's destructive power to end hostilities into a single attack, and thus leave no opportunity for bargaining, nuclear war did not fit into Clausewitz's conception of war. Although some (in particular, Schelling, with his notions of intrawar deterrence) would challenge this formulation, ultimately, Brodie and Howard came to the view that nuclear war marked the end of classical Clause-witzean strategy because it could not be used as an instrument of policy. Wohlstetter agreed, but parted company with them in his conviction that nuclear *weapons* could be politically useful, and rejected the argument that expending intellectual and material resources on remedying strategic vulnerability would lead to dip-lomatic polarization and a hopeless arms race. Although he con-sidered the Soviets intolerant of coexistence and at home with "subversion and intimidation," he doubted that they would attack the United States as long as it remained strong.[42] This belief made Wohlstetter less demonizing than either the Central Intelligence Agency or the U.S. Air Force. He did, however, conclude that the Soviets would value surprise attack in some situations, and there-fore would not foreclose the possibility of that form of under-handedness. Thus, Howard's notion that Wohlstetter sterilized his view of nuclear war of human circumstances and political context is not entirely valid. For Wohlstetter, the human factor did creep into the calculus of nuclear war, but did so asymmetrically: more on the American side than on the Soviet one. His sense was that American officials were in general morally incapable of actu-ally initiating a preventive nuclear first strike, and his rigor de-manded that U.S. nuclear planning therefore should not embrace any such possibility. Programs that did he dismissed as "silliness."[43] It was this conviction of U.S. moral—and not just prudential—constraint that bolstered his advocacy of ballistic missile defense: U.S. strategic invulnerability would discourage a Soviet attack without encouraging an American first strike even though such a move might now be militarily advantageous. At the same time, his deep mistrust of the Soviets made stabilizing deterrence, to Wohl-stetter's way of thinking, an extremely difficult and expensive en-deavor.

Schelling and the Nuance of Nuclear Strategy

Between the Brodie/Howard and Wohlstetter camps there evolved in the United States, through RAND and academic institutions enamored of its precise and searching methodology, a third way: a formal theory of strategy custom-fit to the nuclear age. The most comprehensive and inventive of the formal strategists was Schelling, a self-described "errant economist" and, according to Howard, "the cleverest of the lot."[44] Although a base-level presumption of common rationality carried the day for most of the Cold War, strategists persistently stressed technology over psychology. This bias was tempered only once Schelling's ideas took shape, in the early to mid-sixties.

Born in Oakland in 1921, Schelling's own peripateticism started in college. In 1940, when he was nineteen and enrolled at Berkeley, he decided to take a year abroad. Europe was out because of the war, so he opted for Chile. The university there was a "washout," but he wanted to stay and learn Spanish, so he got a job at the U.S. embassy in Santiago as a night watchman. On December 7, 1941, for a few hours, he was the only American in Chile who knew that the United States was at war with Japan. He soon became assistant to the resident FBI special agent. In 1943, however, Schelling got sick and was sent home on a merchant ship. Diagnosed with stomach ulcers—then classified as a psychiatric disorder—Schelling was deemed too vulnerable to stress and therefore ineligible for military service. He was disappointed, and applied for the American Field Service, which, among other things, sent volunteers to war zones—most famously, Ernest Hemingway to Italy in World War I—to perform noncombat functions such as first aid. But even that organization would not take Schelling on.

The upside was that, with nearly all college-age men in military service, Schelling was afforded very close personal acquaintances with virtually every member of Berkeley's economics department. After six months of graduate work, he took a job in Washington at the Bureau of the Budget, then in 1946 went to Harvard to complete graduate studies. They were interrupted by stints with the Marshall Plan missions to Copenhagen and Paris (for which he forsook a prestigious fellowship). During this period, at the behest of a friend, in his spare time Schelling started devising ways to use algebra to solve macroeconomics problems. His jottings eventually grew into a book, *National Income Behavior,* which was published by McGraw-Hill and accepted by Harvard, in 1951, as Schelling's doctoral dissertation. Meanwhile, the head of the Marshall Plan's Paris office, Averell Harriman, was invited back to the White House to be President Truman's foreign policy adviser. Schelling then had a choice of either going to the White House to work on the staff of the National Security Council or joining the staff of the new Council of Economic Advisers. Despite his academic provenance, Schelling chose the former position and first worked for Harriman, whom Truman named Director of Mutual Security in the Executive Office of the President, and then for Harold Stassen, who succeeded Harriman in Eisenhower's first administration.[45]

In 1953, Schelling left government in favor of Yale University. It was there that he began, in earnest, to apply economics to strategic problems. At Yale, and during a year at RAND in 1958–59, he produced the articles that would form his most elegant theoretical work, *The Strategy of Conflict,* published in 1960. Schelling's method, showcased in that book, was drawn from game theory, and his intellectual preoccupation was not military victory—on which deterrence paradoxically relied—but rather strategic stability. That is: given that deterrence depended on the other side's perception that initiating a war would mean defeat, Schelling wanted to ensure the durability of that perception. As an economist, Schelling was by training and disposition concerned with the equilibrium and control required to ensure that no one parameter of macroeconomic health—unemployment, inflation, growth—ran rampant and upset the orderliness of the national economy. But what made Schelling's theorizing anything but a sterile intellectual exercise in "the dismal science" was his searching eclecticism. He drew, in various nontrivial ways, from economics proper, sociology, and Gestalt psychology. Nevertheless, game theory—a specialized branch of economics— was his primary structural inspiration.

Until Schelling came along, most of the work in game theory as it applied to nuclear strategy had focused on two-person "zero sum" games of pure conflict, in which one side's loss was simply the other's gain. To Schelling, the Cold War strategic confrontation resembled oligopolistic competition, in which relatively few players both compete and collude to reach an equilibrium price. Freedman called the strategic analogue "incomplete antagonism."[46] Thus, adversaries in Schelling's world face the "perpetual . . . need to resolve the vacuum of indeterminacy."[47] The mutual release of some information through bargaining could lead to more agreeable outcomes for both sides. This approach was extremely constructive in vividly dramatizing the basic dilemmas facing the two superpowers. The two seminal games were the Prisoner's Dilemma, which implicated military relationships, and Chicken, which suggested political ones. In the Prisoner's Dilemma, the police are separately questioning two men suspected of jointly committing a felony. If both stay silent, each will receive a light sentence. If one confesses and the other stonewalls, the one will get an even more lenient sentence while the other will be punished for his dishonesty with a lengthy one. If both confess, they will get moderate sentences. Although the best joint outcome would be for both suspects to keep their mouths shut, because the individual outcome for one confession is potentially better, neither can be sure that the other won't double-cross him. Lacking the opportunity to conspire, assuming both suspects were thinking rationally, both would confess. Chicken reprises a "game" in which two macho young men are driving their muscle cars toward each other; whoever swerves first loses. If both swerve, both players stay alive but nobody gets bragging rights; if neither swerves, both die but leave a legacy of true grit. If one swerves, he is humbled while the other gains status. Lacking the confidence that the other will cave, each driver chooses to swerve.* These respective solutions constitute the best of the worst possible outcomes, and for that reason are termed *minimax*.

Both solutions dictate stalemate. The minimax solution to the Prisoner's Dilemma implied the futility of a nuclear arms race. The Chicken solution suggested that nuclear brinkmanship ultimately raised incentives for both sides to relent, but discretion remained as to how long to wait before doing so—before, figuratively speaking, turning the wheel, hitting the brake, or easing up on the gas pedal. That calculation would depend on each player's perception of the other's degree of recklessness, which could in turn be theatrically manipulated in any number of ways—declaratory policy, military deployments, and choices of weapons systems, to name a few. Compounding this difficulty

---

*A variation on Chicken occurs in the 1955 movie *Rebel Without a Cause*. James Dean's character and his antagonist play a game of nerve in which each of them drives a car toward a cliff, and the first of them to jump out of his car loses. Dean's antagonist "wins" (i.e., dies) because the strap of his leather jacket gets caught on the handle of the car door. That dramatization illustrates and confirms one of the salient risks of brinkmanship: even if one intends only to flirt with disaster, unforeseen circumstances can precipitate it.

was a countervailing incentive to hang tough in one confrontation for fear of being susceptible to coercion in subsequent
ones. Losing a game of nuclear Chicken did not necessarily entail
nuclear war but more likely would mean backing off—or "blink-
ing"—in the apparent recognition of the winner's superior military strength. That, in turn, it would involve a loss of prestige
that reduced the leverage of the loser's nuclear weapons over
world affairs and, consequently, its freedom of action. The
upshot was indefinitely escalating military expenditure to ensure
maximum flexibility in as wide a range of contingencies as
possible—and perpetual danger. Schelling and others recognized
that in light of these disturbing wrinkles in the game-theoretical
characterizations of the nuclear standoff, the West needed a strategy of *stable* conflict.

Given the fundamentally bipolar nature of the Cold War strategic situation, the simple two-person assumption made sense.*
Schelling himself comments that "the intercontinental strategic
nuclear confrontation was about as simple as any confrontation
since maybe the Peloponnesian War. It was essentially bilateral;
it didn't involve knowing in detail anything about the adversary;
it involved a very limited variety of weapons—essentially, nu-

---

* Schelling has also expressed wistful frustration that for all of his and his strategic brethren's supposed creativity and intelligence, "how in the world could it
have taken so long to straighten out such simple little issues?" Only in 1958,
when Schelling and Wohlstetter, among others, were preparing a U.S. delegation
for negotiations in Geneva on preventing nuclear surprise attack did they drive
home the point that "the problem of surprise attack was that you couldn't deter it
if you could be surprised—that you had to be either sure of your warning or sure
of your invulnerability. There was no way to be sure of your warning, and therefore you had to think about the invulnerability of the force. That may have been
the first time that anybody in State or Defense or the White House ever thought
of surprise attack as essentially the problem of SAC vulnerability. Eventually,
that gave rise to Eisenhower's putting in an airborne alert system, under which
there would always be some aircraft safely in the air in case of an attack on the
bases. Now, that is a very simple idea." Author interview with Thomas C. Schelling,
Bethesda, Maryland, March 9, 2004.

clear explosives and long-range delivery systems or, in Europe, intermediate-range. It allowed—for me at least—analogies with a whole variety of deterrence issues: crime, family, business relations, labor-management relations. So there was a big literature on deterrence that people could exploit in thinking about East-West relations. And despite the importance of classified information, there wasn't a lot of *vital* theoretical importance that was secret."[48]

As simple as Schelling himself may have regarded the intellectual task, he approached it in a way that nobody else had thought to do. He challenged the notion implicit in the zero-sum assumption that the United States and the Soviet Union could not have shared interests—the most obvious one being the avoidance of humanitarian and social catastrophe. Consequently, he concentrated on two-person *non*-zero-sum games, which had a cooperative as well as a competitive dimension. The most powerful criticisms of this methodology carried over from the attacks on Wohlstetter's use of conflict systems. For one, it assumed the rationality of the actors involved, failing to account for the subjectivity and emotional stresses that occurred in real-life situations of conflict—part of Clausewitz's friction. One of the most vivid and alarming aspects of the Cuban Missile Crisis, which resembled a game of Chicken, was that at least one of the principal participants—Soviet premier Nikita Khrushchev—had a well-deserved reputation for *irrational* behavior, which he seemed to have burnished precisely by deploying the nuclear missiles in Cuba. If the very players of the game had initiated it through irrational conduct, why should they subsequently be expected to behave rationally? And the game construct artificially assumed a static set of values and interests when in fact emergent circumstances often, if not always, dictated shifts and mutations in values and interests. The Kennedy administration did not in principle countenance nuclear bargaining with the Soviets, but undertook it—albeit secretly—in agreeing to dismantle its Jupiter missiles in Turkey sometime after the Soviets withdrew their missiles from Cuba for the sake of avoiding nuclear war. Schelling, however, eluded the full force of these criticisms in noting that game theory's utility lay not in predicting actual strategic behavior but rather in providing a framework whereby strategists could distill past military conduct into an essential dynamic that could then be applied to a nuclear context for which there was no real experience to draw from.[49]

He reflects:

If the question is, can an understanding of game theory help you think about strategic issues, for me the answer is yes. If you asked, does game theory itself—other than providing a few concepts and a few ideas about how to organize the quantitative aspects of a problem—really ever solve an important problem, I think the answer is no. I would never have dreamed of approaching Robert McNamara and using game theory to explain anything to him. But I often tell my students that if they understand some game theory, they'll often find it quite illuminating in thinking about a given subject. There are things discovered through game theory that might not have occurred to people. The prisoner's dilemma is an esoteric situation, but I always try to show my students that analytically it is really a pervasive situation that doesn't inherently have to do with whether you want criminals to confess and all that. I often argue that the greatest invention in all of mathematics was the equal sign, the greatest invention in business management was double-entry bookkeeping, the greatest invention in economics was national accounts, and the greatest invention in game theory was the payoff matrix. It's just a way of ordering things. So I tell people to learn to put a problem—if it's a two-person problem—into a matrix because you'll often discover that the situation that you thought was unique turns out to have two or three or four different ways of appearing; or sometimes when you have two things you think are different, when you make up a matrix, you discover they're identical; or sometimes you think of three possibilities and if you put them into a matrix you discover a fourth possibility."[50]

In short, game theory's utility lay in its very abstraction, insofar as that abstraction was premised on empirical facts that otherwise had no systematic link to the untrammeled ground of nuclear war. But, continues Schelling, "I would say if you asked Albert Wohlstetter or Herman Kahn or Bernard Brodie, they would say that strategy had little to do with game theory."[51]

Schelling's main theoretical work on game theory as a basis for nuclear strategy was *The Strategy of Conflict,* published in 1960, but *Strategy and Arms Control,* which he wrote with Morton Halperin and appeared in 1961, and *Arms and Influence,* which emerged in 1966, exerted the heaviest influence on actual policy. True to his notion that games inspired solutions to real problems rather than directly prescribing them, these latter books contained very little overt game theory. In any event, while the formal strategists did not point toward resolving the U.S.-Soviet conflict or military victory, they did hold out a concrete possibility of strategic stability—an urgent need since Wohlstetter's demonstration of the delicateness of the nuclear balance—until what Snyder called the "balance of resolve" shifted decisively in favor of the West. To wit, Schelling came around to the view that introducing cooperation into bilateral relations between the two superpowers could lower risks of escalation to the nuclear level and still allow both sides a given level of security.

Schelling's strategic revelation turned on the distinction

between what he called brute force and the power to hurt, which correspond roughly to counterforce and countervalue capabilities. He observed that in military terms, brute force for taking out an enemy's war-fighting capacity was fundamentally offensive: a first-strike capability. The power to hurt people, on the other hand, was strictly defensive: a second-strike capability. The policy implications were profoundly counterintuitive: nuclear weapons that imperiled mainly populations were to be *encouraged,* those that jeopardized military targets *discouraged.* Moreover, from the standpoint of stability, this held for both sides, not just one. The practical consequence of these conclusions, elucidated by Schelling and Halperin, was arms control—a form of bargaining whereby the two sides could agree to force structures that favored defensive weapons over offensive ones and therefore minimized the temptation to strike first and reinforced deterrence. Among the corollaries to such an approach was a preference for very large nuclear force structures: the greater the redundancy of retaliatory countervalue weapons, the more daunting any prospect of preemptively eliminating them, and the more difficult it was for the other side to increase its advantage through cheating at the numerical margins. Thus, arms control was anathema to both disarmament and brinkmanship—a feature that enabled both the military and the liberal establishment to warm to the idea.*

Wohlstetter would never have disputed Schelling's eminence

---

*By exalting avoidance of nuclear use as the very purpose of nuclear arsenals, this ambivalence also took the wind out of the sails of nuclear abolitionists who argued that nuclear weapons breached the West's tradition of civilized warfare and the principle of proportionality enshrined in the laws of armed conflict. Still, the abolitionists tended to insist that the mere possession of nukes—however they were characterized—was immoral in that it implied at least a contingent intention to use them. Any protestation that they were needed simply for the sake of retaliation was arch, they added, because retaliation for the abject devastation of a first strike would be meaninglessly gratuitous.

as a synthesizer of basic research, but regarded his own work on vulnerability as the root of mature nuclear strategy. Writing to Howard in 1968, Wohlstetter commented that this stance of his "is not to minimize the importance of Schelling's keen analysis of the relations of the problems of surprise attack, deterrence, and disarmament. His essay [i.e., *The Strategy of Conflict*] was an illuminating example of the sort of basic clarification that can proceed without new empirical effort on the foundation of intuition, common sense, and previous empirical work. But the discovery of the vulnerabilities of strategic forces owes its primary debt to the tradition of operational research and empirical systems analysis" perfected at RAND in the 1950s.[52] Having made that assertion, Wohlstetter would have had to concede that Schelling endowed nuclear strategy with a level of nuance and policy sophistication that it would not otherwise have possessed.

There were significant elements of pragmatism in Schelling's approach, as there were in Wohlstetter's. But Schelling's was a more expansive and searching form of pragmatism that at least at times seemed to verge on questioning the wisdom of Western absolutism and intolerance if the alternative was nuclear holocaust. As Freedman noted, "the prospect of an all-engulfing nuclear war reminded the super-powers that they should not push their differences over ideology and geopolitical interests too far. The issue was how far was too far."[53] There was always, in the ether, the risk of self-marginalization in flirting with any position that smelled like a "better red than dead." Schelling did not question the overarching validity and necessity of deterrence, nor the latency of nuclear weapons in world affairs. Against the backdrop of constant tension between the moral disasters of nuclear use and geopolitical capitulation, Schelling put a multiplicity of ideas to man's practical use—avoiding nuclear holocaust being of arguably the ultimate practicality—without insisting on theoretical elegance or stricture when it clashed with common sense. He was not naive enough to believe that second-strike deterrence—pristine as it was in theory, entrenched as it was in doctrine—would stave off subnuclear conflicts that nonetheless had the potential to spiral to the nuclear level; any such notion was discarded with the deconstruction of massive retaliation. Thus, his work on bargaining and Kahn's and Halperin's on escalation converged to address the problem of "intrawar deterrence."

Schelling's single most important contribution to the theory of intrawar deterrence was his observation that those engaged in conflict would usually develop a common symbolic focal point— perhaps a physical or geographical point, perhaps a distinctive operational level of warfare—that dictated boundaries and limits. This phenomenon was particularly vivid in the Korean War, in which the Yalu River represented what Schelling called a "mutually identifiable resting place" from which each side would neither retreat nor advance for fear of appeasement or escalation, respectively.[54] Such a combination of resiliency and restraint constituted a form of tacit bargaining. As he wrote, with typically deceptive simplicity, "The Yalu was like the Rubicon. To cross it would have signaled something."[55] For Schelling, if arms control consolidated the stability of prewar deterrence, resting places did the same for intrawar deterrence. Schelling's theory was couched in elastic general concepts, and therefore was susceptible to nuanced application in a wide variety of situations. It justifiably prevailed over modified notions of massive retaliation under which preannounced threatened limited nuclear reprisals were supposed to hold a conflict at the conventional level. Since such threats would not be credible absent conventional forces to maintain the status quo during bargaining, adequate conven-

tional forces remained indispensable for keeping a conflict from
going nuclear.

Schelling's ideas seemed most useful for generals and planners in actual battle, as opposed to strategists constructing an elegant scenario-based theory. One such theory—Herman Kahn's
"escalation dominance"—implied that one side's deterrent would
be assured in the broadest range of situations if it enjoyed superiority at each level of escalation. The problem was that such
superiority would tempt the side with the edge to exploit its advantage, and cut against the overall emphasis on parity as the
pinion of stability. To deal with this fissure in the theory of stable
deterrence, Schelling's notion of "the threat that leaves something
to chance" was available.[56] This species of threat was primarily
an instrument of intrawar "compellence"—a term coined by
Schelling meaning one side's inducement to another to act rather
than, as with deterrence, to refrain from acting. This could mean
anything from giving up a few prisoners to handing over territory gained. The implementation of such a threat was contingent
on circumstances outside the control of the threatening party.
Like deterrence itself, this species of threat had the paradoxical
quality of rationally deploying the possibility of irrationality. It
was a way of saying, "If X doesn't occur, I cannot be responsible
for my actions." The objective was to "relinquish the initiative"
for escalation to the other side and, conversely, to afford it the
"last clear chance" to avoid it.[57]

This amounted to tactical brinkmanship, and Schelling was
aware that it could transmogrify superpower military confrontation into a choreography of competitive risk-taking—a game of
Chicken. But its saving grace, he suggested, was that it gave the
weaker party an opportunity to save face. And that, he said famously and, at first blush, counterintuitively, "is one of the few

things worth fighting over," for "'face' is merely the interdependence of a country's commitments; it is a country's reputation for action, the expectation other countries have about its behavior."[58] The crude application of such reasoning—disregarding Schelling's admonition that saving face also required a country not to encourage gratuitous tests of its credibility where vital interests were not at stake—led to excessive commitments to Vietnam, while a more sensible iteration produced a better result in Korea. In the more immediate context, the threat that left something to chance reintroduced an equalizer into potentially nuclear war scenarios without negating the desirability of escalation dominance. And indeed, manipulating perceptions of risk to enforce a certain kind of behavior seemed far more realistic and sensible than actually using nuclear weapons or moving closer to their use.

Says Freedman:

> Schelling remains my hero because he was never trapped by his own methodology. There was an intellectual subtlety and imagination. You can still read him now and want to take notes and think about how his work applies to contemporary issues. Wohlstetter, I think, you can admire because he was incredibly systematic and rigorous if you accepted his starting premises, but his starting premises weren't always well thought out. Schelling had a better feel for the fluidity of political life and the possibilities of misinterpretation. And there's sort of a playfulness in his work that some people may find improper, but I think it's what all academics are supposed to do: they're not in fact the policymaker, and what they're supposed to do is challenge the public or the policymaker to look at issues from a different angle. I think he was always able to do that.[59]

Most crucially, though, Schelling took Wohlstetter's primal concern—strategic vulnerability—and made it the centerpiece of strategic nuclear stability. At the time, his dispensation addressed Wohlstetter's chief worry while leaving the fundamental problem of vulnerability nakedly unremedied. Intuitively, this seemed a perverse and retrograde outcome, and the fundamental strategic debate shifted from how to establish stability to whether vulnerability was a morally and politically appropriate basis for it. Significant members of the strategic community believed that it was not. The most conspicuous, if not the most influential, was Herman Kahn.

Herman Kahn's Nuclear Celebrity

During the 1950s, Nevada was essentially a proving ground for atmospheric atomic explosions, the United States was obliterating entire Pacific islands with hydrogen bomb blasts, and the news routinely carried aerial photographs and footage of the fireballs and the mushroom clouds. Fallout shelter drills for schoolchildren—described as such by the teachers but never satisfactorily explained—became as common as fire musters. In 1961, the Soviet Union's attempt to take full control of Berlin nearly triggered a ground war in Europe between the two superpowers that was commonly viewed as the first step to nuclear war, and prompted the United States to contemplate seriously a nuclear first strike. In 1962, the Cuban Missile Crisis brought the Soviet Union and the United States even closer to nuclear war, as the United States resorted to a naval blockade to compel the Soviets to withdraw nuclear missiles from Cuba. These real-world near catastrophes brought home to the common man the soul-racking tension of, in Kennedy's phrase, "humiliation or holocaust."[60] In that psychic environment, with real war such a horrible proposition and the avoidance of war crystallizing into official policy, think tankers were running a virtual battlefield on which the most inventive thinking about nuclear war-fighting was teased out. Most chose, discreetly, to do so away from easy public view. Herman Kahn was the exception.

Kahn's family rues the fact that his principal identifying feature remains his obesity rather than his brilliance. But it was really both, along with his off-color wit, that made him nuclear strategy's first celebrity. A culture of doom and a socialized paranoia were on prominent display in popular media—soberly so in novels like *Fail-safe,* satirically so in Stanley Kubrick's movie *Dr. Strangelove or: How I Learned to Stop Worrying and Love the Bomb,* which appeared in 1962 and 1964, respectively. Kahn's physical mass and somewhat geeky cast—he wore thick glasses, perspired, spoke very fast, and often stammered—seemed to reflect these feelings and all their shades. He appeared resolutely professorial and physically inept, and thus unable to function as any kind of soldier (though he had, in fact, been one). This countenance reinforced rising myths. World War III would be planned not in briefing rooms by generals but in armchairs by mad geniuses, and fought to conclusion—if ever it was—not on battlefields by soldiers with guns but from underground bunkers by sinister men pressing buttons. And it would be they who survived, as everyone in the cities and on the surface of the earth perished. Herman Kahn did not exactly exploit these grave existential worries, but he did embrace them with a certain salacious intellectual glee. His stock-in-trade consisted of discursive statistic-laden analyses of the consequences of nuclear war, often breezily qualified by covering phrases like "barring bad luck and bad management" (his favorite), and culminating in obtusely cold-blooded rankings of trade-offs that involved tens of millions of lives. What gained traction in the American mind was not tailored force structures, controlled rules of nuclear engagement, or arms control. Most people just couldn't wrap their heads around the idea that fine-tuning the policies dictating the use of something as destructive as a nuclear bomb could really make them any safer if the United States and the Soviets decided to duke it out. It was civil defense that provided the greatest comfort. The most vigorous advocate of civil defense was Herman Kahn.

Kahn's arrival at RAND in 1948 was almost as serendipitous as Wohlstetter's three years later. Born in 1922 to working-class Jewish immigrants in Bayonne, New Jersey, Kahn was raised in the Bronx until his parents divorced when he was ten, whereupon he moved with his mother and siblings to Los Angeles. He went to college at UCLA, during World War II served in the Army (famously scoring a record high on its intelligence test) as a communications NCO in Burma, and attended graduate school at the California Institute of Technology. There he pursued a doctorate in physics until he ran out of money, at which point he planned to go into the real estate business. Sam Cohen, an old friend who had become a physicist, then suggested that Kahn instead offer his services to RAND. He was hired to work in the physics division, and toiled mainly on bomb design and the effects of nuclear explosions into the mid-1950s. Only later, spurred by Wohlstetter's basing studies, did he tackle broader nuclear strategy.

The all-engulfing scope of nuclear strategy suited his large appetite, while its gravity and sobriety afforded his obtuseness maximum effect. "No one could tell Herman not to do anything," reflected Wohlstetter in 1989, and "he would do anything to be outrageous."[61] Andrew Marshall—at whose wedding Kahn was best man—recalls that Kahn had persuaded Edward Quade, who developed a RAND course on "appreciation" of operations analysis for Air Force officers, to incorporate into the course a lecture by Kahn on the pitfalls of exactly that kind of analysis. "Herman was an immensely bright, quick-witted, humorous guy, and a terrific success as a platform speaker." From that enterprise,

Kahn became interested in civil defense. "There had been an earlier study at RAND by [economist] Jack Hirshleifer, but the RAND management was not very supportive of civil defense. The Air Force attitude was negative—that it was a diversion from thinking about offensive systems."[62] At the time, admonishes Harry Rowen, Kahn "was not a dominant figure at all. He was just a very energetic, irreverent life force, and great fun to be with. But he had a lot of competition. The talent pool was deep."[63]

Kahn couldn't shake the appeal of first-strike deterrence coupled with civil defense. The prevailing view was that as long as the United States could guarantee that enough of its nuclear force would survive a Soviet first strike to fire back a crippling second strike, the Soviets wouldn't dare attack in the first place. This was second-strike deterrence, and it became entrenched in RAND thinking. Civil defense was not inherently inconsistent with second-strike deterrence, but the Air Force frowned on it in significant part because it would drain money from offensive programs. And the Air Force was RAND's most prized client. While RAND management was entrepreneurial in urging the Air Force to rethink operationally contraindicated plans—such as the forward basing arrangement—it was far less inclined to press for shifts in thinking that were inessential to a basic strategy with which it concurred. RAND also would not jeopardize its relationship with the Air Force by shopping ideas that the Air Force didn't like to other federal agencies or competing services. Later in the sixties, when the Office of the Secretary of Defense jousted with the Air Force for RAND's affections, RAND agreed to change its practices so as to avoid any conflict of interest.[64] Suffice it to say that at the beginning of the decade, nobody at RAND was willing to join Kahn in challenging Air Force priorities.

For Kahn, the marginalization of civil defense was not just

some minor casualty of intramural resource competition. Among rather few others, he was skeptical of the tendency of American strategists to mirror image. He was convinced that the Soviets' own seriousness about civil defense reflected a greater willingness than the Americans to contemplate nuclear war. They seemed to believe that their society and infrastructure could survive a nuclear strike. If so, they might well take the risk of striking first and enduring the promised retaliation if pushed to the brink. In that light, mused Kahn, the United States had to change its tune with more robust civil-defense programs of its own to mirror Soviet resolve and strengthen its deterrent. That is, the American people as a whole, mobilizing collectively, had to convince the Soviets that they were resilient enough to absorb a first strike and then some, so as to cast doubt on any Soviet calculations of a quick total victory and put them on the defensive, in fear of an American first strike. This dispensation would not only produce a reliable deterrent, but also permit the United States greater freedom of action around the world. Being in a constant state of agitated alert was simply the price Americans would have to pay. Reassurance rather than "war hysteria and militarism" would prevail, he declared, from "appropriate precautions taken as a result of realistic fears."[65]

If Kahn could not win his argument within RAND, he might have better luck being heard in the larger world. After a dozen years at RAND, he left to found the Hudson Institute in Croton-on-Hudson, New York. At Hudson, said Wohlstetter, Kahn "was the King and he could do anything he wanted, and aside from Don Brennan [Kahn's deputy at Hudson] . . . there was no one who could really challenge him, whereas Herman got challenged at least five times a day" at RAND.[66] With appreciable Defense Department and private funding, the Hudson Institute became Kahn's mouthpiece for civil defense as he and his acolytes shouted against an American public and defense establishment that increasingly embraced offensive capabilities and the very prospect of nuclear genocide as the linchpins of deterrence. If they were successful, to be sure, there would be no need for shelters; but if they weren't, only shelters would save America. Yet Kahn was anything but a peacenik. Kahn proceeded to antagonize the abolitionists by expressing doubts even about the stability of mutual deterrence as refined through arms control, and stressed the need to strengthen that deterrent by showing willingness to contemplate nuclear war through preparations for nuclear attack. Kahn certainly had the public's ear, if not the Pentagon's. His mission was to savage—with all the bluster and swagger that his 350-pound body could generate—the notion that nuclear equivalence between the United States and the Soviet Union made nuclear war unthinkable. In his view, the United States needed to continue to pose a credible first-strike counterforce threat to keep the USSR at bay. And to do so in the face of increasing Soviet capabilities, Americans had to embrace what it meant to *survive* a retaliatory nuclear attack, and to accept the psychological challenge of that possibility. "It depends on will as well as capability," he noted.[67] It meant taking civil defense seriously.

Kahn had a formidable mind, and made large and lasting contributions to strategy. He was also an irrepressible showman and became something of a huckster for nuclear strategy. His assumption of this role may have catered to a natural public need to give the Cold War a human face. But it also made him a target of both fellow nuclear strategists, some of whom regarded him as caricaturing their field, and their fiercest critics, who saw in Kahn all the hubris and evil of humankind that had brought nuclear weapons into being and tightened their awful grip on daily life. Kahn was the first to insert the word *only* in front of comparative estimates of civilian deaths that ran into the millions; he pondered the "trading of cities"; he asked, "How much tragedy is acceptable?" but also "Will the survivors envy the dead?" While Kahn drew fire for cracking wise about nuclear holocaust (dubbing all-out nuclear conflict "wargasm"), he was also castigated for his "icy rationality" in the face of such appalling prospects of human loss. To this charge, in *Thinking About the Unthinkable,* his popular treatment of nuclear war, he cheerfully responded: "Would you prefer a warm, human error? Do you feel better with a nice emotional mistake? We cannot expect good discussion of security problems if we are going to label every attempt at detachment as callous, every attempt at objectivity as immoral. . . . Technical details are not the only important operative facts. Human and moral factors must always be considered. They must never be missing from policies and public discussion. But emotionalism and sentimentality, as opposed to morality and concern, only confuse the debates. Nor can experts be expected to repeat 'If, heaven forbid . . . ,' before every sentence."[68]

One of Kahn's essential convictions was that an apocalyptic war could be won, and it stemmed from his refusal to divorce human fallibility from strategic calculations. For him, the scenarios that governed policy had to take account of the irrationality of people and their consequent unpredictability. Schelling, who had less extreme and more nuanced views than Kahn but counted him a great friend, "regarded him as someone who was as sincerely interested in avoiding wartime casualties as a person can be. Also, comparing him to Kaufmann, Brodie, and Wohlstetter, Herman was the cleverest of them all. He could think of what you might call games to illustrate strategic principles"—which also happened to be Schelling's métier. If Wohlstetter stood aloof, Kahn stayed in the trenches of humanity. "He was a jovial, happy gourmet," recalled Schelling. "He liked to claim that he knew as much about delicatessens in Manhattan as he did about nuclear strategy."[69] Schelling—short, slight, and steely—may have been Kahn's physical opposite. But where Wohlstetter's chief gift was analytical rigor, theirs lay in bountiful strategic imagination.

Whereas for someone like Brodie considerations of human fallibility suggested mainly that men on the verge of Armageddon would ultimately back off, Kahn and Schelling felt the need to account fully for the second-order possibility that, albeit against intuition and expectation, they might not. Kahn, however, went for the common man's jugular in a way that Schelling did not. While the ominous cast of his books' titles—*On Thermonuclear War* and *Thinking About the Unthinkable*—made them more notorious than widely read, they also made Kahn a figure of popular culture.* He mused about being "one of the ten most famous obscure Americans," and was approached by the Keedick Lecture Bureau to become a client along with the likes of Walter Slezak and Amy Vanderbilt (Kahn politely declined).[70]

Kahn would acquire by far the biggest public reputation and the greatest fame among the nuclear strategists. Wohlstetter had some exposure outside professional circles, but it was limited and fraught. He had written an article for *Life* magazine titled "The National Purpose" (noting that the United States had multiple purposes that sometimes contradict one another) but undoubtedly rued the experience: due to the inaccuracy of the galleys he received, he obtained an injunction against its publication until he could correct certain egregious errors, and had to miss his daughter Joan's high school graduation on account of the mess.[71]

---

*It has been reported that *On Thermonuclear War* sold more than fourteen thousand copies during the first three months of publication. Louis Menand, "Fat Man," *The New Yorker,* June 27, 2005, p. 95. As of fall 1963, *Thinking About the Unthinkable* had sold about fifty-five hundred copies in hardcover. Royalty Statement to Herman Kahn from Horizon Press Inc., October 3, 1963; from the Hudson Institute Papers, National Defense University Special Collections, Fort McNair, Washington, DC.

On balance, Wohlstetter was too exacting an analyst for general-interest media, where Kahn's tendentiousness and ease with sweeping qualification as well as gross generalization suited him to it. He and Wohlstetter were good friends, but it was a testy relationship. Two years after Kahn's death, which had genuinely saddened Wohlstetter, he remembered: "I loved Herman, but he exasperated me. And one of the reasons was that he would always have sets of things which in a Boolean diagram were supposed to be mutually exclusive sets, but they always overlapped with something else. He lectured frequently on the methodology of the base study, and he would say that they [SAC] just had a single strike and return. And I would say, 'Herman, take a look at it. These are campaigns, they cover a month or two!'"[72]

Kahn himself was featured in one of the *New York Times Sunday Magazine*'s personality pieces. He also spoke frequently and published abundantly in popular magazines and Sunday newspaper supplements, which, coupled with his irrepressible penchant for the last word, led him to have an extraordinarily intellectual engagement with the wider public. Responding to a letter from one Carl E. Rosenfeld of San Francisco, who had heard Kahn speak at Berkeley and read an article he wrote for *Fortune* on his escalation ladder, Kahn ominously wrote: "I wish I could assure you, as a 'simple-minded citizen,' that I could be trusted to keep us from an insensate holocaust, but unfortunately nobody can be trusted to do that. But I hope you will accept my assurance that that is what is intended to result from the analysis and that our effort may even be helpful in that endeavor."[73] His efforts were not altogether for naught. Supporters of civil defense were primarily liberals, who viewed it as a less provocative cause than offensive weapons, and they got a boost when Kennedy was elected. By 1961, research was under way on antiballistic missiles, a fallout shelter program was revived with an eye toward saving up to fifteen million lives in a major nuclear exchange, and two million dosimeters (which measure radiation levels) were distributed. That year there were full-page ads in the *Boston Globe* taken out by contractors offering to build customers fallout shelters. During the same period, the school fallout shelter drills peaked.

What bothered policy makers and other strategists about Kahn, though, was his apparent belief that nuclear war was winnable. The man in the street who disdained American defeatism, of course, championed Kahn's moral courage. And Rowen regarded the ascription of "winnability" to Kahn as unappreciative at best. "It wasn't so much winnability. It was that many people would still be alive, and have stakes, interests. One needed to think of any possible use of nuclear weapons as being followed by something else," says Rowen. "What one wanted to do was to make what happened not so catastrophic. There was a lot at stake for round two. And there was an enormous tendency for people not to look beyond initial action. In thinking about nuclear terrorism, we need to ask, how do people react? This remains an unknown."[74] "So civil defense," recalls Schelling, "for a moment looked as if it was going somewhere. But it became not only laughable but also subject to the [criticism] that it's just a monstrous way of taking war seriously."[75]

The theatrical relish that Kahn showed in discussing the prospect of nuclear war also made him a dubious spokesman for civil defense. A letter to Kahn from Muriel S. Short of Marin County, California, reacting to a televised debate on "The Nation's Future" between Kahn and Harrison Brown, exemplified the layman's scorn:

For a man who is on the record as saying that thermonuclear war is feasible, involving as it would the deaths of probably ninety percent of the population at the first attack, your concern for the number of children suffering from mutations was interesting but hardly believable. I also do not believe you when you say the shelter program was set up for humane reasons, when you have stated elsewhere that the [fallout] shelter program is "an offensive weapon," and an adjunct to the military posture. This last statement I do believe. It is also the cruelest deception ever played on any people, an unprincipled hoax which is, however, self-defeating. The civil defense "program" is such a nonsensical chaos, that it is both a source of amusement and shame to this country. . . . It appears, however, that there are many salesmen for the program, but very few customers. The American public is not buying this unscrupulous scheme, which speaks well of their intelligence and pride.[76]

The overriding (if impressionistic) sense of futility on the part of the public, the far greater marginal cost of defense over offense, and the fear that investment in defense would create a false sense of security squelched the civil defense program by 1965. In an exchange with Joseph Romm, assistant director for Civil Defense at the Pentagon, Romm characterized Kahn's more robust proposals for firming up existing programs as "desperate" and "unrealistic." Kahn reacted with his own orthodoxy and his usual energy:

The "desperate" programs do seem "unrealistic" if we are thinking about normal conditions. But as you know the important point is that we are thinking about a situation in which millions of lives are at stake, and we are subjected to an immediate and credible threat. Under these conditions, provided there has been adequate planning and reasonably competent leadership, experience with intense disasters suggests that most people will rise to the occasion. Even if the measures themselves cause great loss of life and property, they still may be counted "successful" under sufficiently desperate conditions. And there is no need to *guarantee* that such an evacuation will work—we argue only that the option seems good enough that it ought to be kept available for the possibility of a situation in which there is nothing better left to try. Personally, I would go further, and argue that disaster studies, experiences in World War II, etc., all suggest that social control would probably remain "adequate," if not "satisfactory," even under desperate circumstances such as a crisis evacuation.[77]

Kahn seemed aware that his vision of possible nuclear futures embodied a certain hopelessness, or at least desperation, and that may have moved him toward a more systematic and comforting way of thinking about nuclear war. Kahn's "escalation ladder," with its celebrated forty-four rungs, defined discrete quanta of escalation with an eye toward ensuring that the United States would prevail in a conflict as hostilities enlarged. Over the full range, Kahn identified six "firebreaks": symbolic thresholds—the most significant was conventional/nuclear—the crossing of which signaled profound changes in the political implications of war. The American ladder leveraged nuclear superiority, the Soviet ladder conventional superiority. The ultimate state of war was a nuclear "spasm" of all-out mutual destruction. Under Kahn's scheme, nuclear use first occurred in the fifteenth stage, although not all subsequent stages involved nukes. This implied the viability of intrawar deterrence at the nuclear level. More particularly, one side's capacity to deter the other side from escalating hostilities to the next stage rested on its perceived military superiority over the enemy within that next stage. This was escalation dominance.[78] It was a useful and clever concept—not so much for guiding the conduct of actual war as an eventual guide to force planning, and inspired the contemporary U.S. imperative of "full-spectrum dominance." The discomfiting wrinkle in Kahn's theory of escalation was that escalation dominance required an asymmetry in capabilities at a given level of escalation, which would tend to embolden the side with the edge and thus be destabilizing. Schelling, as noted, found a way to finesse the problem. Nevertheless, in the fullness of time, Kahn's work has come to be seen as symbolizing an era of intellectual adventurousness and brinkmanship rather than representing the most rigorous and prudent products of that era.

The escalation ladder was a genuine contribution to strategy, but Kahn's own seriously intended work often smacked of self-parody, too. His rococo antireductive tendency came to the fore in his best-known mental invention—the Doomsday Machine—which he articulated in *On Thermonuclear War.* In a tone that was sardonically conversational rather than soberly pedagogical, he wrote:

A Doomsday weapons system might be imaginatively (and entirely hypothetically) described as follows: Assume that for, say, ten billion dollars we could build a device whose only function is to destroy all human life. The device is protected from enemy action (perhaps by being put thousands of feet underground) and then connected to a computer which is in turn connected, by a reliable communications system, to hundreds of sensory devices all over the United States. The computer would be programmed so that if, say, five nuclear bombs exploded over the United States, the device would be triggered and the earth destroyed.... Doomsday Machines are likely to be better than any current or proposed competitor for deterrence.... [But] the Doomsday Machine is not sufficiently *controllable.* Even though it maximizes the probability that deterrence will work, ... it is totally unsatisfactory. One must still examine the consequences of a failure. In this case a failure kills too many people and kills them too automatically."[79]

On War was published posthumously in 1832, but Clausewitz was a long-established military thinker to whom broad respect had been accorded in his lifetime. The fact that he was himself a military officer in an epoch of war, attempting to glean lessons from Napoleon's defeat of Prussia, no doubt promoted admiration rather than disdain. By contrast, Kahn's countenance as a flamboyant egghead, an armchair strategist, in a triumphal pre-Vietnam America, made him an easier target for abuse. Used to avuncular generals like Eisenhower or swashbuckling types like Patton and MacArthur, Americans were unaccustomed to being lectured on war by fat, clever civilians. Thus, despite Kahn's idiosyncratic charisma and a degree of solemn thoughtfulness that his bombastic style often belied, disdain for his brand of apocalyptic thought mounted. In a splenetic review in *Scientific American* in 1961, mathematician James Newman labeled *On Thermonuclear War* "a moral tract on mass murder; how to plan it, how to commit it, how to get away with it, how to justify it," and priggishly questioned Kahn's very existence, archly speculating that he was a figment of government propaganda.[80] As a child, Debbie Kahn, Herman's daughter, was accused by other kids of being the child of a "monster."[81] When Hudson sought influential board members, like former secretary of state and defense Dean Acheson and former assistant secretary of war and World Bank president John J. McCloy, they politely declined.[82]

Kahn himself was sensitive. It is well known now and was at the time that Kahn helped inspire Stanley Kubrick's paranoid, megalomaniacal Dr. Strangelove in the eponymous 1964 movie—its initial working title was *The Delicate Balance of Terror,* after Wohlstetter's seminal article, but changed when Kubrick decided that nuclear war was worthy of satire—and Kubrick's screenplay

lifted whole concepts and passages from *On Thermonuclear War.**
Kahn himself added to the popular conflation of himself with
the fictional Dr. Strangelove when he croaked cryptically that
Strangelove was "too creative" to last even three weeks in the
Pentagon.[83] In 1964, however, the London *Sunday Times* published an article titled "The Prototype for Dr. Strangelove" that
not only portrayed Kahn as such but also snidely stated, alluding
to the movie's subtitle, that "he collects a million dollars for worrying about The Bomb."[84] Kahn took offense and sought legal
advice as to whether he might sue the newspaper under British
libel laws, which accord a plaintiff far greater leeway than their
U.S. counterparts. His New York lawyers consulted London co-
counsel and concluded that the article probably was defamatory.
The Strangelove character—played by Peter Sellers as a sexually
excitable wheelchair-bound scientist with an uncontrollable
black-gloved hand and a vaguely Germanic accent—had been
described as, among other things, a fanatic ex-Nazi. This interpretation would have been especially opprobrious to even an ostensibly secular Jew like Kahn, who "became an atheist before
his Bar Mitzvah, as he aged became an agnostic, was heading to-
wards deism, and thought he might die as a rabbi."[85] But the
lawyers concluded that Kahn would have a hard time proving
damages.[86] At best, Kahn evoked bemused patronization in the
United Kingdom. About a BBC appearance, one critic commented: "The interview was a curious mixture of the apocalyptic
and the homely. There were no signs of death wish on the surface of Kahn, round as a cartoonist's version of a Hollywood

---

*Kubrick consulted Schelling, Kaufmann, and Wohlstetter as well as Kahn, and
all four were chagrined by the fact that a movie that they thought would have an
earnest core ended up a farce. See Gregg Herken, *Counsels of War* (New York:
Alfred A. Knopf, 1985), p. 214.

tycoon. He seemed lapped in domestic bliss, with a wife like an attractive beetle, who believed he was saving the world, and a small son being taught to win at what looked like nuclear halma. For nuclear disarmers it must have been rather like meeting the Charles Addams family."[87]

In 1966, Kahn came under more serious attack from American liberals. While they did not represent the political mainstream, they also were far from members of the lunatic fringe. Their arguments both reflected and fed a vestigial popular impulse toward nuclear abolition. Kahn was the prime target of Philip Green—then an assistant professor of government at Smith College—in his book *Deadly Logic,* which impugned his work as "prophetic science fiction" rather than the scientific systems analysis that it purported to be.[88] Kahn was, as Michael Howard notes, "bizarre" if "wonderfully provocative." He did, concedes Howard, "force people to 'think the unthinkable,' but of course making them think the unthinkable is not the same as making them *wish* for the unthinkable. I never quite knew when he was being self-mocking, but I think quite often he was rubbing your nose in the implications of what you were saying. The deadpan-cool way in which he described what could happen in various stages really did deter one very effectively."

Kahn's role in the history of nuclear strategy had been to expose the dangers of complacency. He fulfilled it with greater élan, but less rigor, than Schelling and Wohlstetter. Once deterrence had putatively been refined and stabilized in the form of mutual assured destruction, his brand of freewheeling scenario-spinning was no longer needed. It is hard to quarrel with Freedman's coda on Kahn: "His work is incredibly dated now. He has been described as a sort of Lenny Bruce—he was a provocateur. Wohlstetter thought he was trivializing what he [Wohlstetter] was trying to do—shocking for the sake of being shocking. A lot of his work was gimmickry."[89] Though Kahn may have been indefatigable, by the late 1960s his interlocutors had grown weary of thinking about the unthinkable.

Schelling cheerfully notes that "most people took Kahn *too* seriously. I can tell you one reason why they might have thought that way. One trouble with Herman is that he had an irrepressible sense of humor, and a lot of people thought he was making fun of either war or the military or the people in his audience."[90] At the same time, Kahn's flamboyance and wit endowed him with the crossover appeal that won the appreciative attention of liberals like Freeman Dyson and even Allen Ginsberg, who had gone to school with Kahn and persuaded a hostile crowd at a Columbia University teach-in during the late sixties to lend Kahn an ear. But this, in turn, made him appear all the more dangerous to the po-faced James Newmans of the world. He was, in short, a polarizing figure. Schelling canceled his *Scientific American* subscription when he learned that the editor of the magazine refused Kahn's request to publish a rejoinder to Newman without heavily editing it on the grounds that *Scientific American* was not open to people who entertained ideas such as Kahn's.[91] That editor, Dennis Flanagan, wrote to Kahn: "In my view, which is not too different from James R. Newman's, nuclear war is unthinkable. I should prefer to devote my thoughts to how nuclear war can be prevented. It is for this reason that we must decline your offer."[92]

Dyspeptic and unadventurous as that attitude was, it won the day. Underlying it were the collective guilt of the scientists who cleaved toward Oppenheimer's view that the military applications of nuclear weapons should be strictly curtailed (and away from Edward Teller's conviction that their robust development and deployment were the linchpin of strategic leverage and eventual victory), and the consequent censoriousness of their rhetoric against contemplating military uses for nuclear weapons. These were among the most formidable intellectual obstacles to Kahn's brand of thinking about the unthinkable. But the main practical impediments, over time, were the strategists' very success in rolling back Armageddon, and the persistence of less spectacular and more empirically familiar forms of violence.

3

Sidelining the Unthinkable

Louis Menand has commented that, even if you acknowledge his brash theatricality, Herman Kahn was merely

a believer. Questioning military policy was his business; questioning the policies that military policy is designed to protect and enable was not. For all the avant-gardism, all the high-powered analytic techniques and "thinking outside the box," Kahn's work was fundamentally in the service of preserving the system, and without cynicism. In this, he was like most of the Cold War defense intellectuals. The attitude was: we are trained scientists. We've studied the situation with detachment and disinterestedness; we have taken nothing for granted, given no hostages to sentiment. And we conclude that the world as it is—in this case, a global rivalry between two nuclear powers in an escalating arms race—is acceptable (provided that the policy changes we recommend are adopted). "On Thermonuclear War" is a preposterous monument to this way of thinking. Complications and qualifications are swatted away like flies.[1]

Whether the book is preposterous is debatable. But Menand's more substantive insight hits the mark. As a thinker, Kahn sat solidly within the prevailing national security orthodoxy. Across a broad cultural spectrum, his imagination was actually quite limited. In 1961, a Louis J. Henrich of San Francisco sent him a handwritten note asking: "Is there anything you can do to help? (I read your very sane remarks in the Science News Letter of Aug. 19.) . . . The program below is a 'natural' one—i.e., taken from Nature. I hope *you* like it, for a consultant wields great power." Enclosed with the note was a typewritten chronological list, entitled "I GO MAD," of Henrich's activities, beginning with "I cut a check mark into my forehead with a razor." His "daily mayhem"—interspersed with observations of the activities of world leaders, votive appreciations of the female peace-loving ones among them (notably Eleanor Roosevelt), a fantastical summit meeting of American and Russian mothers convened by Mrs. Roosevelt and Mrs. Khrushchev resulting in a one-year moratorium on war, exaltations of the female of several species, and laments about the prevalence of destructive male priorities, the insanity of war, and the cost (which he pegs at $40 million an hour) of preparing for World War III—continues for five months, whereupon there is "no more need for it" on account of the author's epiphany. That epiphany concludes: "Sanity can be restored to humanity when the Female attains the same status in human life as she does in Mother Nature. When her values come first, as they should, war will be a thing of the past and the a) Build b) Tear to pieces c) Kill . . . cycles will be ended forever."

Henrich's missive decodes as a caustically facetious pacifist plea—a kind of beat poem incorporating imagined performance art (or, indeed, the real thing if Mr. Henrich actually mutilated himself) and registering the antiwar, feminist, and environmentalist themes that would emerge in large-scale social mobilizations later in the decade. Yet Kahn, either dismissively or obliviously, deposited the letter in the Hudson Institute's

"Crackpot File."[2] Clearly he resisted taking criticism seriously from anyone outside a fairly narrow range of interlocutors. The image of a fearless intellectual bull-in-a-china-shop that Kahn fed so diligently was largely a facade. It's well known that he tried LSD. Less celebrated is the fact that he did so in 1962, before the hallucinogen was illegal.[3] Kahn's LSD experimentation was undertaken with the encouragement, sanction, and clinical interest of Dr. Sidney Cohen, Chief of Psychosomatic Medicine at the Veterans Administration's Wadsworth GM&S Hospital in Los Angeles, and with the knowledge of William Brown and possibly additional Hudson Institute colleagues of Kahn's. Cohen, however, appeared to be rather circumspect, eliciting Kahn's report of his LSD-influenced interpretation of a series of images (which he saw as, for example, a boy studying a violin, a lovers' quarrel, an emergency appendectomy, and spacemen observing an insect studying a spoor) through William McGlothlin, a colleague, who himself communicated with Kahn in private letters.[4]

More generally, the Hudson Institute's correspondence files from the mid-1960s contain a number of letters indicating that Kahn and his Hudson Institute confreres increasingly viewed his colorfulness and visibility and his attempts to engage a wider audience as net liabilities. In a 1961 letter to Patricia Stone, who had written him a letter of qualified admiration about *On Thermonuclear War,* he acknowledged that he had ignored "the moral aspects of this problem," pleaded that the book was basically just "a specialized technical monograph," and despaired that critics who believed that he was advocating either preemptive war or Doomsday Machines were "so full of hostility that they cannot read the typewritten page."[5] At the other end of the political spectrum, on the basis of a conversation about a conversation that a third party had had with Harrison Salisbury, editor of the *New York Times,* Hudson Institute president Donald Brennan in 1965 sent Salisbury a two-page letter with six enclosures beseechingly seeking to correct any notion that the Hudson Institute was a "right-wing organization."[6]

In the realm of national security proper, Kahn's imagination was powerful and his intellectual courage considerable, but his visions were all highly contingent and conditional and his prescriptions maddeningly hedged. In the area of nuclear warfare, he and other strategists could get away with this kind of slipperiness because the truth or falsity of their conclusions and recommendations wasn't likely to be tested in a real war. And while Kahn certainly considered himself pragmatic in the general sense—indeed, fearlessly so against his craven and "ostrich-like" peers—he never doubted that the basic objective of the strategist's endeavor was nuclear deterrence, as a step in advancing American primacy. A true pragmatist would have had his doubts. A true pragmatist might have been at least curious about what effect the Cold War was having on people like Louis Henrich.*

Thus, Menand has also argued that the intellectual tradition of pragmatism was one of the most poignant casualties of the Cold War. Wohlstetter's subordination of pragmatism and RAND's

---

*To be fair, the Hudson Institute did try to enlist people with novel viewpoints that diverged from those held by Kahn and his crew. One was Haverford College physicist William Davidon, who favored unilateral nuclear disarmament. Just as the Cuban Missile Crisis receded, in October 1962, he declined, declaring: "I do not believe that in this capacity, I would be able to further the possibility of the constructive, fundamental changes in U.S. goals and policies I am convinced are necessary." Brennan protested—this time, as well, a bit too much—that he did not think that Davidon "could find a place with more leverage from which to further the possibility." In perhaps an ill-judged jest, Brennan added that he hoped Davidon, who was about to leave for New Zealand, was not emulating the Hungarian Manhattan Project physicist Leo Szilard, who had recently flown to Geneva to avoid a possibly imminent nuclear war. Letter to Professor William C. Davidon, chairman, Department of Physics, Haverford University, from D. G. Brennan, October 30, 1962; from the Hudson Institute Papers, National Defense University Special Collections, Fort McNair, Washington, DC.

lustier embrace of logical positivism lend credence to this view. Pragmatism postulates, in essence, that principles are adopted by men to advance practical ends, and that they must be allowed to adjust to experience. Conversely, principles and ideas could only be valid if the consequences of their application proved them useful and constructive. Pragmatism evolved during the late nineteenth and early twentieth centuries, as the United States consolidated its core values in the aftermath of an eviscerating civil war that called the country's very identity into question. Pragmatism flourished, that is, in a period when Americans felt that their world most needed to heal rather than to triumph. It was also a time in which the validity of the country's founding precepts had been proven tenuous, and were stiffly tested against the ravages of war and commerce. There was a certain empirical logic, then, in the conviction of the great American pragmatists— Oliver Wendell Holmes Jr., William James, Charles Sanders Peirce, and John Dewey—that even the most heartfelt and precious beliefs were just bets on the future. The implicit malleability of this view resides in the notion that odds change as knowledge does.

The Civil War had cast doubt on the view, inherent in ideas like Manifest Destiny, that a future of American supremacy and advancement was etched in stone. Pragmatism's primal message was that the world was unfinished and pluralistic, and that people—not God or physics—determined their destinies. Menand gets to the heart of the matter. "The United States in the 1890s," he writes, "was a society fractured along many lines: the South against the North, the West against the East, labor against capital, agriculture against industry, borrowers against lenders, people who called themselves natives against the new immigrants. In a time when the chance of another civil war did not seem remote, a philosophy that warned against the idolatry of ideas was possibly the only philosophy on which a progressive politics could have been successfully mounted."[7]

Pragmatism surely resonated in U.S. policy and attitudes during the second half of the nineteenth century and the first half of the twentieth, especially with respect to the weighty issues of imperialism, war, and revolution. An anti-imperialist strain reinforced by the pragmatists gave way to hemispheric intrigue, "gunboat diplomacy," and the "open door" policy primarily to secure U.S. access to resources and markets so as to continue its march to economic supremacy. Yet American administrations blanched at outright colonial rule. U.S. aspirations to global primacy were checked by extreme caution in committing U.S. military power in the First World War, a return to isolationism—urged by Dewey, among others—as the storm gathered in Europe during the interwar years, and a reluctance to enter the Second World War so persistent that only the Japanese surprise attack on Pearl Harbor and Hitler's rashness in declaring war on the United States could decisively dislodge it. The pragmatists' rejection of Marxism as absurdly deterministic and rigid in the face of empirical observations that disprove it, and their preference for evolutionary as distinct from revolutionary reform on the basis of trial and error, were evident in the United States' fundamental opposition to Soviet expansion.[8]

But Menand judges that pragmatism was not the philosophy for carrying the United States through the Cold War, owing to two basic shortcomings. First, it provided no way of discriminating among interests except by reference to the consequences of acting on them. Second, pragmatism failed to accommodate the fact that desires and beliefs can lead people to behave in ways that may be very unpragmatic, yet still be noble, admirable, and constructive. "Pragmatism," Menand sums up, "explains everything about ideas except why a person would be willing to die for one."[9] If it could not support an intuitively vital life-and-death struggle between two ideas, the value of pragmatism seemed dubious on its own terms. A kind of compartmentalized positivism prevailed. Precise men and institutions, sequestered from any doubts that might emerge from historical considerations or competing ideologies, applied rational methods in the service of national interests that had been rigidly defined in accordance with a strategy of containment to which there appeared no alternative. This dispensation was deemed better suited to safeguarding the morale and girding the will required for eventual victory. Furthermore, insofar as the Cold War "was a war over principles," it was, at least between the two main antagonists, "a war fought mostly with images and ideas. A style of thought that elevated compromise over confrontation therefore did not hold much appeal."[10] The perceived monolith of communism engendered the United States' near-absolute rejection of any semblance of sympathy toward it—internally, as reflected in McCarthyism, and externally, as demonstrated by the acceptance of "the domino theory" and a penchant for coercive action against any government remotely perceived as adverse to U.S. interests.[11] With so much at stake, the pragmatists' tolerance "had come to seem naïve, and even a little dangerous."[12] And the Cold War never got hot. Deterrence never failed in a big way. The erroneous perceptions of zealous Cold warriors like John Foster Dulles that any left-wing political aspirant was a puppet of Moscow—in fact, many were merely nationalists seeking to reclaim indigenous resources and markets controlled by American business interests—went untested. Experience never compelled the pragmatic downgrading of the policy of containment that all proxy activity served—and which enjoyed the status of a governing principle of international relations—because it seemed to prevent mutual annihilation and preserve American power and influence.

During the 1950s in particular, the U.S. government was searching for a nuclear strategy that would both ensure a stable-enough deterrent to consign the nuclear option to last-resort status and quietly frame the U.S. military superiority in order to foster containment and, ultimately, something more ambitious. That nuclear strategy was nurtured, under mainly the Air Force's sponsorship, by think tanks—primarily RAND. And it was not pragmatic in the sense of entertaining compromise or accommodation with the Soviets in any serious way.* Until détente emerged, nuclear strategy went only so far as to acknowledge that nuclear weapons were not the best means of fighting a war with the Soviets. There was no room for doubt that the Soviets eventually had to be defeated, and that at least the credible threat of nuclear war was essential to achieving that objective.

Within those parameters, nuclear doctrine did not altogether lack subtlety. The deconstruction of massive retaliation made it clear that nuclear options would not usually be the best ones. Nuclear strategy's key function was to deter nuclear war through credible threats, which excluded mutual suicide. Nuclear deterrence could be "extended" both to defend an ally and to keep an opponent from undertaking nonnuclear provocations, but that role was best served if nuclear proliferation was stemmed. Nuclear war, like conventional war, could be rationally conducted

---

* A vivid and egregious example involved a book by RAND researcher Paul Kecskemeti titled *Strategic Surrender: The Politics of Victory and Defeat* (Stanford, CA: Stanford University Press, 1958), a study of the French surrender to the Germans, the Italian surrender to the Allies, the Japanese surrender to the United States, and the German surrender. Several senators and congressmen read an article in the *St. Louis Post-Dispatch* to the effect that RAND studies were oriented toward surrender, and raised concerns about whether anyone was studying such a craven subject at government expense. Senator Richard Russell of Georgia, chairman of the Senate Armed Services Committee, proposed legislation, subsequently known as the "Better Red Than Dead Amendment," forbidding government funding of any study "concerning the circumstances under which the United States would surrender to any aggressor." After debate, the Senate passed the legislation 88–2.

through selective targeting, which called for precision in order to make serious U.S. intent clear and credible to an adversary and thus encourage his rational behavior. Cities didn't have to be threatened to deter or bombed to prevail in a war, but could be held "hostage" in favor of initial counterforce strikes as means of potential or actual war termination. Given that this posture could still, without more, leave preemption an attractive option, offensive forces would be useful deterrents only if they could survive a first strike, which made their protection paramount. There were several ways that survivability could be improved. Passive defenses, like concrete-reinforced missile silos and the repositioning of the strategic bomber fleet, were available. Counterforce strikes were the bolder option. There was a third, highly theoretical possibility: that of active defenses, the principal of which was an antiballistic missile system that could intercept incoming offensive missiles and destroy them before they reached their targets.[13]

By the early 1960s, official U.S. nuclear strategy became more closely aligned with this doctrine. In 1960, the Joint Strategic Target Planning Staff (JSTPS) was established by the Pentagon. Overseen by the Joint Chiefs of Staff, this group was drawn mainly from the U.S. military services, but also included representatives from NATO allies. The JSTPS quickly put together the first Single Integrated Operational Plan (SIOP)—that is, the official determination of precisely how nuclear weapons would be used in a war. The initial SIOP really involved only two broad possibilities: an all-out first strike or an all-out second strike. But presidential candidate John F. Kennedy predicted that a Soviet advantage in ICBMs (later proved fictitious) and movement toward nuclear parity would improve its deterrent sufficiently to allow Soviet conventional strength to degrade the United

States' geostrategic position unless the American nuclear deterrent was refined. This concern and the crystallization of nuclear doctrine at RAND set the tone for a strategically dynamic Kennedy administration. RAND had established the distinction between first- and second-strike deterrence, Wohlstetter had illuminated its broader policy lessons with the publication in *Foreign Affairs* of "The Delicate Balance of Terror" in January 1959, and Schelling had begun to explore their ramifications for actually managing crises.

More than any other single institution, RAND fermented the ideas about the vulnerability of U.S. nuclear forces and command-and-control that led to stable deterrence—and to keeping the Cold War cold until its termination. In doing so, RAND analysts established the template for dedicated and focused strategic thought about how to avoid self-annihilation. They wielded their influence in what had become a fiercely engaged public-private community. A thin layer of high-level interaction was officially sanctioned. In 1956, for example, President Eisenhower established the President's Board of Consultants on Foreign Intelligence Activities—renamed the President's Foreign Intelligence Advisory Board (PFIAB) by Kennedy—which has remained constituted since then, except for a hiatus during the Carter administration. Senior analysts from RAND and other think tanks have almost always sat on the PFIAB, as well as on other advisory bodies, such as the President's Intelligence Oversight Board, the President's General Advisory Committee on Arms Control and Disarmament, and the Defense Policy Board. Typically meeting for a few days every couple of months, these bodies have exercised varying and often considerable degrees of influence over U.S. policy in their respective subject-matter areas.[14]

One of Schelling's anecdotes illustrates the less formal infrastructure of the partnership between government and strategists. Shortly before he and Morton Halperin published their influential little book, *Strategy and Arms Control,* in 1961, they held a Harvard/MIT faculty seminar that met once a month.[15] For the first four meetings, the topic of the evening was simply a chapter from that book. There were about forty regular attendees. They included McGeorge Bundy, who became Kennedy's national security adviser; Walt Rostow, the future head of the State Department's Policy Planning Staff under Kennedy; and Jerome Wiesner, the prospective White House science adviser. "So we made the White House, the State Department and the Defense Department up to date on all of our arms control thinking. That meant not only that people went into government with knowledge of what was floating around academia but that those in government were on a first-name basis with academics all over the country. So academics now had access. The military services also began to send people with the rank of colonel to places like the IISS, Harvard, MIT, Ohio State, Chicago, the Council on Foreign Relations, for a whole year."[16] Furthermore, the war colleges increasingly invited civilians to lecture and teach.

Overall, a nearly seamless connection evolved between the strategists and government. There was perhaps a shard of daylight between them. After 1958, CIA policy barred the distribution of National Intelligence Estimates to contracting firms—including FFRDCs like RAND. As a consequence, RAND based its nuclear deterrence analyses in 1958–60 on estimates of Soviet missile numbers from Air Force or Strategic Air Command intelligence that turned out to be unrealistically high, thus reinforcing the "missile gap" fiction.[17] In the Kennedy administration, however, civilian strategists immersed in the relentlessly analytic, empirically grounded "RAND tradition" ascended to the highest ranks of government. Ted Sorenson, Kennedy's closest adviser, had premised much of Kennedy's missile-gap speech on "The Delicate Balance of Terror." Although Wohlstetter himself disagreed with missile gap assessments, he favored the Democrats' active disposition because the Eisenhower administration had in his view been "very inert" in remedying strategic vulnerabilities highlighted by Wohlstetter's post–base study analyses for RAND which the Democrats were keen to eliminate.[18] Schelling—having taken a year off from Harvard in 1958–59 and spent it at RAND—declined an offer from Paul Nitze, assistant defense secretary for international affairs, to become his deputy for arms control, but remained a close informal adviser to the Pentagon.

Kennedy himself was a student of history, his book *Profiles in Courage* having won a Pulitzer Prize in 1957, and listened carefully to historians—in particular, Arthur Schlesinger Jr., the Harvard professor he appointed to be his special assistant—on matters of policy during his presidency. But the new president was more keenly interested in the ideas of political scientist Richard Neustadt—who became one of Kennedy's key intellectual confidants—about how to increase and optimize presidential power.[19] While Neustadt's theory did stress "contemporary history" and case studies, the more granular details of policy formulation Kennedy entrusted to technocrats like Walt W. Rostow and, as to military matters, Robert S. McNamara. A Harvard MBA, McNamara had been a phenomenally successful executive in the automotive industry, and before that a "whiz kid" in the Army Air Corps' Statistical Control Office during World War II. He believed national security decision-making, like business and military logistics, could be rendered rational and systematic, and thus found RAND's fastidiously analytic approach appealing. As Kennedy's secretary of defense, he made systems analysis the central function of the Office of the Secretary of Defense and populated the Pentagon with RANDites, most of whom shared Wohlstetter's view that Eisenhower's foreign and security policy was too passive.

McNamara's top adviser was Kaufmann, who tutored the secretary of defense on nuclear strategy. Harry Rowen became deputy assistant secretary of defense for international security affairs, Alain Enthoven deputy assistant secretary of defense for systems analysis. Charles Hitch, formerly head of RAND's economics department, was named comptroller of the Defense Department. Daniel Ellsberg, a highly regarded RAND analyst, also took on important posts. Schelling became an adviser to the Arms Control and Disarmament Agency. Wohlstetter, though terminally resistant to formal government employment, became an even closer consultant to the Defense Department and, effectively, part of its A-team. As Colin Gray—himself an influential Cold War strategist—has put it: "A bare recital of important 'names' appointed could understate the new privileged and influential position of the civilian strategists. All the leading civilian strategists who were willing to be consulted were drafted, at least on an ad hoc basis, into the official defense community. Their intellectual dominance in the early 1960's was nearly absolute. Although the administration might dilute or reject a proposal, the mode of reasoning, the terms employed were those popularized by Kissinger, Wohlstetter, Kahn, Schelling and others."[20]

Enjoying unprecedented input into official U.S. policy, the civilian strategists integrated formal nuclear strategy into the United States' nuclear doctrine. Perhaps the most salient nuclear fact in 1961 was that the United States could kill 360 to 450 million people in Eurasia in a few hours. Some kind of restraint needed to be explicitly built into policy. The cost-benefit rationality of the RAND defense intellectuals who had infiltrated government did not trump the political and psychological compulsion to match the Soviets in missile strength, and thus could not preclude what seems in retrospect to have been an absurdly large nuclear force structure.[21] But McNamara and his "whiz kid" advisers—Kaufmann in particular—did declare that a U.S. second strike would initially be confined to military targets. The intent was, in effect, to hold the enemy's civilian population hostage to provide the strongest possible motivation for him to spare Western populations. This was the "no-cities" strategy, and it contemplated a broader brand of limited nuclear war that seemed more plausible than earlier iterations that had cast atomic weapons as mere tools of the battlefield. Thus, in 1962, the SIOP incorporated "flexible response" to give the president greater control and more options.*

While "no-cities" did not actually remove the threat to civilian populations, it made the counterforce peril to military targets an equally important element of a second strike. In the mordant atmosphere of the early 1960s, counterforce had customarily been regarded as quintessentially a first-strike capability. The Soviets, therefore, were unlikely to buy a U.S. emphasis on counterforce as anything but a preemptive first-strike capability regardless of how the United States officially characterized it. McNamara's priority became getting Moscow to change its perspective. He

---

*Both Schelling and Kaufmann argued in favor of the no-cities strategy that McNamara enunciated in 1962. They had very different reasons for advocating it. Kaufmann argued simply that to have any hope of winning a nuclear encounter, the United States would have to launch the most massive counterforce attack possible on military targets, and could not waste resources on cities. Schelling contended that the United States probably could not protect itself with even the heaviest counterforce attacks, so the most important message to send the Soviets was that if they stood down, the United States would not destroy their cities; otherwise, they would retaliate. Only in this way, believed Schelling, could a nuclear war be brought to a close without exterminating entire populations. Thus, Kaufmann's concerns were essentially operational, Schelling's essentially motivational.

wanted the Soviets to sign up to city avoidance as a rule for any retaliatory nuclear attack, as opposed to a first strike. For the offer to be credible, in 1963 he recommended structuring U.S. nuclear forces so that they could take out relatively soft military targets, but not hardened ICBM sites and missile-launching submarines, in a single strike. This would allow Moscow to use those less vulnerable assets to hold the U.S. population hostage to retaliation and deter further American strikes. The idea was to discourage the Soviets from striking first by guaranteeing them a meaningful second-strike target in the form of the American people, which in turn would constrain the Americans from striking first and preserve stable deterrence. Ingenious though it was, the gambit didn't work because the imagined circumstances under which such nuclear bargaining could occur—in effect, a limited and accurate attack on noncritical nuclear weapons—seemed so improbable. Counterforce remained most valuable as a first-strike instrument, which in turn was consistent with NATO's need to offset conventional inferiority with a credible threat of nuclear first use. And a retaliatory Soviet counterforce attack would still entail so much collateral damage that no American commander could afford to assume that it was intended to be limited and exercise restraint in kind.

The Cuban Missile Crisis cast further doubt on the viability of counterforce in U.S. doctrine: Kennedy's initial salvo to the Soviets was the threat of full retaliation, not a limited counterforce strike. After the crisis had thus appeared to reveal the United States' disinclination to use restraint at the nuclear level, Moscow did not benefit from agreeing to such restraint itself. But Kennedy had used the U.S. triumph in October 1962 constructively, to make the nuclear balance more stable, by vigorously orchestrating the Partial Test Ban Treaty, which was signed by the United States, the Soviet Union, and Great Britain in 1963 and over one hundred additional countries shortly thereafter. The treaty banned all nuclear tests except those conducted underground, which stood at least to slow down the arms race. There still remained serious doubts about the reliability of the United States' nuclear umbrella as the sine qua non of the Allied defense of Europe, and about assured destruction—a term first used in 1964—as a basis for nuclear deterrence in general. These worries ensured that the quest for a better means of using nuclear weapons to strategic advantage without destabilizing the strategic balance would continue.

Extended Deterrence

In 1962, Khrushchev's recklessness in Cuba and Kennedy's audacious response also led to public confirmation of overall U.S. military superiority and, in 1964, to Khrushchev's "retirement." Yet despite Western perceptions of Khrushchev as a warmonger, neither he nor other Soviet leaders were as diabolically ambitious as Kahn, Wohlstetter, and probably most Americans sometimes seemed to fear. Not unlike American leaders, Stalin had employed war's possibility to marshal vision and resolve in his citizenry. Marxism-Leninism did not dictate the inevitability of war.

Though Khrushchev's operational thought was somewhat confused and marked by an almost childlike fetish for rockets, Soviet doctrine did not starkly distinguish between nuclear and conventional forces or civilian and military targets, did not embrace the notion of graduated and deliberate escalation regulated by mutually recognized firebreaks, and derided any notion of damage limitation in nuclear conflict. Even post-*Sputnik,* the Soviet position redounded to the status quo: the perpetuation of a nuclear stalemate. That said, Khrushchev really did believe that a conventional war could go nuclear by way of a transcontinental exchange between the Soviet Union and the United States, and that a "balance of intimidation" was therefore required. Indeed, he cut conventional forces prior to 1961, and declared ICBMs the centerpiece of Soviet nuclear doctrine. After the missile gap was exposed as a figment in 1961, however, the balance of intimidation was lost. Although the Soviets were determined to redress the nuclear imbalance between the Soviet Union and the United States after the Cuban Missile Crisis, conventional forces resumed primary importance.

To the Soviets, Europe was the real objective. Its conquest would be achieved through superior conventional forces—and all but negated by the use of nukes on European soil. The Soviets worried about nuclear weapons mainly as impediments to the exercise of their conventional strength and as the ultimate flatteners of the people's morale. Khrushchev thus stressed the overwhelming devastation of a single nuclear bomb; the Soviet Union tested a sixty-megaton device in 1961 when the United States' ICBM warheads were being scaled down to the hundreds of kilotons. The net effect was a Soviet nuclear posture of minimum deterrence, a continued confidence in conventional superiority, the leveraging of the Soviet threat to Europe, and an apparent view that the Soviets might well win a general war against the United States. Recognition of these truths, however, served mainly to steel the leading lights of the first generation of nuclear strategists to shoring up America's deterrent.*

---

*To accommodate the U.S. buildup in strategic capability, which to the Soviets implied an increased first-strike threat, in 1967 the Soviets adopted a "launch on warning" policy whereby, in the event of the United States' initiation of a first strike, the bulk of their nuclear arsenal would be released before American missiles hit their targets. Under Leonid Brezhnev, the Soviet Union caught up with the United States in nuclear armaments. This development stemmed mainly from the domestic political need to demonstrate resolve and the notion—less sophisticated than the American one—that deterrence depended on brute strength. From one perspective, it also reinforced the view of some American officials and analysts that the Soviets tilted toward war-fighting rather than deterrence.

Yet in some ways the debate about a purely U.S.-Soviet strategic confrontation was a kind of tabletop proxy war. Through most of the sixties, the scenario considered most likely for nuclear war involved a Soviet ground incursion into Eastern Europe and then across Europe's central front. If Soviet conventional forces overwhelmed NATO troops, the United States would be tempted if not compelled to go nuclear against communist targets. The Soviet domination of Europe was clearly unacceptable, and Moscow's erection of the Berlin Wall in 1961 made the possibility all the more salient. Strengthening conventional capabilities in Europe, in furtherance of McNamara's general subscription to "flexible response," had been a priority for the Kennedy administration. Schelling recalls McNamara as "a good listener and a strong person. When McNamara decided that he didn't like nuclear weapons, he made it his mission to try to talk NATO into developing enough conventional strength so that it wouldn't have to rely on nuclear weapons."[22] From a strategic point of view, a robust NATO conventional capability would constitute "the threat that leaves something to chance." The stronger the conventional obstacle, the more destructive the effort that the Soviets would have to mount to defeat it. The more destructive that was, the more risky was escalation to nuclear war. The more American soldiers were implicated in a Soviet ground advance, the more credible the threat of American nuclear intervention to stop it. A U.S. conventional buildup in Europe approaching parity with Soviet conventional forces—by the late sixties considered qualitatively though not quantitatively plausible by the RAND alumni in the Pentagon—would thus create a tripwire that would strengthen deterrence.[23]

Civilian strategists generally supported this policy. Bernard

Brodie, then at RAND, was the chief exception. He regarded the "tripwire" line of thought as fundamentally flawed. In his view, the implied threat of nuclear escalation could not be easily dislodged from Soviet thinking, so that going to war with the United States or its allies at all, especially in Europe, remained prohibitively risky, and extended deterrence remained intact—all the more so if U.S. conventional deployments in Europe could not measure up to the Soviets'.[24] This viewpoint dovetailed with European fears that if the United States deployed too many troops and too much conventional hardware on European soil, Washington could become so confident of U.S. conventional forces' independent capacity to deter a Soviet invasion of Europe that it would refrain—implicitly or explicitly—from threatening nuclear retaliation to repel such an invasion, and thus render it more tempting to the Soviets.* At this point, other than the United States and the Soviet Union, the only countries possessing nuclear weapons were the UK and France; China would test its first bomb in 1964. McNamara, too, was concerned about decoupling, but mainly insofar as it would spawn an independent European (i.e., British or French) nuclear option and loosen centralized American control over the West's nuclear weapons and lead to proliferation. The U.S. imperative was to place the power to destroy the world in as few hands as possible. The persistent question in NATO was: Which hands? After France opted out of NATO's Integrated Military Command in 1966, West Germany became the key continental European player in the alliance. The land battle for Europe would be joined in West Germany, and the chances of its emerging intact—especially if tactical nukes came into play—were low. West Germany thus depended on not

---

*In the jargon of nuclear strategy, this was known as "decoupling" conventional and nuclear deterrents.

merely a strong nuclear deterrent but one whose trigger was perceived to be as automatic as possible so as to stave off any pause between crossing the conventional/nuclear firebreak that would permit Warsaw Pact occupation of the country. Automaticity, in turn, would be more credible if the prime stakeholder—West Germany—had some operational part in the decision to go nuclear.

Here Bonn leveraged its singular geostrategic position and orchestrated the barely thinkable prospect of a nuclear-armed Germany. Although it had agreed in 1954 not to produce nuclear weapons, Bonn intimated that its continued resoluteness as a nonproliferator would be bolstered by giving it some decision-making authority over nuclear use. The Kennedy administration's diplomatic response was to propose a Multilateral Force (MLF) of internationally manned missile ships under American command but subject to NATO Council guidance—a compromise between independent European deterrents and a U.S. monopoly. Wohlstetter had noted that such a framework for collegial decision-making created a perception of potential paralysis—quite the opposite of the automaticity that Bonn desired.[25] So did the French strategists Pierre Gallois and General André Beaufre. Foreseeing a political as well as an operational quagmire, the Allies settled on the Nuclear Planning Group—essentially a consultative scenario-building body. The MLF never materialized. The United States retained ultimate control over the nuclear decision.

By the mid-sixties, then, deterrence had come to mean much more than just preventing a nuclear exchange between the United States and the Soviet Union. The concept represented a complex network of interrelated assumptions and capabilities, and determined the strategic and operational behavior of not just the two superpowers but also all of the allies and partners to which the superpowers had extended their respective umbrellas of protection. An immense and diverse array of American military capabilities was required to provide that protection, which was expensive to produce and maintain and would be required for an indefinite period of time. That array included proxy wars like Vietnam, which, as it escalated, was proving anything but easy, benign, or stabilizing, and consuming national blood and treasure at an accelerating pace. The "military-industrial complex" that Eisenhower had identified upon his departure from office came to be viewed as an existential force. The services, the defense industry, and the intellectual infrastructure that mapped out their interaction appeared to have mutually sustaining lives of their own. While necessary, it also seemed dangerous, and outside the spirit of democracy. At home, liberal activists fused American militarism with the civil rights movement to question the integrity of America as a whole. The protest was largely symbolic, but for the most part very serious. While activists at the extreme edge of the protest movement, like the Black Panthers and the Weather Underground, would commit violent acts, those closer to the center were more inclined to lodge earnest complaints about the military-industrial complex or to poke fun at it, so as to inject a note of pause into the martial symphony that the system of deterrence had inspired.

Epitomizing this attitude was the highly inventive liberal disinformation campaign unintentionally inspired by Herman Kahn and the Hudson Institute. Spearheaded by *Monocle* editor Victor Navasky, who later became editor of *The Nation,* this effort featured the infamous 1967 "Report from Iron Mountain," a spurious but not altogether unconvincing hoax account of a study conducted by a fictional think tank on Iron Mountain—"located near the town of Hudson"—that regards détente and conflict resolution as dangerous to the U.S. national interest, and pronounces peace undesirable.[26] Conceived by Navasky and writer Leonard C. Lewin after Navasky noticed that the stock market dipped at the hint of demilitarization, the report was presented as a rueful but morally compelled divulgence by a member of the "Special Study Group"—"John Doe"—that composed the report of a secret government plot to keep the United States on a war footing for the sake of the economy even if doing so required that new enemies be manufactured. Dial Press editor E. L. Doctorow agreed to advance the hoax by publishing the report as a nonfiction book. As originally issued, the document does not indicate the name of the author or publisher or the place or date of publication. Although both Navasky and Lewin long ago came clean that *Report from Iron Mountain* was a satirical invention, into the late 1990s some right-wing fringe groups continued to cast it as a genuine article and to take its prescriptions seriously. This consequence is an odd form of blowback and one in which some of Kahn's sterner critics would likely find vindication: if his actual thinking was so close to morbid parody that extreme hawks couldn't distinguish the two, he must indeed have been dangerous.[27]

The report itself is a masterpiece of satirical subtlety and manipulation: initially half an octave more extreme than actual policy so that it's kind of funny, yet forwarded with an air of such walleyed seriousness that it can't quite be dismissed; then, having hooked and reeled in the lay reader, progressively outrageous. In an "interview" purportedly conducted by Lewin with "John Doe," he notes: "Kahn's books, for example, are misunderstood, at least by laymen. They shock people. But you see, what's important about them is not his conclusions, or his opinions. It's the *method*. He has done more than anyone else I can think of to get people accustomed to the *style* of military thinking. . . . Today it's possible for a columnist to write about 'counterforce strategy' and 'minimum deterrence' without having to explain every other word. He can write about war and strategy without getting bogged down in questions of morality."[28] Satire or not, this assertion was substantially true. Kahn's "icy rationality" is also cited with approval, which leads to an obtuse yet, in the early Cold War context, credible declaration of the need to "deal with the problems of peace without . . . considering that a condition of peace is *per se* 'good' or 'bad.'"[29]

Even in retrospect, some of the report's deadpan assertions seem to describe the manner in which many considered the Cold War an existential phenomenon—and alluded to some Clausewitzean underpinnings of this line of thinking—with a measure of accuracy and insight. "Although war is 'used' as an instrument of national and social policy, the fact that a society is organized for any degree of readiness for war supersedes its political and economic structure. War itself is the basic social system, within which other secondary modes of social organization conflict and conspire."[30] Having seduced the reader with the magisterial tone of this elegant, well-nigh arguable, general statement, the report moves on to more fatuous orwellian pronouncements. "Art that cannot be classified as war-oriented is usually described as 'sterile,' 'decadent,' and so on. Application of the 'war standard' to works of art may often leave room for debate in individual cases, but there is no question of its role as the fundamental determinant of cultural values."[31] The nonmilitary benefits of war—social release, generational stability, ideological clarification, international understanding—are then blithely catalogued.[32] The report's crowning economic conclusion is that there is no adequate substitute for war because nothing else is sufficiently "wasteful" and nonproductive to stabilize supply and demand.[33] The authors rein in the report's recommendations, returning to the realm of the almost-sensible. The chief structural recommendation is the creation of a "War/Peace Research Agency" that would research alternatives to war as well as its optimization. Each of those alternatives, of course, has been shot down in earlier pages. Nevertheless, the ostensible goal is "to maintain governmental freedom of choice in respect to war and peace until the direction of social survival is no longer in doubt."[34] The assumption remained that a war footing was the only one that made sense.

Snide as it was, *Report from Iron Mountain* actually did deal with the meat of many of the arguments advanced by Kahn and others. Somewhat uncharacteristically, Kahn reportedly did not find it all amusing. He regarded it as a juvenile affront—perhaps because it boiled his ideas down to a core cynicism and vapidity in all too engaging a fashion. More earnest critics like Newman shied away from even entertaining their substance, preferring instead to wallow in haughty revulsion over any suggestion that hydrogen bombs could be legitimate military instruments, galvanized by the prospect that operational mistakes could lead to self-annihilation as in *Fail-safe.* They were less formidable opponents. Usually cheerfully, Kahn derided such declamations as "educated incapacity."[35] But in unguarded moments, he also intimated that *On Thermonuclear War,* for all its shock value, might have won him more followers if he had injected less-contrarian irony and more ethical self-consciousness. By contrast, the next big nuclear debate became suffused with genuine passion—not about the morality of the nuclear age, but at least about the morality of nuclear deterrence.

The ABM Debate (I)

The sidelong look at deterrence as a calculus of bureaucratic survival as much as a security policy, provided by the *Report from Iron Mountain,* was not just lefty nonsense. McNamara's deterrence posture depended on threatening cities as well as military and industrial facilities—to be precise, 20 to 33 percent of the Soviet population and 50 to 75 percent of Soviet industrial capacity. Because McNamara and his advisers used worst-case estimates to determine force planning, U.S. capabilities throughout the 1960s easily exceeded these levels. His motive, though, was efficient resource allocation along RAND lines rather than brute intimidation: he aimed to short-circuit hawkish arguments against ceilings rather than to produce a wasteful overkill capacity of diminishing marginal utility, and he phased out conspicuously first-strike weapons such as intermediate-range ballistic missiles in Europe. The most notable aspect of McNamara's post-no-cities dispensation was his refusal to do anything in the arms-control arena to inhibit the *Soviets'* attainment of a matching assured-destruction capability. Ostensibly defensive antiballistic missiles were eschewed, even though prominent strategists—including Kahn and Donald Brennan, his right-hand man—looked favorably on them.

In a famous 1963 article voicing support for the Partial Test Ban Treaty and a prospective comprehensive ban, Jerome Wiesner and Herbert York sought to allay concerns that strategic stability might be disturbed by any curtailment of nuclear weapons research—including exploration of ABM systems. They argued that the more effective an ABM system might be, the more dangerous it would be. These authors, both physicists, were anything but fringe figures. Wiesner had been Kennedy's science adviser and became president of the Massachusetts

Institute of Technology, while York had been cofounder and chief scientist of the Pentagon's Advanced Research Projects Agency, established by Eisenhower. And their argument was compelling. "Such a system, truly airtight and in the exclusive possession of one of the powers," they wrote, "would effectively nullify the deterrent force of the other, exposing the latter to a first attack against which it could not retaliate."[36] They further argued that in the nuclear context, with single warheads so destructive, defensive systems would have to be perfect to be meaningful—a tall and probably impossible order—and that one side could always overwhelm the other's defensive capability at a given moment by building more offensive weapons. In other words, an ABM system was, however paradoxically, a first-strike weapon, and a bad one at that. The upshot was that missile defense likely would not work and, if undertaken, would fuel an arms race.

McNamara was happy enough to premise his opposition to an ABM system on mere technical infeasibility until about 1966. Then three developments increased his burden of persuasion. First, technological progress made missile defense start to look more viable. Second, the Soviets were developing an ABM system of their own. Third, the military was starting to get tetchy about McNamara's domination of U.S. nuclear doctrine. McNamara's riposte, penned by Halperin, was peremptory and powerful, emphasizing that the reciprocal nature of the U.S.-Soviet strategic relationship—what he called an "action-reaction phenomenon"—made offensive parity the only means of maintaining stable second-strike deterrence.[37] As with many of McNamara's arguments, the mechanical elegance of this one wasn't enough to silence critics. Among other things, the argument did not suppress the drive for superiority that instinctively took hold in arms contests.

By the late 1960s, then, a combination of scientifically based hope, strategic rivalry, and bureaucratic politics afforded advocates of missile defense some traction. Joining Kahn and Brennan was Wohlstetter, who had left RAND in 1963 and joined the faculty of the University of Chicago in 1965. An ABM capability would have positive political implications for the defense of Europe: if it worked, it would make the strategic linkage between Europe and the United States more credible by increasing U.S. freedom of action in coming to Europe's aid with tactical nuclear weapons, strengthening the European deterrent against the Soviets. And it would have the added bonus of neutralizing de Gaulle's annoying pretense to an independent French nuclear deterrent. More broadly, for the ABM advocates it was not so much that deterrence was dead; whatever the differences in U.S. and Soviet military doctrines, each side recognized that nuclear war would visit hell on both. What stuck in the craw of many missile-defense advocates were (a) the characterization of mutual assured destruction as a "strategy" when, in their view, it was next to useless once war began; and (b) the sheer ethical and philosophical perverseness of using the vulnerability of one's own population to annihilation as a basis for its continued existence.

Still, an antagonism between civilian strategists and the scientific community—portended by Wiesner and York's 1963 article—also enriched the argument against ballistic missile defenses. RAND and other think tanks had monopolized the ear of government policy makers throughout the fifties and most of the sixties. By the 1970s, though, the scientists inspired by Oppenheimer's guilt-cum-skepticism had become politically savvier and rhetorically subtler about registering their objections to what they saw as technocracy encrusting the nuclear debate. Dyson, for example, conceded that although the Sentinel system would be a good defense against a counterforce strike on the Minuteman

ICBM system in ensuring the survival of about half that arsenal, that ratio would be unacceptable as to the defense of cities; thus, ABM deployment might encourage first-strike population targeting.[38] Some of those who had been in decision-making positions had simply grown weary of the U.S. government's faith in the cold, scientific calculation that civilian strategists had initially imposed. In 1969, McGeorge Bundy—not a man easily moved away from orthodoxy—noted that an "unthinkable level of human incineration is the least that could be expected by either side in response to any first strike in the next ten years, *no matter what happens* to weapons systems in the meantime."[39]

McNamara, though fundamentally opposed to an ABM system, was dispirited by Vietnam, on the verge of departing the Pentagon, and too exhausted to fight with the pro-ABM contingent, who had asserted themselves before Congress. In 1967, the secretary of defense announced that the Sentinel ABM system would be built to protect U.S. cities against China, which was considered less disciplined and more inscrutable than the Soviet Union. This would not immediately degrade the Soviet deterrent, since the USSR had far more missiles than China. But the scientific community still threw up heavy resistance, arguing mainly that a limited system would solidify misplaced confidence in the technical feasibility of missile defense and lead to a more extensive program that the Soviets would perceive as enervating their second-strike deterrent, which in turn would fuel an arms race and general instability. Their fears were realized when the Nixon administration in March 1969 rolled out plans for the Safeguard ABM system, which was to protect American ICBM silos against a Soviet counterforce attack. Although Safeguard was supposed only to preserve the United States' second-strike capability without unduly damaging the Soviets', scientists lodged fears about an arms race and the imminent demise of arms control.

Technocrats like Brennan, however, envisaged a diametric scenario wherein missile defenses would facilitate meaningful, if not necessarily formal, nuclear arms limitations. In testimony given before the Senate Committee on Foreign Relations in March 1969, Brennan allowed:

> I may be the only one you have heard who has a plausible theory of how you can do a lot of strategic disarmament. You can do it with defenses. Let me sketch roughly how it might go, complete with a possible timetable.... We might begin at once with a Soviet-American understanding about a ceiling on offensive forces, expressed in inspectable terms such as gross weight, and an understanding that we might both build up defense. Such an agreement is clearly in the common interest of both the United States and the Soviet Union and should prove realizable. By the mid 1970's [sic], if the defenses are in place and appear to have the capabilities now expected of them, there should be enough confidence in them to begin some gradual reductions in the offensive forces on both sides, reductions which would require only modest inspection because the defenses would (if suitably deployed) sharply diminish the effectiveness of clandestine missiles. The defenses would then become even more effective against the then-reduced offensive-force threat, which would facilitate further reductions in offensive forces. Just how far this process might go would depend on the technological and political circumstances then prevailing, but I should not be surprised to find that by 1980 one might reduce the risk of Soviet-American strategic nuclear war to negligible proportions.[40]

This purported virtuous cycle anticipated Reagan's "Star Wars" vision, as amended with the admonition "trust but verify."

The technical core of the anti-ABM argument was that the United States was the fount of innovation in the sphere of nuclear weapons. Accordingly, the United States had substantial unilateral power both to trigger arms races and to restrain them—that is, to break the action-reaction cycle driven by worst-case assumptions. Schelling counseled that the ABM debate itself was of strategic utility and should not be sacrificed to ideological rivalry within the U.S. defense community. "I am much more concerned," he stated to the House in mid-March 1969, "that the decision on *Sentinel* or any such system be taken wisely than that the decision be the correct one. The decision ought to be tentative—dependent on negotiations with the Russians. It ought not to be a victory for either side in an ideological debate. Those who oppose ABM ought to avoid making it a decision between none at all and an open-ended commitment to a defensive arms race. Those who favor ABM ought not to make it a mortal challenge to all who hope to avoid a defensive arms race. . . . An intelligent decision can go either way. A responsible decision can go either way."[41] Wohlstetter had a somewhat more upbeat view, though it fell well short of Brennan's optimism. "A carefully worked out arms limitation agreement can add something to stability achieved unilaterally," he told the Senate. "I believe that ABM can contribute to such an agreement. By defending the strategic force, it can hedge against changes in the offense, such as increases in accuracy, not likely to be prevented by the agreement. By permitting both sides a light protection of their population, it can offer each some insurance against accidental or unauthorized acts and against desperate acts of countries not likely to sign the agreement. Such acts cannot be foreclosed by treaty."[42]

In a "Summary of Major Arguments" that Brennan composed in 1968, in the "For BMD" (meaning ballistic missile defense) column he included "protect against small attacks (e.g., anonymous)." But the problems in the "Against BMD" column—"likelihood of war," "arms races," "money (wasted or otherwise)," "alliance reactions," and "proliferation"—were far more immediate.[43] Deterrence, though morally awkward, worked. During the height of the ABM debate in 1969, Brennan, in recommending that the procurement bias should be reversed in favor of defensive systems, noted: "We should rather prefer live Americans to dead Russians, and we should not choose deliberately to live forever under a nuclear sword of Damocles."[44] And Wohlstetter himself was fond of ridiculing the notion that it was moral to fire missiles at people but not at other missiles (to which Schelling scoffs, "That's no argument"[45]). Brennan was ultimately a tragic figure. He had started out as a liberal arms controller, then ended up as a thwarted advocate of a large-scale ABM system at the Hudson Institute. He committed suicide. Perhaps he was dismayed that the contradiction between stable deterrence and a "moral" nuclear posture meant that practicality would prevail over moral considerations time and again. Practicality, however, could mean disparate things. It could and did mean the rejection of a nuclear posture that did not emphasize risks to populations. But it might also mean an appreciation that many, if not most, strategic interests had little to do with military matters in general and nuclear weapons in particular.

The Vietnam Effect (I)

McNamara's domination of U.S. nuclear strategy straddled the Kennedy and Johnson administrations, and its architects were almost all prominent alumni of the RAND Corporation. The key constituents of that strategy were initially the concepts of "second strike," "counterforce," and "flexible response."[46] The former two were replaced by "assured destruction" and "damage limitation" by 1966, and the nuclear devastation thus contemplated became more explicitly quantified so as to erode the early preference for counterforce.[47] To be sure, the Vietnam War, a conventional conflict, became the test bed for a fully extended "flexible response" doctrine: the Americans tried a range of devices short of nuclear arms—counterinsurgency, limited war, controlled escalation using airpower, nation-building—to thwart the communist takeover of South Vietnam. But Vietnam was still a proxy war fought precisely because the United States and the Soviet Union could not afford to confront each other directly on the battlefield for fear of winding up in a nuclear exchange. The pivotal importance of nuclear arms in foreign policy, then, was not only retained but enhanced during the 1960s. Yet it was in the domain of conventional war that the great Cold War strategists got their comeuppance.

RAND's preeminence as a source of strategic wisdom stemmed from two peculiar circumstances. First, professional soldiers were not expert in nuclear war, which left room for civilian strategists to shine. Second, the matter of nuclear deterrence lent itself to the highly technical and quantitative analysis at which the civilian strategists excelled. But professional soldiers could claim supremacy over civilian strategists with respect to a conventional conflict like Vietnam, which ultimately turned much more on the messy psychological realities of insurgency and counterinsurgency than on the sophisticated, quasi-scientific matching of arsenals and trading of body counts and cities. Furthermore, once the leading civilian strategists were in government and consumed with the day-to-day implementation of policy, like those they had once advised from on high, they lost the intellectual luxuries of time and distance that had yielded their strategic and operational innovations.[48] Although formidable minds—Wohlstetter, for example—

remained at think tanks or in academia, their influence waned owing to the new strategic priorities that had evolved. Winning a conventional war had supplanted securing the nuclear deterrent as the issue of the day. McNamara and the civilian strategists were extraordinarily sound on nuclear strategy. But in the end, the Vietnam War eroded not only McNamara's standing but also the authoritativeness and prestige of those strategists.

The leading civilian strategists steered a safe middle course between withdrawal and escalation in Vietnam, and did not—collectively or individually—enunciate a single strategic concept to guide the prosecution of the war.[49] From a historical perspective, this dispensation was not acutely incriminating. But if the strategists had succeeded admirably in staving off nuclear war and stabilizing nuclear deterrence, they were also proven fallible by their overall support for the Vietnam War and their disinclination to illuminate the flaws of U.S. policy. This discrepancy suggested to some of their doubters, later echoed by Menand, that theoretical scenarios had desensitized them to real-life, low-tech flesh and blood. Herman Kahn's defrocking constitutes perhaps the starkest example of this phenomenon. His slow demise as a strategic player began with the success of the scientific community—predominantly through the *Bulletin of the Atomic Scientists* and *Scientific American,* Kahn's great antagonist—in rallying a consensus against any defensive ABM system, which Kahn and Brennan strongly favored. But thereafter, in the late 1960s, Kahn's catholic intellectual sensibilities—he was, to put it bluntly, a know-it-all, if a very talented one—prompted him to insinuate the Hudson Institute into the Nixon administration's restrategizing of the Vietnam War. He made some headway at an intermediate level, but was essentially rebuffed as he got nearer to the top political-military echelon and the White House.

In February 1968, Philip Worchel, deputy science adviser for Military Assistance Command, Civil Operations and Revolutionary Development Support (MACCORDS)—the CIA-led rural pacification program—in Saigon, wrote to Kahn, who was planning a visit to Vietnam.

> Frankly, I am glad that you were not here during the Tet offensive. We will fill you in on this when you get here. I really believe that the GVN [government of South Vietnam] really rose to the occasion. Of course, they did miss some good psychological opportunities, but Monday quarterbacking [*sic*] is always so much easier. . . . I still feel that you minimize the psychological factors while emphasizing the economic and military tactics. The VC [Vietcong] certainly put much greater stress on involvement, organization, human dignity, and interpersonal relationships. Their PsyOps, without any sophisticated research, is damned effective. I wonder when we will learn to use the message.[50]

Shortly after this communication, Kahn, along with four other Hudson colleagues, published their respective essays in a volume titled *Can We Win in Vietnam? The American Dilemma.* Kahn's personal answer was yes, provided forces were wisely reallocated and the escalatory American policy through which the North Vietnamese were supposed to be battered and depleted into submission—dubbed "attrition–pressure–ouch" by Kahn—rethought. He proposed that the American and South Vietnamese armies concentrate on preventing the direct invasion of South Vietnam or the seizure of territory by a major North Vietnamese force and establish secure areas within which intensive police operations could be executed to counter the Vietcong insurgency. In a review in the *Washington Post*, Amrom H. Katz, himself a RAND research analyst, characterized Kahn as "a man for all problems" destined to weigh in with "neither civilian modesty, humility nor equivocation."[51] John Mecklin, a former public affairs officer at the U.S. embassy in Saigon, was less deferential, calling Kahn's contribution "turgidly pompous" if also "fresh" and "important."[52] In any event, within a few months Nixon was elected in part on a promise to draw down American involvement in Vietnam and conclude the Paris peace talks with a satisfactory deal. To Kahn, this meant that to salvage the U.S. effort in Vietnam, robust remedies had to be undertaken before political pressures to withdraw became irresistible. In an audacious five-page, single-spaced letter to General Creighton Abrams, who had replaced General William Westmoreland as the U.S. commander in Vietnam, Kahn set forth a four-point plan—emphasizing rural area security, beefed-up regional forces, and combined American-Vietnamese operations leveraging U.S. Special Forces—for turning the tide. Kahn also wanted to set up a small Hudson Institute office in Saigon to conduct studies, advise CORDS, and stay on top of developments in South Vietnam—a possibility he had discussed with an apparently receptive William Colby, who was then the director of CORDS.[53] Simultaneously, he sent a letter to Secretary of Defense Melvin Laird.[54] Enclosed with each letter were twelve pages of "annexes" fleshing out the four-point strategy. One element of Kahn's vision was a five-year peacetime development program dubbed—ironically, in retrospect—the "1975 ideology"; it was supposed to demonstrate positive U.S. contributions to Vietnam.[55]

Frustrated at Abrams and Laird's silence, three weeks later Kahn sent a ten-page memorandum to Henry Kissinger, who was then national security adviser. After laying out Hudson's proposals, he asked that Kissinger, Laird, or one of their assistants importune the Joint Chiefs of Staff or General Abrams to consider them seriously.[56] Scarcely ten days later, Kahn sent another letter and two memoranda to Kissinger, veritably pleading for a high-level audience. "As far as I can see," Kahn wrote, "the Vietnamese war is the central issue facing the Nixon Administration and the nation. Assuming that the ideas presented in the attached memos have any serious possibility of 'salvaging' what is rapidly becoming an intolerable situation, it simply does not make sense not to give these ideas serious and adequate consideration. This attitude is not due only to egocentrism on my part. This conviction about the potential value of the suggested program comes as much as a result of a great deal of discussion with almost everyone in the system as from any original biases and assumptions of my own."[57] Memoranda followed to General Earle G. Wheeler, chairman of the Joint Chiefs of Staff, on July 23, and to Kissinger again on October 24.[58] He wrote another letter to Kissinger (copied to U. Alexis Johnson, Melvin Laird, David Packard, and Elliott Richardson) in April 1970, outlining inspirations he'd had during a week spent in Saigon as to explicitly marshaling the Nixon Doctrine* to support "sustained if limited U.S. intervention in Cambodia."[59]

Finally, with yet another missive to Kissinger in mid-August 1970, Kahn appeared to have exhausted himself on the subject of Vietnam. While it is clear that Kissinger and others acquiesced in Kahn's epistolary approaches, the tone of his letters—at once increasingly ingratiating and increasingly defensive—suggests a man of waning influence angling in substantial futility to get it back. The last letter concluded: "I am having this particular letter delivered by hand by somebody who is going to Washington so that you can at least be aware of what I hope could be done. Again, I will be available next week and would be

---

*The Nixon Doctrine, enunciated in 1969, provided a foundation for détente. The doctrine called broadly for a decreased American presence in the Asian theater and rapprochement with the Soviet Union and Communist China. Kahn's suggestion that it justified expanding the war to Cambodia was evidently a stretch.

delighted to meet with any of your people or with yourself if you have time."[60]

In their basic contours, Kahn's ideas for winning in Vietnam tracked the post-Westmoreland counterinsurgency strategy that was being developed at the time Kahn and colleagues' book came out and was applied during the Vietnamization period, so they may have seemed to government insiders like extraneous (if unobjectionable) sermons to the converted. But the more pronounced reaction was probably that Kahn was in essence an armchair nuclear strategist who had no business delving into the messy operational province of ground warfare and counterinsurgency. On this score, Amrom Katz's 1968 *Washington Post* review of the book was remarkably perceptive. He made special note of the fact that the great nuclear strategists had conspicuously tried to stay away from Vietnam. He offered a compelling explanation. "The cruel paradox of 'wars of national liberation,'" wrote Katz, "is that they are simultaneously much less consequential to the world and a thousand times more complicated to understand and wage than is the fatal but simple thermonuclear war."[61] Having said his piece on nuclear strategy and encountered frustration in prescribing counterinsurgency strategy, Kahn vaulted from nuclear strategy to futurology. It was a field that many scholars and experts then (less so now) consigned to hacks. Yet predicting the future may have been the only calling grand enough to satisfy one of the original wizards of Armageddon. In this disposition, Kahn was emblematic of his colleagues. When writing the first edition of *The Evolution of Nuclear Strategy* in the late 1970s, Lawrence Freedman admits, he did not fully understand the range of strategic issues—especially nonnuclear ones involving counterinsurgency and the Third World—that the United States had to confront during the Cold War. "Vietnam crept up on me like everyone else."[62] Nuclear strategists in general were not inclined to grapple with the vicissitudes and complexities of nationalism, religion, and ideologies other than those falling under the broad contours of communism and democracy. But their resistance to immersing themselves in these problems did not absolve them from blame. Those who refused to recognize the Vietnam policy as a failure were guilty of extreme obtuseness, those who ignored it of intellectual cowardice.

The Vietnam War was a kind of slow-motion political apocalypse for the United States and America's worst strategic failure of the Cold War, and it involved not missiles in silos but boots on the ground. With respect to actual war-fighting and threats more insidious than world incineration, the Cold War strategists faltered. Overall, RAND itself had a workmanlike but hardly inspiring record in Vietnam. Schelling had offered a defensibly circumspect assessment of President Johnson's retaliation for the supposed North Vietnamese attacks in the Gulf of Tonkin as a measured reprisal designed to demonstrate American resolve while encouraging the adversary to relent.[63] RAND researchers bootstrapped Schelling's analysis into a doctrine of graduated escalation that ramified as heightened U.S. provocation, like the "Rolling Thunder" bombing campaign against North Vietnam that began in 1965. In turn, such moves were sterilely characterized by the civilian strategists that McNamara had recruited as "signaling."[64]

While nobody associated with RAND crucially influenced the conduct of the Vietnam War, neither did any RAND analyst or alumnus do anything notable to ameliorate the mistakes that were made. In time, failure in Vietnam was associated most resonantly with McNamara, McNamara with systems analysis, and systems analysis with RAND. At least indirectly, then, the war tainted RAND and the community of civilian strategists and knocked them from the perch to which they had ascended on the strength of their contributions to nuclear strategy.[65] But RAND's greatest Vietnam legacy, albeit unintended and unwanted, was Daniel Ellsberg.

Ellsberg's affiliation with RAND ran from 1959, when he joined as an analyst, to 1970. He embodies both thesis and antithesis of RAND's underperformance in the area of conventional war, having evolved from hard-nosed strategic thinker, to in-country Pentagon adviser in Vietnam, to antiwar activist and revealer, in 1971, of the Pentagon Papers. In graduate school at Harvard (where Schelling was his doctoral thesis adviser) and at RAND, stimulated by the Cuban Missile Crisis, Ellsberg's preoccupation was decision-making under conditions of uncertainty, especially as applied to ordering nuclear strikes. More broadly, he felt that the advent of nuclear weapons necessitated a better understanding of implementing policy during crises in general. On the basis of that belief and a robust professional relationship he had established while at RAND with John T. McNaughton, assistant secretary of defense for international security affairs under McNamara, he became McNaughton's special assistant in 1964. Ellsberg's task was to go to Vietnam and analyze the American intervention—which McNaughton portrayed as "one crisis after another"—from the inside, on an ongoing basis.[66] For bureaucratic reasons, Ellsberg transferred from the Defense Department to the State Department for this mission, yet he lived in Vietnam substantially as a soldier. As a Marine Corps platoon leader and company commander in the mid-1950s, Ellsberg had not seen combat. In Vietnam from mid-1965 to mid-1967, however, he was often with combat units to observe and evaluate U.S. counterinsurgency operations—in essence, the pacification and political indoctrination programs designed to win "hearts and minds." Then supervising the programs was the legendary former CIA officer Edward

Lansdale, the prototypical "ugly American" whose reputation had been burnished by his oversight of a highly successful counterinsurgency campaign in the Philippines.

During the most critical phase of the Vietnam War's escalation, then, Ellsberg was part of the Vietnam quagmire. But he did not like what he saw, and was extremely critical of the U.S. civil support efforts and more aggressive attempts to isolate the Vietcong from the rest of the South Vietnamese population, concluding that the president should not expect substantive progress by the end of 1966—"if ever."[67] He also gathered testimony from that population that it had lost confidence in South Vietnam's military rulers, and counseled the Johnson administration to promote civilian leaders, which it declined to do.[68] Once home from Vietnam in 1967, Ellsberg elected to return to RAND rather than continue in the State Department's employ, and his slow but steady conversion from praetorian intellectual to war protester proceeded in earnest. Ellsberg became dismayed over the United States' cynically brutal aerial bombing of Vietnam. Military Assistance Command, Vietnam (MACV)'s inaccurately low estimates of enemy strength—unsuccessfully contested by the CIA—also alarmed him, and he leaked secret documents revealing this fault to the *New York Times* in March 1968, shortly after the Tet offensive.

In early 1969, after Richard Nixon was inaugurated, the National Security Council tapped RAND to provide studies and recommendations on Vietnam options, and Ellsberg was chosen to head the project. Meanwhile, Halperin, deputy to McNaughton and his successor, Paul Warnke, and Halperin's assistant, Leslie Gelb, were supervising a sweeping top-secret study—initially commissioned by McNamara before his 1967 departure from the Defense Department—styled the "History of U.S. Decision-making in Vietnam, 1945–68." This study would come to be known as the Pentagon Papers. Just before Nixon took office, Warnke, Halperin, and Gelb arranged with Harry Rowen, now president of RAND, to have two sets of the complete study stored after they left government in RAND's Washington office as classified documents, but under relaxed safeguards.[69] Ellsberg was immersed in a "Lessons of Vietnam" project, for which he had produced a number of internal RAND documents on the feasibility of U.S. objectives in Vietnam. He first read the Pentagon Papers in September 1969, and they moved him to abandon any hope that the United States could, or should try to, win in Vietnam. Despite Nixon's campaign promises to get out of Vietnam, it was not at all clear then that he would do so expeditiously. In early October, Ellsberg and five other RAND researchers, duly identified as such, submitted a letter on RAND letterhead to the *New York Times* and the *Washington Post* urging the Nixon administration to resolve to withdraw all American forces from Vietnam within a year.* On October 8, the *Times* published a news article about the letter, and four days later the *Post* printed the letter in full. To no resistance from RAND's leadership, Ellsberg voluntarily terminated his employment at RAND effective April 15, 1970, retaining a suitcase containing the forty-seven volumes of the Pentagon Papers. The Nixon administration, meanwhile, made no decision to pull out of Vietnam. Ellsberg tried in vain to have Senators Fulbright and McGovern promulgate the Pentagon Papers and then, as a last resort, handed them over to the *New York Times,* which published them in June and July 1971.

RAND had long sought to transcend its evolved role as consultant nonpareil to the Air Force and Pentagon to a similarly

---

*The other five were Melvin Gurtov, Oleg Hoeffding, Arnold Horelick, Konrad Kellen, and Paul F. Langer.

privileged position in the White House, and its recruitment by the NSC may have been a factor in skewing the organization's critical eye.[70] Over the course of the Vietnam War, RAND, on balance, promoted U.S. policy in Vietnam without informing or challenging it much. For example: Robert Komer, the former CIA officer who first headed CORDS, recruited two RAND researchers for his staff. That effort would have controversial elements—such as the notorious Phoenix Program, which sometimes involved assassination—and produced at best transitory successes. Komer later joined RAND, and wrote an upbeat assessment of the program.[71] And an influential RAND study dubiously predicted that a U.S. withdrawal from Vietnam would produce a massive bloodbath by the Vietcong, and reinforced resistance to such withdrawal into the 1970s.[72] Ellsberg, for his part, was indicted for unauthorized disclosure of government information under the Espionage Act. The charges were dismissed, in significant part due to the manner in which he had been victimized by the Nixon team's "dirty tricks."

Ellsberg emerged as a people's hero and a transitional public figure through whom the civilian strategists as a group became publicly humanized and accountable—and, at the same time, more fallible and vulnerable. His release of the Pentagon Papers from RAND's custody also directly reduced RAND's trustworthiness and credibility in the eyes of its government customers. Furthermore, Vietnam on its own merits drove home the limits of an aggressive containment policy, and gave rise to détente, which suggested a realist "balancing" solution to the riddle of peaceful coexistence. The resulting stability, partly attributable to the evolved manageability of nuclear deterrence, made thinking about serious disruptions to the international order recede. The fact was, after the tingle of thinking about the unthinkable had worn off, the arms-control champions' approach was more comfortable: their offer of stability was a compelling alternative to the uncertainty of the extremes. After one decade of nuclear dread and another one of conventional fiasco, national leadership settled into a risk-averse posture that made a priority of dealing carefully with the devils it knew.

Détente

In the 1970s, Henry Kissinger—first as national security adviser, then as secretary of state—became the dominant force in U.S. strategy. Kissinger, though a RAND consultant during the 1960s, was never on staff and in fact resented RAND's skepticism about limited nuclear war, which he had notably advocated.[73] Remaining first and foremost a professor of government and international affairs at Harvard, he also looked askance at RAND's proclivity for promoting technical solutions to political problems. Kissinger spent the 1950s and 1960s mainly as an observer of international politics, developing the "conceptual basis for political action" that he believed competent statesmanship required.[74] Once in government, and a major player in international affairs, he set about boldly putting this framework into practice. His ideas cleaved to the point of view that military challenges were a subsidiary aspect of the strategic rivalry.* "What Kissinger did was that he reminded everybody that having a

---

*He did, of course, remain concerned about perceptions of U.S. power and, with Nixon, inherited an extraordinarily difficult perception problem in Vietnam. These factors help explain why he was dilatory in ending the Vietnam War, attempting by the invasion of Cambodia and heightened aerial bombardment throughout Indochina to buy time (a "decent interval") for the South Vietnamese to build sustainable political and military capacity before a U.S. withdrawal. As a realist, Kissinger also naturally worried about the overall geopolitical balance, which suggests why he indulged Nixon's determination to engineer a coup in Chile and felt compelled to confront the Cuban troops in Angola. Nevertheless, Kissinger was less inclined than his predecessors to micromanage geopolitics.

good or bad nuclear strategy, having nuclear weapons, was not going to affect the basic political problems that really create the tensions in the modern world; and if only we could get away from the emphasis on nuclear weapons, we could get somewhere. And he had this amazing capacity for sitting next to the Russians and telling them this."[75]

Kissinger was a staunch realist, and as such subscribed to a worldview that recognized the tendency of states to collectively check powers perceived as dominant to establish workable international stability—which, given both the variability and the persistence of human cultures and the fallibility of national leaders, was all humankind could reasonably ask for. His driving epochal idea was détente, which involved the United States' politically isolating the Soviet Union through reengagement with China. This geopolitical gambit—initiated by Nixon's historic trip to China in February 1972—introduced a new, overarching strain of pragmatism into U.S. foreign policy. But its sweep was strictly limited by Soviet ideas about the role of nuclear weapons in international affairs. If they differed from Kissinger's, his views, however compelling, were unlikely to substantially diminish the influence of nuclear weapons.

And they did appear to differ. By the early 1970s, the Soviets had caught up with the United States in numbers of ICBMs and were gaining in submarine-launched ballistic missiles (SLBMs), and later enjoyed numerical superiority in both, though they remained behind in deploying multiple independently targetable reentry vehicles (MIRVs), which enabled a single missile to deliver warheads to several targets. The Soviets' greater launcher numbers suggested better survivability with respect to its nuclear force, which in turn meant an improved second-strike capability. U.S. superiority in MIRVs but not in launchers, however, implicitly made a first strike more attractive. McNamara had been broadly unconcerned with this trend in the belief that mutual destruction would in any case stay assured. Kissinger was less sanguine. The Soviet buildup made him unconfident that unilateral American restraint in effecting qualitative advances in nuclear weaponry would, by itself, produce reciprocal forbearance on the part of the Soviet Union, and worried that the Soviets still sought a superior nuclear war-fighting capability. Against this backdrop of insidiously destabilizing deterrence, in the early 1970s, Brennan snidely labeled mutual assured destruction "MAD."[76] Kahn himself cast MAD as "a suicide pact" and, consequently, an uneasy basis for coexistence. How to maintain nuclear stability remained the central challenge of U.S. strategic policy. Thus, arms control with the express purpose of curtailing the arms race was required, and Moscow's relative geopolitical weakness in the wake of the American rapprochement with China was supposed to make Moscow more amenable to arms control. Perhaps it did. But détente still complicated rather than defused the ABM debate.

The general wisdom of détente seemed to be confirmed by the Soviet Union's clearer appearance as a relatively cautious power, which had been conditioned to an extent by MAD. Yet this caution did not extend to Third World proxy wars—for instance, in Angola—designed to enlarge the Soviets' sphere of influence. The strategic safety of these wars was reinforced by the very taboo on direct superpower confrontation that détente enshrined as well as encouraged by the United States' humbling in Vietnam. Kissinger revived the Strategic Arms Limitations Talks (SALT), which had effectively been suspended for several years on account of the Soviet invasion of Czechoslovakia in 1968. Through those negotiations, he intended to rein in Soviet nuclear leverage that actually tended to underline parity. This led to an emphasis on the nuclear triad as solidifying the capacity to strike back, and to force structures large enough to permit plenty of innovation beneath very high warhead and launcher ceilings. Arms competition and arms control, it seemed, could coexist. The ABM Treaty limiting U.S. and Soviet antiballistic missile deployments to two hundred each had been signed in 1972 as part of the SALT process. But supporters as well as opponents of antiballistic missiles could still mount strong arguments. Their gist was: even if we have stability we're not getting anywhere in terms of diminishing the quality or quantity of nukes, so a technological dynamic that has some prospect of diminishing their salience in world affairs ought to be pursued.

Détente, though undeniably effective in diminishing the influence of nuclear weapons on world affairs, assumed the permanence of the Soviet Union as a rival power. In the mid-1970s, that was a reasonable assumption. But it deprived détente of the satisfying moral clarity of the Truman doctrine or containment. Conceding that Soviet rivalry was an existential fact also seemed to obviate the need to plan for facing a different enemy or a shift in the venue or modality of strategic confrontation. Many of the best minds were uncomfortable with détente, but they remained nearsightedly focused on the Soviet threat. Wohlstetter— proving Schelling's point that he himself was always at his best when presented with a target to attack—returned to center stage. In a series of caustic, hard-hitting articles in *Foreign Policy* appearing in 1974 and 1975, he contended that U.S. strategic forces had been declining, that American intelligence had consistently underestimated Soviet strategic capabilities, and that therefore the simple action-reaction phenomenon thought to reconcile arms competition and stability did no such thing.[77] He also reemphasized the moral discordance of MAD, and the euphemization of the nuclear debate by means of terms like *countervalue*. On this score the strategic orthodoxy was indeed vulnerable: it was well and good to point out that guaranteed suicide was an effective deterrent in that it psychologically distanced nuclear arsenals from actual use; but the failure of NATO to build up conventional forces and to operationalize its purported "flexible response" concept meant that the West still had to rely on the nuclear threat to repel something *less* than a strategic attack on the United States to a much greater extent than did the Soviets. This was not a new observation, but it was a persistently poignant and troubling one.

Fred Iklé, soon to become director of the Arms Control and Disarmament Agency, made perhaps the most impassioned and outraged plea for an alternative to deterrence. The "narcotic" language of U.S. strategy, he said, "fosters the current smug complacency regarding the soundness and stability of nuclear deterrence. It blinds us to the fact that our method of preventing nuclear war rests on a form of warfare universally condemned since the Dark Ages—the mass killing of hostages."[78] His policy prescriptions—making U.S. forces less vulnerable and capable of considered and discriminate response under testing psychological and operational conditions—were unprepossessing, harkening back to the late 1950s. Furthermore, these sorts of arguments still turned on confidence in the efficacy of new technologies that the McNamara-tutored establishment could not muster.

The moral weight of the arguments endured, but did not immediately inspire a feasible doctrinal alternative. Scientists like York agreed with Iklé, but could offer only the bland and unsatisfying remedy of reducing the degree of nuclear overkill via deep cuts in force levels. The net effect was that while SALT succeeded in capping defensive systems (by virtue of the ABM Treaty) on a wholesale basis, its regulation of offensive ones was marginal by design. Technological advances made doing so more rather than less difficult, as they often had offsetting effects on strategic planning. For instance, while improvements in ICBM precision guidance and MIRVing enabled force reductions, they also made ICBMs more feasible as first-strike weapons—a phenomenon that would perpetuate an arms race—leaving relatively inaccurate SLBMs the only pure second-strike strategic weapon. SALT at least had the virtue of codifying the reality that more weapons would not produce greater security, and, by declaring what Freedman calls "an honourable draw," establishing a cooperative atmosphere that could pay dividends in diplomacy in general and managing crises in particular.[79] An interim five-year deal struck a rough trade-off between American technical and bomber superiority and the Soviets' numerical missile edge, capping U.S. ICBMs at 1,054 and SLBMs at 656, and Soviet ICBMs at 1,409 and SLBMs at 950, further specifying a maximum of 308 "heavy" ICBMs. In 1974, the two sides contemplated a permanent accord limiting all nuclear delivery vehicles to 2,400 and MIRVed missiles to 1,320. But the unilateral introduction of highly accurate nuclear-armed cruise-missiles by the Americans and the *Backfire* bomber and SS-19 ICBM by the Soviets rendered the trade-offs more intricate, draining congressional support for a SALT treaty. The Soviet invasion of Afghanistan in 1979 sealed its fate.

Of what use, then, *were* nuclear weapons? An unconsoling answer shook out: they still defined the worst case, and the worst case was still plausible because men could always behave irrationally. This epiphany did not obviate the need for nuclear parity. Rather, coupled with concerns that a steady Soviet buildup may have shifted the strategic balance, it dictated an institution-alized recognition that any subjective outside perception of So-viet superiority in any sphere could lead to the unnecessary capitulation of an ally ("Finlandization") or adventurism on the part of the Soviets themselves. Thus, in the mid-1970s the Penta-gon began to emphasize nuclear parity on a broader range of criteria (called "essential equivalence") and flexible and selective options. Nuclear arsenals would at least serve as indices of political will. As the crowning wisdom of the nuclear age, such a conclusion was a pronounced anticlimax.

Nuclear Ennui

The debates over antiballistic missiles and the Vietnam War represented the first pitched battles in the nuclear age between the military and the defense industry, on one hand, and America writ large, on the other. Until those controversies, what was good for the Air Force and Lockheed was presumptively good for America. The American people deferred to the military-industrial complex—and to the think tanks led by RAND—despite Eisenhower's earlier warnings. As a consequence, a military-industrial bias evolved in favor of procuring the most advanced weapons regardless of their effect on strategic stabil-ity. Invention, as Lawrence Freedman quipped, became the mother of necessity.[80]

In the ABM debate, however, those in favor of developing the new defensive weapon could credibly assert the moral high ground in declaring that deterrence, based as it was on the vul-nerability of civilian populations, was fundamentally perverse and arguably immoral. As the debate unfolded, though, the moral qualms seemed increasingly beside the point, which was simply to prevent nuclear war from happening. It became evident that neither U.S. leaders nor their Soviet counterparts saw any political utility in resorting to nuclear war because of the overriding humanitarian and moral shock that doing so would entail. This grand constraint had prevented nuclear deterrence from extending down to the subnuclear level. Given that both sides were horrified with the prospect of nuclear war, the Soviet Union could in fact be quite aggressive. They had gone into Afghanistan as well as Ethiopia and, via Cuban troops, Angola. For the United States, the limited functionality of nuclear deterrence in prosecuting foreign policy had less agreeable ramifications. The Vietnam War was a disheartening experience that strengthened the view that the United States should not throw down the gauntlet to the Soviet Union whenever challenged but should rather more discriminatingly determine, on the basis of regional political considerations, where defendable American interests lay and pick its spots accordingly. Détente enshrined these attitudes and circumstances, and marked the point at which the civilian strategists' Cold War–era grip on U.S. policy loosened.

The so-called first Cold War—the period between World War II and détente—marked the first time in modern American history, and probably any country's modern history, that civilian strategists rose above military professionals in influence and importance. The reason was that strategy had become more a matter of determining the adversary's calculations about the nature and objectives of war itself—and in particular, when not to engage in it—than one of positioning armies and navies for victory. That is, strategy became more intellectual than operational. Given the stakes of nuclear war, there was an incentive to keep it that way that tended to guarantee the civilian strategists' primacy. Sir Michael Howard, one of Clausewitz's most perspicacious interpreters, warns that "it must not be forgotten that Clausewitz was a soldier writing primarily for soldiers: that he looked forward to the continuation of war as something natural and inevitable; and that his teaching was intended for successive generations of patriotic Germans fighting for their Fatherland—not for world statesmen conducting international politics in an age of nuclear plenty."[81] For that, civilians were more appropriate because they were likely to be more sensitive to political context and nuance. They delivered. Against the disdain of many of those professionally involved in the nuclear debate, the great strategists indisputably made the world safer.

By demonstrating that the nuclear "balance of terror" was in fact rather complicated, and turned on a number of fairly subtle trade-offs, the strategists also short-circuited abolitionists and pacifists. A viable architecture of deterrence—along with its building blocks, the nuclear triad (strategic bombers, land-based ICBMs, and SLBMs)—was put in place. With the bombers on twenty-four-hour alert, the missiles MIRVed and in hardened silos, and the missile submarines able to hide for months at a time, the triad was a rich mixture of offensive and defensive capabilities, sufficient both to threaten realistically and, by the same token, to deter with substantial assurance. What this meant was that as Cold War reality become protracted and quotidian, "the unthinkable" in the form of nuclear destruction became entrenched and fixed in strategy. Whereas the fifties and early sixties was a period of unequaled technological change, which fermented equally extraordinary thinking about the implications of new technologies, during détente strategic thinking lost its edge. A dialectic occurred: what was once novel and enterprising had, by the early 1980s, become conventional and staid—domesticated and normalized. The civilian strategists, for better (on the nuclear side) and worse (in the conventional sphere), had thought themselves out of the loop. The problem was that the perpetual rethinking of U.S. strategy, nuclear and conventional, political and military, was an important and unappreciated component of maintaining its viability.

4

Intellectual Dislocations of the Cold War

The United States' mission in the 1950s and 1960s centered on integrating nuclear strategy into grand strategy—that is, the American plan for establishing the world order that it preferred. The nuclear strategists concluded, and persuaded the Pentagon and successive administrations and Congresses, that nuclear weapons were useful for deterring the Soviet Union from attempting to change the existing order in one apocalyptic stroke, and were an emblem of American primacy and resolve. But because they morally should not—and practically could not—be used to any effect that would yield a better world, nuclear weapons would be unable in and of themselves to roll back Soviet influence, as instruments of outright victory in actual combat. For that, the economic and political superiority of democratic capitalism and selected limited conventional military engagements would be required. On the latter, the Vietnam War was a cautionary gloss. If the fifties and sixties were mainly about finding the proper role and limitations of nuclear weapons, the seventies and eighties should have been predominantly about doing so for low-intensity warfare and counterterrorism.

Unfortunately, most of the strategists and policy makers in the U.S. government missed this point. There were three main reasons. First, Vietnam had devalued the currency of the civilian strategists and left the government bereft of the robust intellectual support that had powered the development and refinement of nuclear deterrence. Second, to the extent that the diminished policy research establishment could be of help, its capacity remained absorbed by the unanswered question of how to get beyond the perverseness of deterrence—that is, of holding millions of people at risk of incineration as a matter of policy. Third, the United States' defeat in Vietnam had left American civilian and military leadership institutionally averse to pursuing or perfecting counterinsurgency, and committed to reserving the conventional armed forces mainly for major wars against strategic adversaries and, implicitly, for deterrence. This aspect of "the Vietnam syndrome" made U.S. government officials and policy intellectuals alike reluctant to think of conventional warfare as anything but a subsidiary dimension of containment. Under this self-limiting approach, potential conventional enemies were presumed to be controlled by the Soviet Union or China and therefore ultimately subject to nuclear deterrence; undeterrable free agents that might require innovative uses of force or dissuasion in response to their provocations were out of sight and mind.

The Vietnam Effect (2)

Early in the Cold War, the terror and novelty of nuclear weapons had concentrated academia on the challenges of nuclear strategy. The result was a healthy competition between think tanks and universities that effectively enlarged America's supply of high-quality strategic analysis. Think tanks and universities also fertilized one another. Research organizations tapped professors, focused their minds, and extracted insights. Then they sent them back to the academy where they trained the next generation,

which continued the cycle, or to government, where they trans-
formed ideas into policy.[1] The Vietnam War's primary impact on
this state of affairs was to erode the credibility of civilian strategists in both think tanks and academic institutions, and decrease
their intellectual clout in government circles.

Although the work on Vietnam was performed almost exclusively by the social scientists (i.e., political scientists and economists) at RAND, the leak of the Pentagon Papers tainted the
entire organization, including hard scientists (in particular, nuclear physicists and chemists), in the eyes of the Defense Department. As a result of this development, and the fact that a number
of RAND's leading scientists, à la Herman Kahn, sought a more
exclusive and lucrative limelight, several of them chose to leave
to start for-profit "beltway bandit" firms. One prominent one was
Pacific-Sierra Research Corporation (PSR), started in 1971 by
Frank Thomas, who had been a key member of the physical sciences department at RAND. Ironically, Thomas had come to
RAND in early 1967 from the Pentagon, where he had been assistant director of nuclear programs under the Director for Defense Research and Engineering (DDR&E), in part because he
was disenchanted with the Vietnam War and wished to distance
himself from it. Thomas undertook nuclear test detection research at RAND, for the DoD's Advanced Research Projects
Agency (ARPA). He was "happy" at RAND, even though those
heading the physical sciences department—Albert and Richard
Latter—were "a little hawkish" for his taste with respect to Vietnam. In the summer of 1970, RAND experienced substantial budget cuts and reductions in staff. These stemmed from budget
reductions at the Air Force, which in turn had been necessitated
by the costs of the Vietnam War. Although RAND's physical sciences department "had more work than it could handle" from
other agencies, primarily ARPA, Harry Rowen, then president of

RAND, decreed that all parts of the organization had to "share the pain."[2]

Many members of the physical sciences department resented this dispensation. In the late 1950s and early 1960s, RAND had contracts with the Atomic Energy Commission and the national laboratories (Los Alamos, Lawrence Livermore) that required a Q clearance—that is, top secret as applied specifically to nuclear weapons—which most of RAND's other work did not require. Accordingly, the physical scientists were physically and in a way socially separated from other RAND researchers, and indeed felt as though they were a separate organization within the mother ship. In early fall 1970, many in the physical sciences department decided that they did not want to "share the pain" and began to consider splitting off from RAND. These included the Latters and Thomas. They put out feelers to some of their government customers to determine whether they would do business with them even if they were not with RAND. They answered in the affirmative. After the infamous "RAND letter"—characterized by Joseph Kraft in a *Washington Post* column as "breaching the code"—was published in October 1969, the physicists feared that all at RAND would be made to "share the blame" and lose funding even further. The letter thus provided the final impetus for them to leave. The Latters started Research and Development Associates (RDA) in early 1971, and Thomas started PSR with four employees plus an ARPA contract.[3]

Firms like PSR, RDA, and Braddock Dunn & McDonald would cream off a substantial share of subsequent leading-edge research work in science and technology for the government. While RAND initially retained a fair amount of business from ARPA (renamed the Defense Advanced Research Projects Agency, or DARPA, in 1972), it slowly diminished.[4] RAND's reputation had been built substantially on its science-and-technology prowess, its ability to translate intricate data into coherent and elegant strategic policy. Even though its post–Pentagon Papers brain drain had ultimately stemmed from the conduct of a social scientist working on low-tech counterinsurgency and conventional warfare in Vietnam, the loss of talent meant that RAND did not recover its reputation, within government, as a leader in science and technology.

Although think tanks flourished and proliferated in the 1980s, their relationships to the Pentagon were less intimate than they had been, and their priorities and missions were correspondingly different. Outfits like the American Enterprise Institute (AEI), the Brookings Institution, the Council on Foreign Relations (CFR), the Carnegie Endowment for International Peace (CEIP), the Center for Strategic and International Studies (CSIS), the Cato Institute, and the Heritage Foundation became bigger and richer. The CEIP (founded 1910), CFR (1921), and Brookings (1927) long predated RAND. They were old and familiar, seeded with old money by patricians with a strong sense of public duty; while all three had the formal conceit of nonpartisanship, they also developed a generally liberal political tilt. AEI was established in 1943, mainly to lobby against government intervention in the free-market economy. Other outfits arose after RAND: CSIS in 1962, the Heritage Foundation in 1973, and the Cato Institute in 1977— the former at the height of the Cold War to address what were perceived as existential national challenges, the latter two as détente took hold explicitly to promote counterbalancing conservative public policies. If some were not immediately or exclusively focused on foreign and security policy, all evolved a substantial interest and expertise in it. But none of these organizations was, by statute or by aspiration, a federally funded research and development center (FFRDC). Though they might receive government support for specific studies or events, their funding came mainly from private sources like the Carnegie Corporation of New York, the Ford Foundation, or the Rockefeller Foundation, or from self-generated revenues from membership dues or publication sales. They did not, for the most part, deal with classified information, and most of their researchers lacked government clearances. Virtually all of the studies that these organizations produced were intended for immediate public consumption, even if many also targeted a particular agency in governmental constituency.

Most of these new institutions certainly remained analytic in approach. But they also tended to adopt political biases either to the right (AEI, Cato, Heritage) or to the left (Brookings, CEIP, CFR, CSIS) of center—the primacy of Reagan Republicans in government meant that identifiably conservative think tanks grew at a faster pace than liberal ones from the mid-seventies through the mid-nineties—and endeavored to provide rhetorical fuel to one political "side" or another.[5] They also functioned as "holding pens" for former government officials displaced by changes in administrations, but awaiting the return to power of their party or policy elite. Overall, their effect on policy was far more attenuated than RAND's had been in the 1950s and 1960s.

These advocacy think tanks, then, added a new dimension to the architecture of U.S. foreign policy, functioning largely on their own, without any standing or formal connection with government agencies, with an eye toward influencing but not directly determining policy. Thus, their contribution was more to the process of public debate and the aesthetic of policy formulation than to the actual substance of government policy. To the extent that they did garner singular influence in the corridors of government power, it was generally because they focused intensely on narrow "niche" issues—for instance, Middle East security—rather than anything so broad as U.S. strategic priorities or grand strategy.[6] Insofar as they cleaved to partisan viewpoints, they further submerged the vestige of pragmatism in American public discourse and policy analysis: strategic values became petrified in hardened political positions. The "principled" expert gained distinct favor as an idealist over the "pragmatic" expert, who tended to be viewed as weak or morally compromised.[7] The net effect was a diminished interest in thoroughgoingly analytic and fully investigated studies with which to inform policy.[8]

At the same time, FFRDCs like RAND, having been integrated into the U.S. national security establishment during the Cold War, became increasingly limited by their own intellectual and bureaucratic strictures. They had become symbiotically bound to government clients whose concerns—once the niceties of stable nuclear deterrence had been worked out—were more and more mundane and workaday. The leading FFRDCs "ossified," comments Schelling, and lost the "pioneering spirit."[9] The routinization of deterrence and progressive emphasis on procurement during the Cold War diminished the bold creativity that emerged from RAND in the 1950s and 1960s. By the 1970s, noted Richard Betts, RAND had evolved into a "bureaucratized contract research organization as much as a think tank and was no longer the hothouse of theoretical ferment it had been in the 1950s."[10] As the other FFRDCs gained favor, they all were forced to clamor for government contracts, and each institution had to focus more tightly on more immediate priorities, to tailor output to very specific contract requirements, and to account precisely for every nickel spent. They became micromanaged. Because they could retain people only for existing or proposed contracts—or out of their own revenue—FFRDCs could develop intellectual capital and effectively stockpile it only with some difficulty. RAND's voice remained significant, but its avenue of influence veered from broader issues of strategy toward more particular aspects of defense policy—for example, whether the F-22 fighter is essential to maintaining U.S air superiority capabilities, or how the next generation of tanker aircraft should be procured.[11]

Amplifying the politicization and atomization of the research endeavor was the Reagan administration's preoccupation with reducing the size of the federal government by outsourcing as much work as possible to the private sector. Although the defense budget rose for countervailing reasons, the Pentagon remained under persistent pressure to reduce in-house expenditures. As a result, government tasking to FFRDCs became all the more exacting and increasingly geared to short-term operational concerns that would previously have been the province of the government agencies themselves. After the Cold War ended, military spending diminished. While in 1995 some 82 percent of RAND's $114 million budget—by far the largest among think tanks—came from the federal government, a substantially lower proportion was for national security.[12] RAND analysts like Bruce Hoffman and Brian Jenkins did, to be sure, perform top-notch examinations of terrorist threats well before 9/11. But against an expanding array of more immediate and momentous state-based threats, terrorism was not a government priority. The intelligence community arguably had greater responsibility than the Pentagon to anticipate threats that were over the horizon, but its capacity to focus on deeper research questions diminished. Government interest in terrorism was therefore too sporadic to keep it well funded, and it was supported out of RAND's own pocket or as a distinctly subsidiary aspect of Pentagon-funded studies of "low-intensity conflict."

In sum, RAND and its institutional brethren could no longer afford the luxury of anticipating and thinking about the next strategic challenge when they were being paid to attend essentially to current operational ones. There were considerable amounts of money to fund new open-ended research, and much of it went to the "beltway bandit" offshoots of RAND and other FFRDCs that had proliferated in the 1970s. PSR, for instance, pioneered the use of new modeling techniques in relating intelligence data to working hypotheses about how the Soviets moved their nuclear weapons and forces during peace, crises, and war, in order to exploit vulnerabilities in Soviet doctrine. This tasking facilitated a better understanding of intelligence-based warning, and expanded wartime targeting opportunities.[13] Such work, however, still involved issues that were tightly bound to an assumed operational objective, and far more circumscribed than the uninhibited inquiries that RAND had undertaken in the 1950s.*

The Vietnam War also had a second-order impact on academia that was more subtle and pervasive. In retrospect, a historian of ideas might have expected Vietnam to have a wholesale effect on American intellectual leanings comparable to that of the Civil War, which spawned pragmatism and a rejection of what Menand calls the "idolatry of ideas." Along those lines, Vietnam, viewed as a grotesque consequence of bipolarity, might have fueled a consensus repudiation of containment and deterrence in favor of a radically more conciliatory approach. But the perils of Soviet domination—even when the prospect had substantially diminished—had apparently become too deeply ingrained in the American psyche to permit any such epiphany. Instead, the political establishment hedged, settling on a strategy of détente that did seek to ease tensions between the United States and the Soviet Union but declined to reject the fundamental tenets of the first Cold War. Those for whom Vietnam repre-

---

*Some of this work was also done by highly specialized Department of Defense organizations, such as Harry Diamond Laboratories and the Defense Nuclear Agency.

sented an intolerable moral blight opted out of the mainstream policy world, engendering a broader anti-"establishment" liberalism that found its most fertile ground, as protest movements often had, on college campuses. By the late sixties—well before the United States would stop deploying troops in Vietnam, long in advance of the Paris Peace Accords—opposition to the war among America's intellectuals was widespread, and their recommendations had shifted from measured policy alterations within accepted legal and policy channels to public defiance of the government by way of draft and tax evasion and mass protest.[14] The "long-run effect," noted the late Richard Rorty, a prominent contemporary pragmatist, was "to separate the intellectuals from the moral consensus of the nation rather than to alter that consensus."[15]

This militant liberalism strained the bonds between the federal government and academia that were initially forged in World War II, achieved a defining strength with the Manhattan Project, and were consolidated during the Cold War up to détente. The war as well as the Church Committee's revelations in the mid-1970s of intelligence excesses also made many academics wary of working on national security issues for the U.S. government. New intellectual trends spurred by the 1960s' philosophical ferment, particularly in Paris, reached the western side of the Atlantic. "Postcolonial" studies and gender studies triggered by the civil rights and feminist movements crystallized wariness of prevailing political views into outright opposition to them. Deconstructionists, in their skepticism about purported objectivity and their belief that there can be no value-free judgments, contributed to a broadly subversive mind-set.

These antiestablishment groupings decried what they saw as a kind of elitism whereby those anointed as eminent in their respective fields imperiously but insidiously incorporated their own political and ethical values into analyses presented as "value-free" and objective, in the process suppressing various forms of "otherness."[16] Within the U.S. academy, while deconstruction-ism got started with literary criticism—in Europe, where it originated, it was a broader anthropological and philosophical response to structuralism—it seemed to spawn the most enthusiastic American practitioners in the realm of jurisprudence.[17] There was considerable merit to the upshot of the basic arguments: it appeared indisputable that an exalted intellectual cadre elevated by an entrenched political and intellectual hierarchy would be psychologically prone to view alternatives as inferior, that this tendency would inevitably skew even the most neutrally intended assessment, and that successive iterations of a given mode of analysis would only amplify bias. And in fact, the generational conversation that morphed from hyped debates about "political correctness" into more nuanced discussions of multiculturalism has produced a much greater appreciation of cultural differences and the legitimacy of their expression throughout American society.

But thirty years ago, the strategic brotherhood, as it had developed during the Cold War, epitomized just the sort of exclusionary white and predominantly male club that angered the new thinkers. There was no portal available through which the two camps could constructively and pragmatically interact, and this mutual impermeability was reinforced by the former's unbending commitment to "the West" and the latter's primal ire over the perverseness of that commitment, manifested by the Vietnam War. Furthermore, deconstructionism seemed to imply intellectual nihilism, or at least an intractably atomizing pluralism and an irremediable relativism. Jacques Derrida, one of its founders, insisted, for instance, that "deconstruction is justice."[18] This peremptory dispensation telegraphed the futility of attempts to reharmonize revealed cultural or ideological divergences, which discouraged collegial debate. In the event, a widespread academic refusal to perpetuate Western (particularly American) hegemony, and a postmodernist commitment to using the father's tools to dismantle the father's house, emerged on university campuses. To undermine putatively authoritative orthodoxy became the aim of what came to be known as "critical scholarship" and "postcolonial theory."

None of the social sciences or humanities was immune to this dimension of the zeitgeist. Although there were arguably overriding reasons for opposing Soviet communism and expansion, an ideological perspective developed that minimized Soviet (and other) transgressions and impugned Western civilization. Political science in general, and Middle Eastern studies in particular, became especially politicized and polarized. Those engaged in Middle Eastern studies were inclined to target what they perceived to be pro-Israel, anti-Arab U.S. foreign policy. The late Edward Said's powerful Orientalism thesis, first put forward in 1978, furnished potent ammunition. From a broad analysis of literature and commentary, Said advanced a bruising critique of the academic discipline of "Oriental studies" that developed in the United Kingdom, France, and the United States. Basically, he argued that a collective psychology driven by colonialist self-interest had made white Europeans regard Arabs and Muslims as culturally homogeneous and inferior.[19] Many American Middle East scholars found Said's argument compelling. To give substance and amplitude to his charges of misguided cultural essentialism, they attributed Islam's decline and humiliation to Western imperial policies and scholarship, and used that interpretation to justify Muslim victimology and rage.[20] The Palestinians were cast as the latest victims, and the Israelis the unmerited beneficiaries, of the Orientalist bias.

As it matured, this hostile attitude antagonized an intellectual minority consisting mainly of so-called neoconservatives. The neoconservative movement began in the 1980s, when Daniel Bell, Irving Kristol, Daniel Patrick Moynihan, and Norman Podhoretz led an intellectual revolt against what they considered the excessively timid brand of realism that Kissinger's détente had spawned. They drew inspiration from the work of political scientist Leo Strauss, whom they read as championing a well-ordered, militarized, and judgmental Platonic state, and from Allan Bloom, a professor of philosophy at the University of Chicago and Strauss's foremost contemporary interpreter.[21] They sought to restore the primacy of American values, as distinct from interests, into U.S. foreign policy.* On Middle East matters, neoconservatives—latterly under the auspices of Campus Watch, a self-appointed Internet-based group dedicated to "monitoring Middle East Studies on campus"—railed like nineteenth-century pamphleteers against alleged "apologists" for radical Islam and related political violence. They, in turn, fired back with their own broadsides, eventually making the Middle East Studies Association an effective platform, and by boycotting scholarships offered under the National Security Education Program (NSEP) to students who wished to serve in U.S. defense and intelligence agencies and demonizing institutions whose students sought NSEP support.[22] Fruitful systematic collaboration between government and the academy was dampened by the rejectionism of Said's followers, who came to dominate Middle Eastern studies, and the corresponding trepidation of his reactive opponents.[23] During the Cold War, American Middle East experts

---

*The traction of neoconservativism in government waxed and waned, reaching a peak in Reagan's stridency, losing currency with George H. W. Bush's cautious though opportunistic term, resting in healthy equilibrium with Clinton's more pragmatic instincts, and transmogrifying into a kind of militaristic idealism under George W. Bush.

made precious few contributions of lasting value to U.S. policy making over the course of a generation.* Said's *Orientalism* and the climate of academic protest that nurtured it, albeit particularly resentful and energized, amounted to a true iteration of pragmatism: these phenomena certainly reflected, in Menand's phraseology, "skepticism about the finality" of a "particular set of beliefs."[24] The extreme political polarity that the Cold War engendered and the disinclination of the anti-Orientalists to work within the system, however, foreclosed the possibility of reconciling the two points of view and effectively conceded the balance of inside policy influence to the neoconservatives.

The absence of synergy between government and academia on strategic matters involving Islam also failed to spur the U.S. government to enhance its collective understanding of Middle East political, ethnic, and religious dynamics. Though denied political control of Arab states by authoritarian regimes, since the 1967 Six-Day War radical Sunni Islamists had steadily gained popular political momentum, and Arab paperback apocalyptics had conjured visions of devastating attacks on New York and visiting mass destruction on the United States.[25] Radical Islam as a global force first reared its head in 1979, when the Ayatollah Ruhollah Khomeini, the charismatic Shiite Muslim cleric, led the popular overthrow of the Shah of Iran and directed his wrath most immediately on the Shah's former patron, the United States.

At that point, regional security issues—particularly those in the Middle East—were becoming as important as nuclear strategy in think tanks and academic institutions. But the lack of intellectual depth on Middle East matters in the U.S. government,

---

*A conspicuous exception was William Quandt's important role, as member of President Jimmy Carter's National Security Council staff, in formulating the Camp David peace agreement between Israel and Egypt. But the very singularity of that example serves to underline academia's broader futility.

government-friendly think tanks, and universities limited the scope and imagination of their research. The Iranian revolution continued the trend of Islamist ascension with the ouster of a corrupt and brutal U.S.-backed secular regime by a pious Muslim revolutionary. But Iran was merely demonized as the fount of Muslim evil. The superpowers quickly placed the upheaval in Iran in the existing Cold War context. The Ayatollah Khomeini's regime was both anti-American and anticommunist. Accordingly, the 1979 revolution induced the United States to cultivate Saudi Arabia and Iraq—Sunni Muslim powers—as its new geopolitical proxies in the Persian Gulf. It also increased pressure on the Soviet Union to invade Afghanistan to prop up a faltering pro-Soviet regime and thereby prevent energized Islamic nationalism from spreading into Moscow's sphere of influence, expand its influence in Asia, and safeguard its access to Gulf oil.

Although the first Islamist terrorist attack of the era may have been Hezbollah's Marine barracks bombing in Beirut in 1983, U.S. officials saw no larger prospective significance in the incident. It simply involved Islamic extremists, and so, as Harry Rowen puts it, "there was an assumption that only local crazies were involved. The notion that this was a systemic threat took a long time to develop. We also were saddled with something that might sound prejudicial but I think is defensible, and that is the fact that the scholars of Islam available in the West—certainly in the United States—were a pretty sorry lot."[26] Somewhat clearer insights about Muslim radicalism in the Middle East ensued as Hezbollah became a standing challenge to Israel in south Lebanon and the Sunni militant group Hamas arose in the Palestinian territories in the late 1980s, but American perceptions were still skewed by the United States' preoccupation with Iran. The 444-day hostage crisis reinforced American perceptions that radical Shiite rather than radical Sunni Islam was the overriding

Muslim threat, and to American eyes tended to crystallize the global Muslim problem into the identity of a single state. There were a few voices warning that the "bureaucratic panic" exhibited by the evacuation of American personnel from the region would produce a kind of official introversion that would damage U.S. relations with the Islamic world. "We will find it harder and harder," said one NSC staff member, "to communicate with Muslims—because we reduce our opportunities for communicating."[27] But for Washington, the prime balancing solution was to bolster a corrupt and brutal secular regime—Saddam Hussein's Iraq—against Iran in a savage eight-year war.

Iran-sponsored terrorism increased, mainly in the form of heftier financing and some training for Hezbollah. But that was because, according to the CIA, "Iran [was] incensed over what it perceive[d] as the active alignment of Western and moderate Arab governments behind Iraq."[28] The CIA's broader line was that Iran did have a transnational agenda of fomenting 1979-style revolutions throughout the Persian Gulf region, often prosecuted with the assistance of the Iranian Revolutionary Guard Corps, but that the Iranian vision naturally privileged minority Shiite Muslims.[29] If, therefore, U.S. policy reconfirmed devout Shiite Muslims' view of America as a corrosive and inimical influence, it also inspired far more numerous Sunnis and Sunni regimes to align themselves with the United States. Furthermore, the apparent persistence of the state as the seat of strategic threats made the prospect of terrorism dip under the strategic radar. Finally, by the mid-1980s the CIA had come around to the view that economic pressures and the war with Iraq had empowered the pragmatists in Tehran and moderated the trajectory of Iran's Islamic revolution both inside and beyond Iran.[30]

Iran would remain a dangerous terrorist sponsor.[31] Iran-backed terrorism, after all, had forced the United States to quit its Lebanon peacekeeping mission in 1984. And the expectation was that U.S.-Iran relations would worsen. But nobody in or outside of government was looking systematically or intensively at the global Muslim situation in the round. No one noticed, for instance, that through Hezbollah Iran was establishing a model for the transnationalization of revolutionary activities that was not inherently limited to Shiite Muslims, or that the brand of self-abnegation and martyrdom—including suicide attacks—that Hezbollah had employed could render asymmetrical warfare more effective. Toward the end of the 1980s, the CIA viewed transnational Islamic radicalism as an Iranian state phenomenon largely subordinate to the extant Cold War strategic architecture.[32] Iran, however revolutionary, had achieved its main objective of an Islamic republic, was recovering from its devastating war with Iraq, had an intense religious and geopolitical rivalry with the Saudis, and thus could be contained. Libya—a secular Arab nationalist regime—appeared to be a more potent actuator than Iran of international terrorism against Americans, as its complicity in attacks in Europe prompted Reagan to order air strikes on Tripoli in 1986. Terrorism, on the whole, continued to be viewed as perhaps an intensifying threat to U.S. assets and personnel overseas and in the skies, and stimulated better physical protection and an assertive "no-concessions" policy, but was not considered a strategic threat to the functioning or integrity of the government.[33] And radical Sunnis came to be viewed not as enemies but, quite to the contrary, as anti-Soviet—hence pro-American—proxies.

The ABM Debate (2)

The continuing primacy of the Soviet Union in the array of threats facing the West further blinded Washington to the coming "defensive jihad," and made it focus again on the nuclear balance. At first blush, reviving the nuclear debate seemed pointlessly disruptive. Deterrence seemed to work as a mechanism of social control as well as military strategy. The fixed place that mutual assured destruction had in the structure of international security had, in the paradoxical way that marked deterrence, calmed populations about the perils of nuclear war and WMD in general: the very destructiveness of nuclear weapons, and the fact that each side had enough of them to waste the other many times over, comfortingly paralyzed both sides. MAD had also produced remarkable continuity and consistency in nuclear strategy and operations. Through the Nixon, Ford, and Carter administrations, "there was some progression as to how [SAC operators] got guidance from the SIOP," but "what you were doing was basically just adjusting target categories and emphasizing one thing more than another," notes Michael Wheeler.[34] Confident that both the Americans and the Soviets were hypersensitive to the horror, the world came to trust them not to let things roil into Armageddon.

When NATO agreed to deploy an intermediate nuclear force (INF) consisting of 572 Tomahawk cruise missiles and Pershing-2 ballistic missiles in five European countries in 1979, however, many European observers interpreted it as the beginning of a "second cold war."[35] Recalls Sir Michael Howard: "On tactical nuclear weapons, we more or less reached a consensus"—namely, that the very notion was oxymoronic. The INF reopened the issue, "and that was almost entirely political."[36] Advocates of the deployment naturally and defensibly considered the INF an improvement in flexible response, and therefore a fortifier of deterrence and reassurance to Europe about the quality of the American commitment to its defense. It was interpreted by some of the more extreme European disarmament advocates as proof that the United States regarded war in Europe as an element of a plausible limited war scenario, and Europe, therefore, as expendable.[37] Even among political moderates in Europe, the INF was considered needlessly provocative. Antinuclear protests—restimulated by the neutron bomb controversy a few years earlier—burgeoned in Europe, and were soon echoed in the United States.

The furor over the INF provided opportunities for both hawkish conservatives and dovish abolitionists. These camps shared an abhorrence of mutual assured destruction as a basis for security. They parted company on the matter of remedies. By cultivating a decisive American edge in defensive weapons, the conservatives wanted to change the makeup of the U.S. arsenal such that it did not imply reciprocal annihilation if used but rather only Soviet annihilation; the abolitionists simply wanted to do away with nuclear weapons as even theoretical war-fighting tools and settle on nonnuclear means of maintaining security. Led by the Committee on the Present Danger, certain key strategists who had been relatively quiescent during détente—including Wohlstetter* and Paul Nitze—and disciples like Richard Perle and Paul Wolfowitz placed the central putative assumption of deterrence—MAD—in doubt. For them, the Soviets' emphasis on counterforce and civil defense still suggested that they sought the capability to win a nuclear war, which they could use to force the United States to back down in a crisis without ever having to fire a shot—or at least a missile.[38]

In parallel, a nuclear freeze proposal—advocating a stark halt to the testing, production, and deployment of nuclear weapons—attracted many followers and grew into a national movement. One of them, psychiatrist Robert Lifton, observed in Americans a kind of

---

*Wohlstetter, though not formally a member of the Committee on the Present Danger, sympathized with its concerns and approach.

"psychic numbing" that had made them all too comfortable with the existential specter of nuclear annihilation. This insight led to dire expositions that intended to force the public to rediscover nuclear horror.[39] In popular culture, the doomsaying reflected in films like *Fail-safe* and *The Bedford Incident* in the late 1950s and early 1960s was reprised. Sober, graphic movies like *The Day After* (U.S.) and *Threads* (UK) forcefully brought nuclear holocaust, which MAD had rendered latent in the popular imagination, back into collective consciousness.* Jonathan Schell's series of articles in *The New Yorker* (later constituting a book titled *The Fate of the Earth*) also made a considerable impact in depicting in minute detail both the immediate and the lingering effects of a nuclear explosion, but the author's naive and inconsistent political arguments—starting with world government, then switching to more insular state sovereignty—and what Freeman Dyson called his "gross exaggeration of the fragility of civilization" limited the persuasive staying

---

* As an antidote to the Reagan administration's perceived bellicosity and recklessness, a kind of gallows humor also emerged. A group of New York writers sharply parodied government civil defense pamphlets with *Meet Mr. Bomb: A Practical Guide to Nuclear Extinction*. In a preface titled "A Special Message from President Ronald Reagan," the notional chief executive mused that "ever since my good friend Mr. Bomb was born people have been referring to nuclear war as 'unthinkable.' Well, they're entitled to their opinion, but I think it's time—and I may be wrong—to reverse that trend of the last 40 years. It's time to start thinking positively. It's time to start thinking the 'thinkable.'" The writers glommed onto both the idiomatic logic of deterrence and popular gloom, as their ersatz president continued: "Now there's been a lot of loose talk about Mr. Bomb. Some folks who must be a lot cleverer than me, I'm afraid, have even said that Mr. Bomb exists only to prevent his own use. What does that mean? Gosh, how would it sound if some other useful invention was talked about that way? You can imagine what people's reaction would be if you said: 'This blender exists only to prevent its own use.'" What ensues is a gleefully puerile, snide, and funny catalog of pre-, intra-, and postapocalyptic guidelines for living under such headings as "Your Home Is Your Casket," "Americans Keep Falling on My Head," "One Nation: Underground," and "Your Shelter or Mine? 'With-It' Dating Tips for Post-Nuclear Teens." Tony Hendra and Peter Cohn, eds., *Meet Mr. Bomb: A Practical Guide to Nuclear Extinction* (New London, NH: High Meadow Publishing, Inc., 1982).

power of his thesis.[40] Physicist Carl Sagan's "nuclear winter" hypothesis added flourish and fast-burning fuel to the abolitionist fervor, but the worst-case assumptions it entailed amounted to rhetorical overkill. The meltdown of the Chernobyl nuclear plant in Ukraine—which caused widespread contamination—ultimately did more to underline skepticism about the possibility of controlling the military use of nuclear energy.[41]

What the Committee had not fully realized was that President Reagan, though not strategically sophisticated and therefore susceptible to being "handled" by his advisers, was at heart a resolute nuclear abolitionist himself. This fact goes a long way toward explaining the schizophrenic character of Reagan's policies through his eight-year tenure. Initially, the hawks held sway. Reagan denounced the freeze proposal, saying that it would play into the Soviets' hands because they had nuclear superiority. The Pentagon accelerated Carter-era programs including the MX ICBM, the Trident SLBM, and comprehensive cruise-missile development, and reinstated the new long-range bomber, the B-1B. They also rejected Carter's "countervailing strategy," which turned on denying the Soviet Union limited nuclear options, in favor of developing such options for the United States. This reversal of emphasis was stark: the operational art was to be applied to nuclear war scenarios that they had believed had been lost in the widening maw between strategy and tactics that had characterized nuclear strategy in the MAD epoch. Nuclear war was to be made winnable after all. To sustain momentum behind this push, the conservatives largely ignored less-alarmist assessments of Soviet military strength and subtler interpretations of the Soviet mind-set. Reagan's 1982 "Evil Empire" characterization reflected his malleability and the entrenchment of the conservatives' attitudes in his policy team.

The liberal counter was in essence a status quo argument that spurned the abolitionists as well as the hawks: the threat of

mutual assured destruction adequately curtailed the political utility of nuclear weapons and was a source of geopolitical stability.
The message was basically to leave well enough alone, and stop
pretending that operational and logistical details significantly affected the superpowers' strategic calculations. There was no need
to query what would happen if deterrence failed, because it
wouldn't. This was no more satisfying to either the hawks or the
abolitionists now than it ever had been. At the same time, the
hawks had painted themselves into the corner of advocating a
revived nuclear war-fighting capability while also having to acknowledge that there was no morally acceptable outcome to a
nuclear war.

The debate thus acquired some modesty. It became more technical than philosophical. The hawks still insisted that Soviet
ICBM advances, unrestrained due to the deferral of the SALT II
treaty, were eroding the United States' ballistic missile deterrent.
While moderates (in particular, the bipartisan Scowcroft Commission) acknowledged the problem, they noted that the other
two legs of the nuclear triad (strategic bombers and SLBMs) left
second-strike deterrence essentially intact. Furthermore, making
the MX missile mobile was expensive and entailed unacceptable
environmental disruptions in the western interior of the United
States. Solutions to U.S. ICBM vulnerability—from clustering
the missiles together to smother the effect of all Soviet strikes
after the first ("densepack") to dispersing single-warhead missiles to inhibit a preemptive strike ("Midgetman")—were proposed, but none were convincing. With the MX infeasible and
alternatives uncertain, the various existing systems were most
useful as bargaining chips vis-à-vis the Soviet Union.

Despite Reagan's personal belief in the abolition of nuclear
weapons, a large-scale reduction in forces (theoretically down to
zero), though a dream of his, received far less emphasis from the

key members of his administration. Instead, they angled for nuclear superiority. However inconsistent this policy was with Reagan's heartfelt beliefs, it chimed with his celebrated view of the
Soviet Union as the "Evil Empire." Containment was not merely
reinvigorated but advanced to "rollback." The Reagan administration took the view that the lessons of Vietnam had been learned
too well, and revived modest and measured activity in proxy
wars—especially in Latin America and the Caribbean, and also
by supporting Islamic fundamentalist mujahideen against the
Soviets in Afghanistan. On the nuclear front, dire warnings of
the earlier strategists suddenly struck a loud, atavistic chord. In
the posthumously released *Thinking About the Unthinkable in the
1980s* (1985), an update of his 1962 classic, Kahn wrote: "It is
unacceptable, in terms of national security, to make non-use of
nuclear weapons the highest national priority to which all other
considerations must be subordinated. It is immoral from almost
any point of view to refuse to defend yourself and others from
very grave and terrible threats."[42]

Indeed, this blast from the past supported those who opposed
arms control, and argued that vulnerability was an illogical and
morally flawed basis for strategic stability and that military revolution via missile defenses—rather than strategic stagnation in
reliance on offensive systems—was the way out of prospective
Armageddon. By the 1980s, the United States had established a
technological edge in nuclear weapons design and variety—or
certainly the Soviets perceived as much—and became emboldened. The Strategic Defense Initiative (SDI or "Star Wars") contemplated an American antiballistic missile network that could
thwart a Soviet nuclear attack by repelling all incoming nuclear
strikes and thus neutralize the Soviets' nuclear war-fighting capacity. In rolling out the initiative, Reagan told the nation in a
national address on March 23, 1983, that nuclear weapons would

become "impotent and obsolete." Freedman encapsulates the idea well: "SDI sought a Great Escape from the nuclear dilemma... from mutual assured destruction to mutual assured survival."[43] Congress more or less fell in line, giving the administration three of the four billion dollars requested for SDI in 1985. Although this was a very small proportion of the total defense budget, the amount was large for what was as yet only a research program. And unlike the ABM program's funding, SDI's was primarily a result of popular pressure rather than a debate between strategy experts and elites.[44]

The political, technological, and legal impediments to implementing Reagan's vision of abolition facilitated by high technology were immense. Even assuming SDI could work, the Soviets had to be convinced of the technical capabilities of the system to avoid testing the United States' will. Strategic stability also required survival to be mutual. Thus, technical secrets would have to be shared with the Soviets. Mutual distrust, evolved over thirty-five years or more, and Soviet opposition to Star Wars made this a dubious proposition. Moreover, the scientific community thought the very concept was ludicrous, and that absent refinement through extensive public discussion, it would be doomed. Recalls Freeman Dyson: "When [Lieutenant] General [James] Abrahamson was running the 'Star Wars' program, Edward Teller and I went to the Pentagon to talk to him. We disagreed about lots of things, but we agreed about what we'd say to General Abrahamson. He knew that we were both sort of friendly to 'Star Wars,' but we went to him and we said, look here, this program is so bad technically that the only way to rescue it is to bring it out into the open so it can be properly criticized. You've got to get rid of secrecy—then it has a chance. With secrecy, it has no chance. That was the message we took."[45] If *Sentinel* and *Safeguard* were unlikely to work against limited nuclear strikes, what chance did a purportedly airtight system have? Absent strong a priori evidence that SDI would be cheaper than offensive systems designed to overmatch it, all it would precipitate was an arms race. In any case, the development and deployment of such an advanced system, even if it were workable in theory, would take decades.

Furthermore, the ABM Treaty seemed to bar anything beyond research on ballistic missile defenses. In 1985, however, RAND analysts argued that the classified negotiating record indicated that article V of the treaty prohibited only the deployment of, and not research on, ABM technology. The administration's interim solution was to recharacterize all ABM components as "subcomponents" and all of the United States' ABM-related activity as "research," and eventually to argue that the Soviets had never accepted any limitations on mobile ABM systems utilizing future technologies.[46] This bordered on sophistry. Yet SDI scared Gorbachev, who sought to confine the program to the laboratory by matching Reagan's stunning offensive concessions at the summit in Reykjavik, Iceland, in 1986. The two leaders' pronouncements, by their literal terms, would have effected a ban on ICBMs. Both governments soon retrenched, however, blunting the hypnotically pacific impact that SDI had briefly had.[47] SDI wound up producing exuberant research but barely any development, and lost congressional support before the end of Reagan's second term. Schelling's coda on the project seemed to sum up the tacit consensus on "Star Wars": "It was crap, and everybody in the Defense Department knew it, I think."[48]

During this period, Freedman brought perhaps a uniquely historical approach to analyzing nuclear policy, and identified with the neoconservatives, who would have a bigger role in the 1990s. In the late 1970s and early 1980s, he recalls, "the neocon stuff was a general critique of détente." In rejecting the aspects of détente that required the West to be deferential to the Russians on human rights issues and to ignore their often alarming statements of doctrine, he agrees,

> the neocons made perfectly valid points. So I had sympathy with their moral critique of the Soviet Union, but I also thought détente nonetheless made sense. I was too much of a European to be wholly won over by their argument. In a number of respects, though, I put some distance between myself and standard Euro-détente liberals. Then, when the great nuclear debate broke out in the early 1980s, I just thought a lot of the antinuclear arguments were specious. I had no trouble saying these weapons were wicked. But when they started to get into first strikes and second strikes and arms race stability, they were supposed to be rigorous and they weren't. There was, for instance, a very good case to be made for cruise missiles in terms of flexible response, and it was deliberately misconstrued. So I became increasingly pro-nuclear—pretty orthodox in nuclear terms.

On the same basis that he saw the logic of INF, he saw no logic in SDI. If, he argued, deterrence is unstable and untrustworthy, the answer is not SDI but disarmament. Wohlstetter and his followers among the neocons "wished to re-interpret what Reagan was trying to do in terms of a 1960s-vintage argument on homeland defense and protection. That's not what Reagan had in mind at all. He was an abolitionist."[49]

By default, though not without some irony, arms control had regained currency by late 1987. In parallel with the "Star Wars" effort, there had been positive movement toward the Strategic Arms Reduction Talks (START) to reduce offensive warheads by 20 to 30 percent. This was consistent with Reagan's underlying conviction that nukes should be abolished, his advisers' belief that the status quo favored the Soviets, and the consensus that the Soviets cheated ("trust but verify") and therefore should be subject to the deepest possible agreed cuts. On top of these factors, there was a scramble to put Reagan's Pollyannaish views on ICBM abolition back in the box and INF back on the table. The INF Treaty was signed in December 1987, eliminating all intermediate-range nuclear forces. From the Soviet point of view, this "double zero" result meant that Moscow was spared a threat to Soviet territory in exchange for withdrawing a threat merely to European and not to American soil. From the American point of view, Washington eliminated a nuclear threat to NATO and thus strengthened conventional deterrence, improving the American position on the escalation ladder.[50] In addition, the apparent fact that Soviet doctrine did not countenance any nuclear war as "limited" as long as it involved strikes on Soviet soil—regardless of the nature of the target—meant that the INF would not have enhanced the United States' ability to limit nuclear war anyway.

The planned deployment of the INF had also lowered any Soviet expectations that they could fight a limited nuclear war spearheaded by their conventional might and leave the Soviet Union substantially intact. The upshot was long-awaited doctrinal convergence between the United States and the Soviet Union. Neither countenanced limited nuclear war, and both were equally concerned about keeping crises from escalating to the nuclear level. The need for the kind of capabilities-based deterrence that had dominated nuclear strategy and arms control during the first Cold War had diminished. Soviet conventional superiority and skepticism as to limited nuclear war pushed Moscow toward a no-first-use position. Despite Reagan's failure to eliminate the strategic reality of MAD, Western conventional weakness did not allow a renunciation of first use. But both sides contemplated a longer conventional phase in any East-West conflict. Analytically, the riddle of preserving the United States' extended deterrence of a Soviet advance across Europe's central front remained.

In fact, that threat was not long for this world. Gorbachev saw that the Soviet state was crumbling. But perestroika was too late to save a command economy strained by two generations of increasing defense expenditures and pushed to the limit in over-reaction to Reagan's buildup; glasnost was insufficient to fur-nish legitimacy to a repressive government that had provided only a relentlessly grim way of life while the West had pros-pered. The Soviets' withdrawal from Afghanistan in 1989 politi-cally emboldened the Warsaw Pact countries. The Berlin Wall was torn down in November, the end of the Cold War pro-claimed in December, Germany formally reunited in 1990. By the end of 1991, the Soviet Union had been dismantled, leaving Russia and its poorly secured nuclear weapons and material, which came to be called "loose nukes." The existence of these vulnerable stocks of potential weapons raised the possibility of small states or nonstate groups developing, buying, or hijacking a nuclear device and thus being able to threaten much larger states. But the intellectual and technological efforts of the United States during the Cold War, for all their sophistication and might, did very little to prepare the United States for asymmet-rical threats. American forces had been largely unsuccessful in fighting irregular combatants in Vietnam, and on that account came to abjure any counterinsurgency mission. Ethnonational-ist and ideological terrorist groups grew during the Cold War, but operated primarily in Europe, Latin America, and Asia, and those plaguing the Middle East were viewed primarily as the instruments of anti-American states; there seemed to be no im-mediate need for U.S. intelligence and law-enforcement agen-cies to develop a robust counterterrorism capability beyond instituting better airline and airport security to protect Americans against hijackings. And the notion that nonstate groups might employ WMD was written off as so improbable as to be unworthy of government attention or money.

The Unthinkability of the Undeterrable

In 1963, the only player that the CIA considered to have the inclination and wherewithal to introduce WMD into the United States for hostile use was the Soviet Union itself.[51] During the Cold War, neither the U.S. government nor the civilian strategists whom it consulted worried seriously about adversaries who might be less deterred than the Soviets or the Chinese by nuclear weapons. To an extent, this intellectual timidity was circular: it stemmed from the fact that even if such enemies existed, the United States had no means of repelling such a threat. The dispensation was not to seek a solution but rather to kick the can down the road. In 1969, veteran nuclear strategist George Quester, now at the University of Maryland, wrote a book chapter on nuclear proliferation arguing that one of the most dire ramifications of nuclear proliferation to states was that it would give rise to proliferation within states and with that the risk of nuclear terrorism. A common riposte, he recalls, was that "we shouldn't even talk about that because it's too early and we don't have a solution. I'd say, hey, on the way home stop at the paperback shelf of a bookstore and you'll find six books that have nuclear terrorism as the plot. James Bond: *Thunderball*. There was a movie made in England in 1946, *Ten Days Till Noon*, the plot being about a scientist in a nuclear weapons lab who is dissatisfied that the world isn't peaceful, so he's made a bomb that is going to blow up London unless everybody agrees to get sensible. That's just a year after Hiroshima. It doesn't take much imagination."[52] But Quester admits that he did not even offer a programmatic remedy beyond the default one of nonproliferation itself.

Fully fledged concern about nuclear terrorists, operating beyond the control of a state, appeared to come from outside security circles. In 1973, the noted literary journalist John McPhee published a series of articles in *The New Yorker*, which the following year appeared as a book called *The Curve of Binding Energy*.* The title referred to the graphically plotted magnitudes of forces that hold together the protons and neutrons in the nuclei of atoms from the lightest to the heaviest elements—and the immense energy that is therefore released when light atoms are pushed together (fusion) and heavy atoms split apart (fission). The book highlighted the risk of terrorists' acquiring nuclear weapons through the prism of former government fission bomb designer Theodore Taylor's disaffection and alarm. The book was disconcertingly prescient. It starts with a simple

---

*McPhee was inspired to pursue the book—and Ted Taylor—by Mason Willrich, a law professor and nuclear security expert who had coauthored a book with Taylor on the risks of nuclear theft for the Ford Foundation. Willrich, who initially encountered McPhee in a pickup tennis match while the two men were coincidentally vacationing in Rhode Island, offered a trenchant assessment of the insufficiency of safety and security incentives to the nuclear fuel-cycle industry, which, though structurally a public-private partnership, was still commercially driven to an extent comparable to that of strictly private enterprise. With environmental concerns and higher reactor costs making utilities unprofitable, said Willrich, the last thing they wanted to be bothered with was a problem, like unaccounted-for fissile material, that had thus far had no consequences. Then again, the U.S.-Soviet nuclear confrontation also had produced no war. And indeed, the premise of Willrich and Taylor's book was that government expenditures on preventing nuclear war (billions), reactor safety (hundreds of millions), and safeguarding nuclear materials (less than ten million) stood in inverse proportion to the corresponding risks: nuclear war was highly unlikely, a reactor meltdown somewhat more likely, and the clandestine manufacture of an atomic bomb from stolen material downright probable. This perverse prioritization was perhaps in line with the institutionalized dominance of deterrence in U.S. national security policy. But it also perpetuated Wohlstetter's fallacy of lesser included cases. Mason Willrich and Theodore B. Taylor, *Nuclear Theft: Risks and Safeguards* (Cambridge, MA: Ballinger: 1974).

observation: "There is . . . no particular reason the maker [of a nuclear bomb] need be a nation. Smaller units could do it—groups of people with a common purpose or a common enemy."[53] While at Los Alamos, Taylor himself designed the Davy Crockett, the smallest fission bomb ever made, at less than fifty pounds the proverbial "suitcase" nuke; the Hamlet, the most efficient one ever devised in the kiloton range; and the Super Oralloy Bomb (SOB), the largest-yield fission bomb ever exploded (at Eniwetok, in the megaton range). Taylor knew just how easy—and hard—atomic bombs were to make.

The prospect of terrorists leveling the World Trade Center was a Taylor leitmotif, and it is mentioned no fewer than five times in McPhee's recounting. Taylor remarks that 10 percent of a piece of uranium-235 the size of the stick of gum, or crystals produced from 500 grams of plutonium fluoride, "would be enough to knock down the World Trade Center."[54] Taylor allows later that he would have instructed the Los Alamos and Lawrence Livermore government laboratories to produce a crude bomb based on unclassified information "that could knock over the World Trade Center" so as to gauge the plausibility of an upstart nonstate group making an atomic bomb.[55] (The AEC was never willing to authorize such an exercise.) McPhee himself takes up Taylor's message, noting that "a low-yield bomb exploded inside one of the World Trade Center towers could bring it down."[56] The impact of the fully fueled jetliner that crashed into each of the two towers has been estimated at roughly one kiloton, the figure Taylor contemplated in the 1980s. Taylor did not concern himself with the utility of nonnuclear technology—like fuel-laden commercial jetliners—for apocalyptic terror attacks. But the larger point stood: nuclear weapons gave nonstate actors willing to use them an asymmetrical advantage and a huge margin of error.

Furthermore, Taylor and McPhee were worried about more than just the relative power of nuclear bombs and the resulting theoretical attractiveness they would have to terrorists. In December 1953, with his "Atoms-for-Peace" speech to the United Nations General Assembly, President Eisenhower had established a "swords to plowshares" moral psychology to guide the civilian oversight of nuclear energy. He urged not only that access to nuclear technology be opened to American industry and research institutions, but also that U.S. cooperation in developing the peaceful uses of nuclear power be extended to other countries. Though a well-intentioned product of sublimated American guilt over having ushered nuclear weapons into international relations, the atoms-for-peace dispensation glossed over the dual-use nature of most nuclear technology. By statute, the AEC was charged with helping to control the military applications of nuclear power and with promoting as well as regulating its "peaceful" applications for cheap electricity. The fact that both categories of use involved the same nuclear fuel cycle, and all uses of nuclear energy were therefore double-edged, was often downplayed at the expense of concerns about the proliferation of nuclear material—and, potentially, bombs.

Taylor and McPhee discovered that it was difficult to register the same sense of alarm with those in charge of maintaining the U.S. fuel cycle. The manager of a plutonium reprocessing plant in West Valley, New York, was both thoughtful and hopeless, and encapsulated the institutionalized constraints on assessing any risks that don't seem immediate. "We of the Establishment resist change," he admitted. "But we do the very things that advance it." Yet when Taylor asked him whether he worried about the possible theft of plutonium, he said: "No. Honest to Pete, no. . . . I have so God-damned many real problems. I haven't time to imagine them."[57] James Schlesinger, chairman of the AEC in the early

1970s, cracked that "a self-respecting ambitious terrorist has better things to do than to take nuclear material."[58]

The consensus was that terrorists were not generally terribly "ambitious," and that those few who might be in any case would go after biological or chemical agents. There was also a wishful, subconscious notion that if strategists ignored certain pesky problems, potential enemies might not be alerted to them. Even Dyson—the last person likely to shun the intellectual discussion of remote possibilities—notes that he and other Princeton scientists "had long discussions with John McPhee about whether he should go public. The question in our minds was, did you want to scream about this problem, because maybe you would then make it more likely to happen."[59] The upshot was that the non-state terrorist threat associated with the world's most terrible weapons, though not ignored, was treated not as a political or ideological problem but as a logistical one, along the lines of requiring signed receipts for shipped nuclear material. This the AEC did in 1970, and the move inaugurated a series of required safety measures for the transport and storage of nuclear material and prompted General Accounting Office "red team" exercises that had theretofore been nonexistent.[60]

Stimulated by the protestations of Taylor and McPhee, however, a few enterprising physics students set about to prove how easy it was for amateurs to concoct a crude but functional atomic bomb. One in particular, John Aristotle Phillips, an undergraduate on the verge of flunking out of Princeton, in 1977 persuaded his adviser—none other than Dyson—to let him try to save himself with a term paper on how to build an atomic bomb. He came up with a feasible Nagasaki-type design of ten-kiloton yield, costing only $2,000 to construct, simply by drawing on open sources: Manhattan Project physicist Robert Serber's *The Los Alamos Primer: The First Lectures on How to Build an Atomic Bomb,* available from the National Technical Information Service; and the DuPont Company. The federal government confiscated and classified the term paper, while the Pakistani government tried to cadge a copy. The FBI watched him for a while. For his part, Phillips continued his intellectual entrepreneurship by writing, with his college roommate, an account of his work on the paper jauntily titled *Mushroom: The Story of the A-Bomb Kid.*[61] Shortly thereafter, the U.S. government sued to enjoin *The Progressive* magazine from publishing an article by freelance journalist Howard Morland describing how to construct a hydrogen bomb, but the magazine won the lawsuit by asserting that the material information was in the public domain. The article was published in November 1979.[62] The Princeton and *Progressive* episodes did reflect general government concern about the possibility that nonstate actors or rogue states might develop nuclear weapons. But given that a great deal of crucial scientific information was already out there, the government's response— essentially, to limit the further dissemination of scientific know-how—was dispirited to say the least. Moreover, with respect to atomic weapons, it was inadequate. While the technical challenges facing a nonstate group looking to make a hydrogen bomb may have been insurmountable, those involved in building an atomic bomb apparently were not.

In the distant background, political Islam was in the midst of resurgence. Western economic models did little to check the greed and corruption of Middle Eastern ruling elites financed by oil sales to the United States and Europe, and the Israelis' overwhelming victory over Egypt, Syria, and Jordan in the 1967 Six-Day War—resulting in the loss of Palestine and Jerusalem, Islam's third-most-holy city—drove home to Arab populations the fecklessness and weakness of secular Arab nationalist governments. In the throes of the geopolitical machinations of the Cold War, Muslims inferred that they were being punished for their apostasy in following capitalism and communism alike, and political Islam—especially the Muslim Brotherhood in Egypt—gathered intensity. By the early 1970s, Muslims in the Middle East were becoming more devout and more observant, and economic migration carried this greater piety to Europe and elsewhere. Egypt's strategic, if not tactical, success against Israel in the 1973 Yom Kippur War energized Arab Muslims, proving that they could effectively confront Israel on the battlefield. Saudi Arabia's subsequent oil embargo and the spike in world crude prices demonstrated the power over the West that oil afforded Arabs. Arab, mainly Palestinian, terrorism was on the upswing, and the "Black September" group's massacre of eleven Israeli athletes in September 1972 prompted President Nixon to form the Cabinet Committee to Combat Terrorism, which in turn established a large interagency working group on terrorism-related challenges.[63] But the terrorist threat was viewed essentially not as a strategic problem but as a vicious nuisance involving "dastardly crimes" like kidnapping and hijacking, and not dire enough to warrant wholesale changes in policy. Improved protection of diplomats and basic upgrades in commercial aviation security, policy makers supposed, would be enough.[64]

The surge in terrorism in the 1970s came agonizingly close to institutionalizing vigilance in the U.S. government about grassroots transnational Islamist terrorist movements of strategic moment. By the middle of the decade, Robert H. Kupperman, chief scientist of the U.S. Arms Control and Disarmament Agency, who had been asked to study the terrorism problem, had broached the possibility of "mass destruction terrorism."[65] Yet a seemingly system-wide resistance kept counterterrorism from becoming a national security priority. One White House staffer, Michael Duval, actually advised that "top White House officials" ought not to be involved in policy discussions about terrorism because doing so only "invites terrorists to target the

United States and latent domestic dissidents to move into action."[66] Nevertheless, while mass-casualty terrorism didn't make it to center stage, "intermediate terrorism"—that is, "a level of terrorist violence lying between mass destruction and the types of assassinations or abductions of medium-grade USG officials or private citizens with which US terrorism policy and the Working Group have been primarily concerned"—did.[67] Among the most gaudy intermediate threats identified was that from terrorists firing man-portable surface-to-air missiles at commercial aircraft, and official concern gathered momentum as the nation's July 1976 Bicentennial celebrations (as well as the Summer Olympics in Montreal and the presidential elections) approached.[68] At this point, Duval significantly changed course, counseling Dick Cheney—who was then President Gerald Ford's chief of staff—that the president should become directly involved in strengthening domestic counterterrorism efforts at NSC level.[69]* The president apparently did act to bolster disaster management for mass destruction terrorism with a national security decision memorandum later in the year.[70] But the absence of terrorist attacks during the events anticipated to prompt them—especially the Bicentennial—meant that threat perceptions on the part of the U.S. government shrank considerably. Thus, two weeks after the Fourth of July, Leo Cherne, chairman of the president's Foreign Intelligence Advisory Board, suggested that Dr. Kupperman recast a classified study titled "The Near-Term Potential for Serious Acts of Terrorism," rather smugly musing: "I wonder whether you have a hypothesis which will explain why no [terrorist] effort was made to take advantage of such unprecedented theatrical moments."[71]

*In 2005, citing the 9/11 Commission report, *Newsweek* reported that no record existed that Cheney ever responded to the memo. Michael Isikoff, "Intelligence: A Warning to Cheney About Terror—in 1976," *Newsweek*, March 28, 2005.

Several studies were completed—including a particularly insightful one authored by Kupperman—and improvements in national counterterrorism capabilities recommended. But no major formal action was taken to put them into effect. Some analysts also appreciated the risk that terrorists would somehow come into possession of a nuke—by stealing material on site or in transit and fashioning a crude device or by hijacking a bomb wholesale. In 1976, for instance, Schelling speculated that terrorists would get hold of nuclear weapons in the 1980s or 1990s in light of the number of countries (including Iran and Brazil) planning nuclear power plants that could produce weapons-grade plutonium.[72] Like Taylor and McPhee, Schelling worried most about fissile material from the Soviet Union getting into the hands of nonstate actors. But the concern was general, premised not on the specific (if then inchoate) designs of revolutionaries but rather on a generic presumption that anyone as unbalanced as certain terrorists would just as soon use an atomic weapon. And nobody, of course, ventured to identify a specific group or pool of terrorists that might exploit the security vulnerabilities that they revealed.

Certain characteristics of Cold War–era terrorist groups were reassuring. In particular, they dimmed the likelihood that terrorists would actually bring down a country or a government. The Provisional Irish Republican Army (IRA) and the Euskadi ta Askatasuna (ETA), for instance, had objectives—a united Ireland expunged of British rule and an autonomous Basque state separate from Spain, respectively—that may have been revolutionary in the sense that they were irredentist, but they were hardly politically inconceivable or abjectly unrealistic. For that reason, the IRA and ETA used violence as a means of political leverage, which they knew they would lose if the bloodletting became too indiscriminate. In campaigns that each lasted roughly thirty years, the IRA killed around two thousand people and ETA about nine hundred—the combined total of which merely approximates al-Qaeda's one-day body count on 9/11—and increasingly targeted security forces to the exclusion of civilians or issued warnings before attacks in public areas. The idea was to put just enough fear into the public to produce political pressure to impel the state to bargain with the terrorists.*

The partial success of such groups moved Brian Jenkins, then RAND's leading terrorism analyst, to observe in 1975 that "terrorists want a lot of people *watching*, not a lot of people *dead*."[73] He also suggested that exaggerating or harping on the threat of nuclear terrorism or the inadequacy of nuclear safeguards, by creating fear in the general public, might only make "going nuclear" more tantalizing to terrorists, who seek to reinforce such fear.[74] He basically maintained these views throughout the 1970s and 1980s, quite correctly characterizing terrorism as "a routine way of focusing attention on a dispute, of bringing pressure on a government," which counsels operating on "the principle of the minimum force necessary."[75] But he also hinted at a dynamic shift in observing that indiscriminate attacks on public areas and carriers aimed for increasingly large casualty figures. Part of the explanation was that the popularity of terrorism as a political tool had made its audience jaded, such that upping the ante was required to get a given degree of responsiveness to terrorist demands. Jenkins further recognized "the religious aspect of current conflicts in the Middle East" as a factor, and in one pregnant sentence encapsulated the general phenomenon of mass-casualty suicide

---

*To an extent, it has worked: the IRA, Northern Ireland's pro-British Protestant majority, and the British government entered into the Good Friday Agreement in 1998, and the Basques have greater autonomy within Spain's majority-Basque provinces than they had when ETA's campaign began in 1975. The IRA has virtually abandoned its armed campaign, and in 1999 ETA began experimenting with cease-fires in earnest.

attacks: "As we have seen throughout history, the presumed approval of God for the killing of pagans, heathens, or infidels can permit acts of great destruction or self-destruction."[76] He envisaged the policy consequences of a hypothetical nuclear terrorist attack in ways that resonate with the aftermath of 9/11, predicting a medley of changes including increased security at nuclear facilities, law-enforcement crackdowns, copycat threats, intense American international engagement, and a more salient preemption option.[77] With the usual caveats, he forecast an increase in terrorism in the 1980s.[78] But he stopped well short of predicting threshold-crossing terrorism, seemingly because he fell into the trap of mistaking the familiar for the probable, of fighting the last war. Wearily he intoned: "Terrorists operate with a fairly limited repertoire. Six basic tactics have accounted for 95% of all terrorist incidents: bombings, assassinations, kidnappings, hijackings, and barricade and hostage incidents. Looking at it another way: Terrorists blow up things, kill people, or seize hostages. Every terrorist incident is merely a variation on these three activities."[79]

This assessment was entirely consistent with the CIA's rather modest threat analysis, which characterized IRA car bombs—they had never claimed more than fifteen people or so, and were increasingly accompanied by telephoned warnings—as "indiscriminate" and "mass-casualty."[80] It also squared with the highly circumscribed experience the United States had had with terrorism directed at air traffic. In January 1972, a lone American named Garrett B. Trapnell hijacked a TWA Boeing 707 bound from Los Angeles to New York, demanding a ransom of $306,800, the release of black militant Angela Davis from custody, and a conversation with President Nixon. Although he was apprehended at Kennedy Airport after an FBI agent shot and wounded him, the Trapnell incident prompted the Nixon administration to mandate metal detectors and carry-on baggage searches at U.S.

airports starting in January 1973.[81] As a result, the theretofore epidemic-like incidence of airplane hijacking dropped to two attempts (both unsuccessful) between January 1973 and January 1974 from one every other week (most of them successful) in 1972.* By the 1980s, domestic hijackings had all but disappeared. Libya-assisted terrorists blew up airliners in the 1980s and 1990s. Nobody predicted that nineteen terrorists would combine five of the six tactics adduced by Jenkins to claim mass casualties.

In 1982, Schelling did lodge a less sanguine viewpoint than had Jenkins, recognizing the need for a new strategy to deal with actors who might actually be inclined to use nuclear weapons if they should get hold of them. Harkening back to Hiroshima, he noted that nuclear weapons were almost inherently terrorist.

> It is worth remembering that on the only occasion of the hostile use of nuclear weapons, they were used in a fashion that has to be considered "terrorist." There was a nation that had a very small capacity to produce nuclear bombs. The need was sufficiently urgent that it was decided to go ahead with "revelation" when only two were in hand. The hope was to stun the enemy into surrender, or to create such a tremor that the government would change into one disposed to surrender. The possibility of a harmless detonation in an unpopulated place was considered

---

*In February 1974, Samuel Byck attempted to commandeer a Delta Airlines DC-9 from Baltimore-Washington International Airport and crash it into the White House to kill Nixon. A troubled man convinced that Nixon was oppressing the nation's poor—and the inspiration for the Travis Bickle character in Martin Scorsese's movie *Taxi Driver*—Byck killed an airport policeman and shot both pilots of the aircraft before being wounded and committing suicide in lieu of allowing himself to be captured. By the time the Byck episode had occurred, however, the post-Trapnell federal measures were in place. Byck's unsuccessful venture was thus considered aberrational, and U.S. commercial aviation practically invulnerable. Andreas Killen, "The First Hijackers," *New York Times Magazine*, January 16, 2005, pp. 22, 24.

but rejected on the grounds that the demonstration might fail (possibly through incomprehension by the witnesses) and in any event would deplete the stockpile by half. The weapons couldn't be wasted on a remote battlefield; and even military destruction in the Japanese homeland would be incidental compared with the shock of an anti-population attack. With a modest pretense at military-industrial targeting, the industrial city of Hiroshima was chosen. No warning was given that might have allowed interference with the demonstration.[82]

The prime lesson he drew from this very limited history of nuclear use was that "nuclear weapons . . . are too valuable to waste."[83] Accordingly, he proposed that "terrorist nuclear threats have a comparative advantage toward deterrence," which entails inducing the adversary *not* to do something, as opposed to compellence, which involves inducing the adversary *to do* something.[84] Terrorists would prefer to retain nuclear weapons to keep their threat alive over using them on the poor bet that a finite series of strikes could bring the United States to its knees.

On the other hand, it is worth noting that Hiroshima and Nagasaki might also be cast as the greatest military acts of compellence ever perpetrated in that they induced the Japanese to surrender unconditionally (though some historians argue that it was the Soviet Union's agreement to join the Pacific war that really did the trick). The most extreme of the Islamist terrorists want to compel the United States and the West, at the very least, to withdraw wholesale from Muslim lands. It is not inconceivable that some of them would bet—albeit imprudently—that a few nuclear detonations in the right Western cities would force a choice between the abhorrent slaughter of innocents and a tacit drawdown of Western influence in Islam, and that the United States and its partners would choose the latter. And Schelling acknowledged that "eventually we may need a domain of strategy for coping with these lesser nuclear threats" that was "likely to be different from the principles and ideas" developed during the Cold War in light of the "utter lack of symmetry between the United States and any such nuclear adversaries."[85] Jenkins, for his part, in 1987 took the view that nonstate actors faced prohibitive technical hurdles in constructing a bomb and equally daunting political ones in that mass destruction would harden governments against bargaining and thus thwart the primary aim of terrorism.

Ambivalent Legacies

After it was all over, Cold War nuclear strategists could point, as Schelling does, to "two spectacular accomplishments": nuclear proliferation slowed to a virtual halt, and nobody launched a nuclear weapon after Nagasaki. Yet Freedman concluded, with considerable force, that the sophistication of nuclear deterrence was largely illusory, and that the sheer horror of nuclear war was the real deterrent all along. He wrote, in 2003:

> Any risk of being on the receiving end of a nuclear attack was an enormous constraint. Western and to some extent Eastern strategists became adept at manipulating this risk, with occasional and timely hints of dark possibilities without ever quite spelling out how they would be realized in practice. So long as the weapons were around even a skirmish between the great powers seemed extraordinarily dangerous in its escalatory potential. Strategy required working with and around this danger. The durability of containment encouraged the view that at this level the strategy worked and at a crude and basic level it did. The Emperor Deterrence might have had no clothes, but he was still Emperor. For both sides, from the early 1950s and in the face of

thermonuclear weapons, prudence was the better part of valour. This strategic relationship turned out to be sufficiently robust in its essentials to survive new technologies and doctrines.[86]

Now he quips that his own intellectual enterprise "was nihilistic, in the end."[87]

After Vietnam, the weakened condition of the United States' conventional force structure and the strategic uncertainties stemming from the decline of American power did give rise to an apparent reconsideration of nuclear war as a legitimate option. In 1977, for instance, the Carter administration asked the Defense Nuclear Agency (DNA) to assess how much war-fighting capability U.S. forces in Europe would retain after a Soviet first strike targeting U.S. theater nuclear forces, and force survivability was reemphasized. In the same year, the Warsaw Pact's joint "Zapad" (meaning "West") exercises were held to determine its ability to deal with NATO's heightened conventional combat readiness. As part of the exercise, the Soviet generals seriously entertained a preemptive nuclear first strike, involving three hundred nuclear warheads, against NATO military assets, and emerged with a relatively optimistic assessment of the notional result.[88] While the United States had genuinely pondered nuclear first use during the Cold War, it had done so far earlier—during the Kennedy administration. Yet "Zapad" was, after all, only a game. Indeed, during the same time period, NATO conducted an exercise in which it decided to go nuclear in response to a Warsaw Pact conventional attack. Thus, the United States also had not foreclosed its first-use option. Both Washington and Moscow were most likely using that option in war games to send a signal meant to reinforce their respective deterrents. However notional, first use was part of each side's declaratory policy, and scripted into its exercises. The DNA's inquiry was defensive rather than strategic in orientation.[89] While the Soviets probably remained marginally more inclined than the Americans to use nuclear weapons through the 1980s, by then most Soviet analysts no longer really believed that nuclear weapons could achieve anything tactically or operationally meaningful on the battlefield and were turning to Western strategic thought for guidance in determining nuclear missions and force structure.[90]

Thus, Freedman concludes, persuasively, that the great strategists

> couldn't solve the basic problem of nuclear strategy, which is how could you credibly threaten to use this stuff when you were likely to get blown up in response. But the faint chance that you might did support deterrence. I don't think anybody ever really improved on that. In the Fifties and early Sixties, it was hard to work out how this could develop. The technologies were still being worked through, and it was reasonable to assume that things were technically possible that turned out not to be. It was still hard to say that [nuclear strategy] didn't have a point. You were still left with the problem of, well, what do you do? Do you say it's all pointless, or do you have to keep up the charade because it's the charade that makes deterrence work?[91]

The Cold War ended before the ABM debate had reached a resolute conclusion. But it did seem clear that even if the threat to use nuclear weapons was really empty, nobody was willing to put that hypothesis to a serious test. "You could ask," says Schelling, "why didn't Golda Meir use nuclear weapons in 1973? The Egyptians had two armies north of the Suez Canal, there were no civilians around, the armies were perfect targets, and the Israelis were known to have nuclear weapons. They never used them." It was, he says, "one of the most spectacular things that didn't happen." Truman in Korea, Johnson in Vietnam, Margaret Thatcher in the Falklands and, "unbelievably," the Soviets in Afghanistan did not use nukes.[92] In 1991–92, Schelling was visiting professor of national security strategy at the National War College. He gave a seminar involving fifteen officers from all four U.S. services as well as an Israeli colonel. Each student had to posit a scenario, and one of the most intriguing envisaged Saddam Hussein, having reconstituted his army in 2005, racing across Kuwait and gobbling up everything on the south shore of the Gulf, including Saudi Arabia. The United States establishes air bases, positions aircraft carriers, and lands Marines in the new theater of war. All of a sudden, Iraq launches nuclear missiles at these targets and destroys them. What, the students were asked, should the United States do? "I just sat back and listened while they talked for an hour and a half. They unanimously decided that the United States should declare war on Iraq, go in the hard way, and defeat them with conventional forces. I thought, 'Boy, have they been brainwashed.' I'm glad of it. The most important thing we had to protect was the unwillingness to use nuclear weapons."[93]

If it was so critical to avoid using nuclear weapons, didn't it follow that conventional capabilities for enforcing international legal and political standards had to be all the more versatile? Yet it was not a priority to make them so. Vietnam, to be sure, did prompt the United States to choose targets of military intervention more carefully, and to conduct counterinsurgency more competently. The United States stayed closer to home, mainly in Central America, and Army Special Forces enjoyed some success in bolstering El Salvador's foreign internal defense capabilities in a way that they had not done for South Vietnam's. But the emphasis remained on firepower rather than the small-unit patrol operations favored by counterinsurgency practitioners. It was only reinforced by the interpretation of Reagan administration defense secretary Caspar Weinberger and General Colin Powell's requirement—inspired by the Vietnam debacle and the United States' desultory and ultimately disastrous peacekeeping effort in Lebanon—of a wholesale political and operational commitment to any American military intervention as the imperative of "overwhelming force." The U.S. interventions in Grenada in 1983 and Panama in 1989 were simply straightforward applications of the Weinberger-Powell Doctrine.[94] The 1990–91 Gulf War—a high-intensity, high-technology blitzkrieg—extinguished any residual institutional enthusiasm for hands-on involvement in messy Third World conflicts. "Fighting the nation's wars" again became the national military priority, with "low-intensity conflict"— later rebranded the even more sedative "military operations other than war" (MOOTW, or "mootwa," in military argot)—strictly subordinate.

The end of the Cold War notwithstanding, deterrence remained the only game in a nuclear-armed world. And it skewed strategic ontology. Although the initial popular perception in 1945 was that large numbers of nuclear weapons would be unnecessary, the subsequent materialization of redundantly massive nuclear arsenals resulted from the increasingly dominant role of the weapons as symbols of power rather than tools of war.[95] Because buying the weapons and sustaining such global jeopardy required more concrete justification than mere symbolism, however, strategists had to think and speak in terms that made nuclear war seem more likely—and therefore acceptable— than it actually was. The "organizational thought-styles" that thus evolved were to characterize nuclear weapons as functionally comparable to conventional ones, to apply oversimplified criteria to nuclear plans, to remain self-consciously vague about the relationship between nuclear policy and strategic goals, and to use the possibility of an adversary's actual "irrationality" in a crisis to support servicing his perception of one's own irrationality or using that perception to keep the adversary at bay.[96] In this light, it is perhaps not so surprising that the United States failed to hone its nonnuclear options more finely than it did, so as to account for more than conventional major-war capabilities and to lay greater stress on the nonmilitary aspects of international security. "Hearts and minds" were neglected. By the same token, it is hardly shocking that the United States gave rather short shrift to the prospect of nonnuclear but nonetheless threshold-breaking terrorism. In the 1970s and 1980s, it is true, U.S. agencies considered chemical and biological terrorist threats more salient than any potential nonstate nuclear ones, and took on board the uniquely "terrifying" psychological effect that mass-casualty weapons had on civilian populations.[97] But such threats still did not loom large in American security planning. From the government's narrowly state-based perspective, chemical or biological threats emanated mainly from governments with major military capabilities and only those nonstate groups that they might directly sponsor. The Soviet Union or its communist "surrogates" were seen as posing the primary threat, with an occasional nod given to China and to certain Arab states.[98] The remote possibility was raised that the latter might supply Palestinian "guerrillas" (the word "terrorist" was not used) with chemical or biological weapons.[99] Specific scenarios, developed mainly by the U.S. Army Test and Evaluation Command at the Dugway Proving Ground in Utah, usually involved area attacks by the Soviet Union and the Warsaw Pact on U.S. or NATO territory, with at best a token discussion of terrorism.[100] Among the few point targets for chemical or biological terrorist attacks identified by the Army were U.S. Navy submarines.[101] In 1986, the government's perceptions of the threat seemed to edge upward.

Test and Evaluation Command disseminated an incisive technical note identifying the "alarming trend" of indiscriminate terrorist violence and the inevitable terrorist temptation to use chemical or biological weapons, which the note, quoting a 1984 Institute for Foreign Policy Analysis study, portrayed as "a far greater threat to American national security" than nuclear terrorism.[102] "Even an independent terrorist group (not state supported) should be able to produce and weaponize small amounts of some chemical and biological agents, enough for terrorist type attacks," said the paper.[103] It ended on an ominous note: "Most terrorist groups have probably contemplated the utility of increased violence, and have generally rejected this option. However, the constraints on terrorism are basically political rather than technical, and are generally imposed by the terrorists themselves. The increased proportion of terrorist events directed against persons rather than against property reflects the growing willingness of terrorists to kill."[104] Yet as late as 1990, the General Accounting Office, while acknowledging the highly toxic effect of the Army decontaminant DS2 (to be used, ironically, to decontaminate military hardware after a chemical-weapons attack) and the public's exposure to the compound via errant sales to civilians, made no note of the corresponding potential for terrorist acquisition and use.[105] Evidently, the U.S. government had not thoroughly assimilated the terrorist chemical and biological threat or, perforce, the greater strategic threat that terrorists might come to pose. It was not prepared for what was to come.

5

The Halting Leap Forward

Freedman's charade, it turned out, had to be maintained. Even after the immediate threat of self-annihilation had passed, the strategists had done such a good job of selling the fear that no one could stop thinking about it. In 1995, France, on the pretext of preparing for a test ban, undertook a series of nuclear tests in the Pacific. The abolitionist movement resurfaced. The hard-nosed experience and seniority of the players—some from unexpected quarters—gave the movement a gravitas that it had lacked forty years earlier. They included Oxford professor Robert O'Neill, a native Australian and former director of the IISS, and General Lee Butler, commanding officer of the Strategic Air Command as the Cold War ended. Others hailed from respected think tanks like the Stimson Center in Washington. These people had understood the grim necessity of deterrence before the Soviet Union disintegrated. Nuclear weapons, they now argued under the auspices of the Canberra Commission, were no longer needed to prevent war between major powers, to backstop security guarantees, to deter the use of weapons of mass destruction, to establish political status and leverage, to deter aggression at low cost, or to respond decisively to large-scale conventional attack. The utility of nuclear arms, they concluded, consisted solely in deterring their use by others—so why not just get rid of them altogether? The problem was that since the mere possession of nuclear weapons would enable any state to hold an adversary in check, a degree of simultaneity and verifiability in disarmament was required that did not seem realistic.

Failure of Imagination

President George H. W. Bush was a realist ill at ease with abolitionist idealism. Realism dictated caution. Bush may have talked about a "new world order" in which state boundaries might be penetrated for the direct benefit of the people who dwelled inside them—that was the motivation, ultimately frustrated, for the U.S. intervention in Somalia. But in fact, he adhered more closely to old notions of state sovereignty. In the most dramatic case, he refrained from toppling Saddam Hussein's regime after removing Iraq's threat to Kuwait, primarily in deference to traditional Westphalian principles of sovereignty and nonintervention enshrined in the UN Charter. He and his advisers still believed that bilateral state-to-state relations made the world go 'round, and remained focused on state actors rather than nonstate groups as the sources of major threats.

Even in hindsight, Bush's position was far from silly. Though the United States' biggest state adversary had faded away, and Russia's gross domestic product was now equal to Belgium's, it was still geographically the largest country in the world and possessed nuclear weapons. The American assumption was that it would remain an important international actor, but one that would cooperate with the United States. The progress of arms-control talks tended to support this assumption. START I was signed in July 1991, reducing deployed U.S. and Russian warheads from 13,000 to 6,000. Bush and Russian president Boris

Yeltsin agreed to reduce that number to 3,000–3,500 by 2003 under START II, Clinton and Yeltsin to further reductions to 2,000–2,500 by 2007. In September 1991, Bush announced the United States' intention to eliminate tactical nuclear weapons through informal mutual force reductions, canceled new development programs, took strategic bombers off alert, and stopped targeting Eastern Europe and the former Soviet republics. Within two weeks, Gorbachev reciprocated. Because Washington had swiftly and unilaterally deemphasized nuclear weapons, the three quasi-nuclear former Soviet states—Belarus, Kazakhstan, and Ukraine—eventually denuclearized. Russia's dearth of resources for conventional forces also held out a real prospect for NATO's conventional parity, which enabled the elder Bush to cancel plans to enhance theater short-range nuclear missile capabilities and to modernize U.S. nuclear artillery shells. The NATO position finally did become minimum deterrence: it would maintain the lowest and most stable level of nuclear forces needed to secure the prevention of war.

In the early 1990s, the world was quantitatively a safer place. But, as Freedman noted, it was qualitatively still subject to nuclear peril: both sides were allowed to keep undeployed warheads warehoused, and deployed warhead ceilings were not terribly different from the pre-MIRV launcher numbers of three decades earlier.[1] The main difference was that Russia's overall military capabilities could no longer compete with the West's, and therefore could not support any ideologically based geopolitical ambitions that clashed directly with American ones and produced the most acute nuclear risk. Some risk, however, remained. In addition to India and Pakistan, Iran and North Korea came to view nuclear weapons as indispensable. The latter two states had interests adverse to those of the United States and for them a minimal nuclear capability would be an invaluable means of restraining the only superpower. In that light, there seemed to be a legitimate role for a practically insuperable Western nuclear arsenal as a deterrent to the proliferation of all forms of weapons of mass destruction—possession of which Western conventional superiority tended to promote—and a source of authoritativeness useful in maintaining global order. So Clinton, in his second term, declared that the U.S. nuclear deterrent was intended to prevent chemical and biological attacks, which precluded a no-first-use declaration on the part of either the United States or NATO. Furthermore, in 1999 Moscow reinstated extended nuclear deterrence by reserving the right to use nuclear weapons "in situations critical to the national security of the Russian Federation and its allies."[2] After the international system had digested the end of the Cold War, the consensus settled on the marginalization of nuclear weapons rather than their abolition.

Meanwhile, NATO's U.S.-led Balkan interventions gave the Atlantic alliance a post–Cold War mission, and they highlighted the instability attending the breakdown of bipolar alignments and the new security challenges of subsovereign conflict. The multipolar world that seemed on the verge of emerging in the 1990s did not quite materialize. Germany's struggles with unification and Japan's endemic recession kept them from challenging the United States economically. Russia became bogged down in corruption and criminality. China's political and economic growing pains would delay its coming of age as a world power. While the European Union became an economic rival of the United States, the stickiness of national identities and priorities and the burden of expansion inhibited its capacity to conjure a truly supranational foreign and security policy cohesive enough to check American power.

Jenkins and Schelling had provided the bases for some comfort that nonstate nuclear use, even if nonproliferation regimes failed, was unlikely. But if true believers unbeholden to any particular government, territory, or people would *probably* refrain from using nuclear weapons, there was still vexing doubt as to whether they would forbear from unleashing other WMD—in particular, biological ones. While chemical weapons had been used on the battlefield in World War I and more recently in the Iran-Iraq war, and would probably be too unwieldy to be readily employable as anticivilian mass-casualty terrorist devices, biological weapons were small, concealable, and easily transportable—and their use was infrequent in modern times and therefore laden with premium shock value.* Furthermore, crude toxins, at least, could be manufactured by any number of trained scientists in an inconspicuous room with commercially available laboratory equipment and biological agents. This grim truth implied not only access to technology and know-how but also an estimable capacity for repeat attacks ("reload").

In late 1989, RAND analyst Jeffrey D. Simon issued a qualified warning: terrorists were less likely to use nuclear weapons than biological ones.[3] Given Jenkins's position, and even Schelling's view that terrorists were less inclined to use nuclear weapons than to threaten their use, this was not an earthshaking stance to take. But Simon also noted trends—more spectacular terrorist attacks, an increase in state sponsorship of terrorism, and a rise in religiously based terrorism—that did suggest a greater disposition among terrorists to cross thresholds and inflict mass casualties. Dialing back on the implied urgency, he noted: "Since biological weapons are less controllable than conventional bombs, they would claim far more unintended victims. This may be a risk that even the religious extremists are unwilling to take."

---

*The Japanese used biological agents (including bubonic plague, cholera, and anthrax) against Chinese cities in the 1930s and 1940s. Peter Williams and David Wallace, *Unit 731: Japan's Secret Biological Warfare in World War II* (New York: The Free Press, 1989).

Thus, fear of backlash among supporters and personal risk are among the four chief factors that Simon cites as constraining terrorists from using bioweapons.[4]

Simon's principal referent for religious extremists was Hezbollah, which had in 1983 killed 241 U.S. Marines in a single suicide truck-bombing. While Hezbollah's objectives—the elimination of the state of Israel and the Islamization of Lebanon—could hardly be called limited, they were local rather than global and it exercised operational self-restraint. These factors distinguished Hezbollah from the Sunni Islamist groups, the most prominent of which was al-Qaeda, that would arise during the next decade. Even so, there was an appreciation for Hezbollah's transnational infrastructure and reach: the Defense Intelligence Agency identified Lebanese Shiites in West Africa as funding sources and potential recruits.[5] Hezbollah was also involved in the bombing of the Israeli embassy in Buenos Aires in March 1992 and the Jewish Community Center there in September 1994. Over the 1980s and 1990s, however, Hezbollah's overall focus increasingly narrowed on Israeli military targets in south Lebanon. Simon did acknowledge that terrorist groups with broader and more vague geopolitical ambitions and consequently "amorphous constituencies" were relatively impervious to the public backlash constraint.[6] But two other considerations might counsel hesitation about using biological weapons. One was fear of an undesirably strong response from a target government. The other was that terrorists are reluctant to try unfamiliar weapons when conventional ones will serve their purposes.* Knowing

*Today's Islamist terrorists have basically combined conventional techniques (e.g., hijackings and car bombs) and equipment (e.g., fertilizer-based explosives) to unconventional effect. At the same time, they have shown a plain operational interest in unconventional weapons. For example, a jihadist cell in the United Kingdom had made a small quantity of ricin from castor beans and was apparently planning to make more, when it was rolled up in early 2003. Insurgents in

what he knew then, Simon made the right call as far as it went: "Since the technological, logistical, and financial barriers to the use of biological agents are not insurmountable, a key determinant in the potential use of such agents will be the willingness of terrorists to engage in this new type of violence. Therefore, efforts to improve intelligence regarding terrorist group strategies and capabilities will become increasingly critical in the future."[7]

Failures of deterrence against troublesome states—Iran, Iraq, and Libya, in particular—also concerned the United States, as the government remained worried about "whether the substantial nuclear and chemical retaliatory capability of the United States is sufficient to deter Nth-country attacks employing WMD."[8] Military vulnerabilities of the stronger state, as well as extreme, desperate, or idiosyncratic motivation and factual misperceptions, were considered the main conditions for attacks by smaller states. "Psychopathological leadership" and "crazy state" cultures that could involve religious zealotry also increased risks.[9] Barry Wolf, another RAND researcher, in 1991 arrayed the Barbary Pirates, American Indians, Iranian revolutionary extremists, and Lebanese terrorists (Hezbollah was not named) as those who exploited large-power vulnerabilities in low-intensity conflicts.[10] And, in quoting Palestinian leader Abul Abbas's declarations that "there is an Arabic saying that revenge takes 40 years" and "some day, we will have missiles that reach New York," he heeded the strategic patience, ambition, and ire of certain Muslims.[11] But Wolf's awareness of any potential nonstate actor or Islamic threat was anecdotal rather than integral to his analy-

---

Iraq have turned trucks carrying chlorine gas into precision chemical munitions by dispatching suicide bombers to blow them up. Furthermore, intelligence gleaned in Afghanistan following the U.S.-led intervention demonstrated al-Qaeda's general interest in developing chemical and biological weapons, radiological "dirty bombs," and, eventually, an atomic bomb.

sis, which concluded merely that any U.S. ballistic missile defense system must be demonstrated effective to minimize misperceptions of U.S. vulnerability that could tempt weaker states to attack the United States and to limit damage in case deterrence fails anyway.[12] Wolf pondered enemies launching attacks "even when by any rational calculus such attacks would lead to defeat or even annihilation," setting forth abundant precedent, and he noted that the stronger state's threat of retaliation might lack credibility on account of humanitarian or political concerns. At bottom, however, his study skirted any searching analysis of threats from apocalyptic, decentralized terrorist groups hunkered down in tents in the Afghan mountains.

In 1991, nobody had imagined a group like al-Qaeda. No enemy in history had designated as legitimate military targets all citizens of Western democracies by virtue of having elected their leaders and thus bearing direct responsibility for their policies, as well as those Muslims who merely acquiesce to the rule of "apostate" Muslim regimes. Killing on a massive scale fit well with this ethic. Practically speaking, it would decimate al-Qaeda's adversaries and intimidate their survivors. The proven capacity to visit mass destruction on a biblical scale would also reinforce jihadists' status as God's agents, making their cause all the more compelling to potential believers and recruits. While, notwithstanding the barracks bombing, Hezbollah was not generally prone to suicide attacks, jihadists are, so personal risk would not substantially come into play. Self-sacrifice and support for absolute victory are prerequisites of al-Qaeda membership, and a member in good standing would tend to dismissively attribute public disapproval of extreme measures to weakness and impiety. In fact, al-Qaeda's *shura,* or council, sharply debated whether the shock of attacking the World Trade Center and the Pentagon would be worth the probable loss of Afghanistan as a base, and ultimately was persuaded that it was.[13] So the threat of devastating retaliation against territory that had proven so reliable a deterrent during the Cold War was unavailing against al-Qaeda's most powerful leaders. They seemed to view not only the destruction of 9/11 but also the robust U.S. response as a catalyst to a self-perpetuating and intensifying jihad that would somehow realize the group's violent eschatological vision of an America destroyed. In that light, any feasible punishment administered by the United States was not merely futile but, in fact, inspiring to the jihadists.

The United States may have been in a position to cripple al-Qaeda after 9/11 by taking down the Taliban regime in Afghanistan and occupying the country. But because the political and moral costs of militarily devastating large portions of the Muslim world were unacceptable, and the United States lacked sound intelligence on just who and where key operatives were, the United States was never realistically in a position to annihilate al-Qaeda. Thus, al-Qaeda did not evince the "magnificent overconfidence" that Arab armies had vis-à-vis Israel in 1948 and 1967 or the French did toward the Prussians in 1870 in assessing America's vulnerability: it could, in fact, pull off 9/11 and still survive in some form, albeit initially weaker. It also did not unduly rely on any state or nonstate allies—two historically salient sources of misperception and vulnerability proffered by Wolf. Furthermore, al-Qaeda's geographical dispersal, adaptability, and recruitment capability might have made even wholesale Western military retaliation insufficient to quell the global jihad. Bin Laden expected retaliation, not extermination. In this light, while the Japanese attack on Pearl Harbor looked strategically senseless, al-Qaeda's calculation as to 9/11 did not.

So, as to why strategists schooled in the nuclear age were caught off guard by apocalyptic terrorists, Quester elucidates,

My own personal answer is that a lot of us said, gee, in the long run terrorism is going to be serious, but let's not talk about it too early because there's no sense in discovering a problem before you can discover a solution. The elementary logic was that a terrorist doesn't have a capital city you can threaten, and you may not even know who he is or what cause he represents. He doesn't have to be Islamic—he can be crazy along some other dimension. People had sat around talking about hijacking airliners before it even happened and said, "Let's not even write this up." The solution to hijacking airliners, we thought, was simply to make it hard, and in the few cases where they succeed, wait 'em out and get the release of the hostages.

Quester also recalls a certain brand of mirror-imaging that some of his colleagues applied to terrorists that bred complacency. He used to ask colleagues, "How come terrorists haven't used chemical or biological weapons? One answer was, they don't know how. Someone else with some expertise would say, sure they do—*I* know how, my students know how. Then someone would suggest that maybe there was some unwritten rule among terrorists that you're trying to become a government, so you behave like a government. Governments aren't using chemicals on each other, terrorists won't do it either to each other. All of that was shattered by 9/11. But others, like Fred Iklé, said that when these capabilities get into the hands of terrorists, we're all in trouble. We won't know how to deter them."[14]

Yet during the 1990s, the West did not face this dilemma with any real imagination. The first full-blooded attempt to grapple with potential large-scale terrorist threats was the Soviet Nuclear Threat Reduction Act of 1991, commonly known as the "Nunn-Lugar Act" after its two sponsors in the Senate. The act established the Cooperative Threat Reduction (CTR) program, under which the United States extended funds and advice to Russia for better security and created legitimate employment opportunities for idled Russian scientists who otherwise might have peddled their knowledge and skills to bad actors. Nunn and Lugar, joined by Senator Pete Domenici, bolstered U.S. preparedness in sponsoring the Defense Against Weapons of Mass Destruction Act ("Nunn-Lugar II"), which was enacted in 1996. The legislation expanded the scope of the original CTR legislation in the former Soviet Union, and required six federal agencies acting in partnership, with the Defense Department in the lead and guided by a "train-the-trainer" program devised by the U.S. Army's Chemical and Biological Defense Command, to train local first-responders to deal effectively with WMD incidents.* And in 2003, President Bush signed the Nunn-Lugar Expansion Act, which extended the CTR program to areas outside the former Soviet Union.

While CTR and Nunn-Lugar II made sense as far as they went, they still reflected relatively shallow preoccupations with essentially bilateral and logistical measures and passive domestic defenses when the evolving threat called for deeper thinking about transnational movements and their motivations. The implication of CTR and Nunn-Lugar II was merely that the best defense against loose nukes and disaffected bomb builders were the standard ones: nonproliferation, physical security, and domestic preparedness. But according to Richard Garwin and George Charpak's pre-9/11 2001 book, *Megawatts and Megatons,* as of March 2000, the United States had purchased eighty-one tons of highly enriched uranium (HEU) from Russia. The largest reported seizure of HEU at that time was only three kilograms—only a tenth of what would be required for a uranium implosion weapon and a mere thirtieth of what would be needed for a gun-

*The other five federal agencies are the Department of Energy, the FBI, the Federal Emergency Management Agency, the Public Health Service, and the Environmental Protection Agency.

type device. Furthermore, during the early 1990s, the vast majority of claims that weapons-usable material had been hijacked turned out to be scams.[15] The net effect of these facts was overall complacency about the ability of terrorists or their collaborators to steal fissile material and turn it into something dangerous. The Pentagon was slow in implementing CTR, which did not gain momentum until Clinton's second term.[16] Garwin, a physicist and leading expert on proliferation of nuclear weapons, in 2001 only tepidly raised the question of whether terrorists might become more inclined to use nuclear weapons and pointedly declined to offer an answer—merely reciting Jenkins's orthodoxy and offering the bromide that "a general remedy to most terrorism is to reduce the level of conflict in society and also the tolerance for violence."[17]

U.S. government agencies responsible for countering terrorism were reluctant to tease out the ramifications of al-Qaeda and its affiliates' actually acquiring a WMD capability. One likely psychological reason was that they were not used to thinking of terrorists as meriting the wholesale political and diplomatic energies of major governments: the U.S. government and most others, as a matter of policy, did not negotiate with terrorists. Accordingly, they simply couldn't come up with anything more creative or sophisticated than a strategy of physical denial. Intellectually, the problem probably involved the kind of pernicious circularity that Quester identifies, whereby a question ought not be pressed if no solution is in view. The difficulty was that technocrats focused on technical problems—locks on doors—when the future threat involved how those who would pry them open were thinking. It was a massive, and collective, failure of imagination. Some new thinking on terrorist threats did emerge, but it was too timid and tentative to move the U.S. government to embrace them as truly strategic problems.

Terrorism and Deterrence

Due to its precipitousness, the Soviet Union's deterioration caught the U.S. national security community off guard. It was left with nascent new threats, bin Laden's included, but no paradigm for thwarting them, which helps explain the buck-passing between the FBI and the CIA and among different CIA units in the 1990s.[18] Notes Quester: "Nobody predicted that the Soviet Union would collapse. The basic logic of deterrence says you shouldn't be delighted if the Soviet Union collapses; in fact, you'd be in deep trouble. What keeps the Soviet arsenal from being used is that they have a vested interest in the future called 'we own Moscow, we own the Soviet Union.' You'd never see anti-communist ground forces in Moscow—write this down, everybody, that's a basic tenet of deterrence—just like you wouldn't have seen communist ground forces in Washington." Quester notes that the behavior of Marshal Sergei Akhromeyev, Soviet leader Mikhail Gorbachev's national security adviser, demonstrates how central the integrity of the state is to the will to conduct war. Akhromeyev was probably an indirect coconspirator in the failed August 1991 military coup instigated by Communist Party hard-liners in the Politburo against Gorbachev and recently elected Russian Federation president Boris Yeltsin. Although Akhromeyev had been replaced as Chief of the General Staff by Marshal Mikhail Moiseev, Moiseev at one point possessed all three sets of launch codes collectively required to initiate nuclear attack that were normally held separately by Gorbachev, Defense Minister Dmitry Yazov, and Moiseev himself.* Yazov and Moiseev were

---

* During the coup, Gorbachev was deprived of his set of codes. Yazov fled Moscow after the coup failed, which evidently left all three codes in Moiseev's possession. Ronald E. Powaski, *Return to Armageddon: The United States and the Nuclear*

both conspirators. Akhromeyev, an old-line true believer, was among the planners of an assault on the parliament building designed to arrest or kill Yeltsin while Gorbachev was under house arrest in Crimea.[19] Akhromeyev might have been expected to use his influence to persuade Moiseev to threaten a nuclear strike against the United States as the coup faltered in order to salvage the effort. Yet there was no sign that he even considered doing so. Instead, he hanged himself, leaving a note to Gorbachev that read in part: "I cannot live when my fatherland is dying and all that I have made my life's work is being destroyed."[20] Without a state—the Soviet Union—to defend, war, fortunately, was meaningless to Akhromeyev.

In Osama bin Laden's eyes, the Soviet defeat in Afghanistan was due in no small part to jihadists' efforts, and had hastened the Soviet Union's larger collapse. This signal jihadist success stimulated bin Laden and Zawahiri to pull together a network covering the broader Middle East that would ultimately become al-Qaeda, committed to upending existing "apostate" Arab nationalist regimes and creating a new sharia-ruled caliphate. At the same time, bin Laden's perception was that the Soviet collapse imbued in the United States a triumphal attitude, whereby the United States became "more haughty and arrogant" and "started to look at itself as a Master of this world and established what it calls the new world order."[21] To him and many other Islamists, the United States' massive invasion of Iraq to repel its attempt to annex Kuwait in 1990–91—even though aimed at a corrupt secular regime—confirmed Islamists' long-held belief, set forth by the Egyptian dissident Sayyid Qutb, that the United

Arms Race, 1981–1999 (Oxford and New York: Oxford University Press, 2000), pp. 128–30. See also Mikhail Tsypkin, "Adventures of the 'Nuclear Briefcase': A Russian Document Analysis," *Strategic Insights*, vol. 3, issue 9, September 2004, http://www.ccc.nps.navy.mil/si/2004/sep/tsypkinSept04.asp.

States was the intrinsic and inexorable nemesis of Islam. Further enriching this turbocharged view of the United States as destroyer of Islam was the Saudi clerical establishment's approval of the deployment of American troops in the kingdom to stage the Iraq invasion, which exposed the royal family and official clergy as infidels as far as bin Laden was concerned.[22]

Bin Laden was developing a worldview that devalued existing Muslim states in favor of a seamless Islamic polity that was as yet completely theoretical and whose birth would inevitably involve revolutionary violence on a large scale. Yet deterrence was founded on the vulnerability of things of value to states—in particular, cities, people, and infrastructure. Because revolutionary nonstate actors would place less value on such things—and nihilistic, apocalyptic ones seeking a new beginning, as bin Laden was, might even assign *negative* value to them—they would not fit familiar frameworks for stable international security, or for deterrence in particular.

Through the Cold War and well into the 1990s, analysts generally assumed that terrorist groups aspired to run or centrally participate in states that had been reoriented according to their demands, which would make them susceptible to deterrence. By the mid-1990s—heightened by the massive car-bomb attack on the Murrah federal building in Oklahoma City by Christian white supremacists and the sarin gas attack in the Tokyo subway system by Aum Shinrikyo, both in 1995—the prospect of WMD terrorism had become less tentative. Terrorism was now officially a major threat, and none of the new terrorist groups presented taking over or controlling a government as a goal. In the lead article in the winter 1996–97 issue of *Foreign Policy,* John F. Sopko took note of a looming paradigm shift. "The familiar balance of nuclear terror that linked the superpowers and their client states for nearly 50 years in a choreographed series of confrontations," he wrote, "has given way to a much less predictable situation, where weapons of unthinkable power appear within the grasp of those more willing to use them."[23] Perceiving "a new arms race toward mass destruction," Sopko chronicled ten events over a period of eighteen months signaling pronounced interests among state and nonstate actors in biological and chemical weapons, dirty bombs, enriched uranium, and plutonium. His tone was far more shrill than Jeffrey Simon's—RAND publications are self-consciously dispassionate, whereas *Foreign Policy* features philippics—but there was substance to Sopko's alarm.

First, the global proliferation environment had changed. The information revolution, the expansion of commercial biology and chemistry, the rising phenomenon of "dual-use" technology, organized crime, and the availability of weapons scientists no longer gainfully employed by the Soviet Union combined to make technical know-how more accessible to nonstate actors, so as to break the presumed nation-state monopoly on WMD. Second, the attitudes of terrorists were becoming more lethal. Acknowledging Jenkins's conventional wisdom, Sopko noted that "for years it was thought that terrorist groups imposed some self-restraint. As espoused by terrorism experts, terrorists or their state sponsors did not want to cause too many casualties, as it would destroy sympathy and support for their cause. By contrast, the new terrorists—whether religious, political, or individual—appear to care little for garnering public sympathy or support."[24] That was not quite right: Islamist terrorists believe that marrying mass-casualty terrorism to an apocalyptic religious vision could generate support and sympathy in the Muslim *umma* (that is, the notional single nation comprising Muslim believers worldwide). But Sopko was generally on target in challenging "past assumptions that those in possession of WMD are rational, informed opponents who calculate the risks and benefits," which don't apply "when these groups are driven by 'divine intervention,' messianic leadership, or suicidal instincts."[25] The 1993 World Trade Center bombing and Ramzi Yousef's plan to destroy a dozen jetliners virtually simultaneously over the Pacific (Operation Bojinka), he allowed, "may be evidence of this trend."[26] Sopko was among the first public commentators to call for improved interagency and intergovernmental coordination on new terrorist threats, to suggest that the Cold War allocation of security responsibilities among intelligence, law-enforcement, and military organizations be reviewed, and to warn that a blinkered national focus on grand strategy could "blind U.S. policymakers to the immediate measures that could help address these challenges."[27]

To some terrorists, no underlying state is necessary to inspire the defense of a religion and ideology. "When people are fencible and their government isn't about to collapse, deterrence works fine, but it's very state-centric," notes Quester. "If you give nuclear weapons to someone who doesn't have a country and who doesn't have any targets to hit, you say, whoops, what do we do now, coach? We hit back at the right target when we knocked out the Taliban because the Taliban cared about maintaining the most Islamic society that the world had ever seen in Afghanistan. So the message to al-Qaeda in the future is that if you find a host who's nice enough to take care of you because you're Islamic and they're Islamic, be careful because you may kill off that host if you lunge at the United States." An identifiable host imposes command-and-control constraints on terrorists comparable to those imposed by the Soviet state in that both valued durability. But "a terrorist who makes a nuclear or super-duper biological weapon in his basement in Hamburg doesn't depend on a sympathetic base that you can punish; he just needs to be invisible and hidden as he launches his attack."[28]

Bill Clinton did not perceive terrorism as a strategic threat during his first term, in part because of more pressing concerns. After strongman Somali president Mohammed Siad Barre was overthrown in a civil war, competing clans commandeered weapons supplied alternately by the Soviets and the Americans during the Cold War to the now-toppled government, and the country degenerated into a Darwinian patchwork of clan fiefdoms without central authority. An ineffectual United Nations mission was unable to ameliorate drought and famine in December 1992, prompting President George H. W. Bush, then a lame duck, to initiate an American-led multinational intervention with the relatively narrow intention of facilitating humanitarian relief in the service of a "new world order." Though well-intentioned, Bush's enterprising policy threatened to draw U.S. ground forces into a guerrilla conflict, for which Vietnam had engendered an institutional dislike in the U.S. Army. In bootstrapping a humanitarian mission into a coercive peace enforcement effort, however, the United States was unable to win the trust of the Somali people or navigate their inscrutable clan-based social and political system. American soldiers instead antagonized Somali clan militias, and their fury culminated in a minor military disaster (known colloquially as "Black Hawk Down"), in which hundreds of Somalis and eighteen U.S. special operations soldiers died as the Americans tried to capture Mohamed Farah Aideed, Somalia's most powerful warlord. The United States soon withdrew, leaving the country in a state of chronic disarray and the task of political resurrection to a UN mission that remained feckless. The Somalia intervention, though a highly discretionary and contingent application of U.S. policy, reinforced the United States' Vietnam-bred distaste for immersing itself in the internal problems of other states when the strategic benefits of doing so seemed remote or attenuated. It also stoked anti-Americanism, and strengthened al-Qaeda's hand in East Africa.[29]

Furthermore, Clinton's standing foreign-policy preoccupations—quite understandably—were stabilizing post–Cold War Eastern Europe and reorienting the international security system to deal with what National Security Adviser Anthony Lake called "the nexus" of nonstate bad actors. While this group certainly included terrorists, the threat was considered a collective one affecting overall stability and order rather than a specific one coalescing around a single figure or directed primarily against the United States and its partners. Although Islamist violence targeting the United States began in earnest with the rather inept 1993 World Trade Center attack, which claimed only seven dead, al-Qaeda had not yet matured as an operational network, and Iran was still the prime focus of U.S. counterterrorism concern. As Clinton's first term progressed, the Aum Shinrikyo attack in 1995 showed that terrorists might have sufficient political abandon to use WMD, and catastrophic terrorism on U.S. soil became a matter of acute official worry.[30] The 1996 Khobar Towers attack in Saudi Arabia, in which nineteen U.S. military personnel were killed, hinted at a burgeoning anti-American Islamist trend. And urgent admonitions to Congress about inadequate security for commercial aviation—deemed "likely to remain an attractive target for terrorists well into the foreseeable future"—also issued from the GAO. Though its central concern was detection of explosive devices, that agency inferred from the 1993 World Trade Center a rising international terrorist threat to the domestic United States.[31] Clinton reacted to the Aum Shinrikyo attack by issuing Presidential Decision Directive (PDD) 39, which centralized federal control over counterterrorism policy. In 1996, he signed the Anti-terrorism and Effective Death Penalty Act, which, among other things, authorized the establishment of a special tribunal that could expedite the expulsion of foreign terrorist suspects from the United States.

At that time, the CIA still tended to characterize bin Laden as a financier rather than an operator.[32] By summer 1998, with the near-simultaneous bombings of U.S. embassies in Nairobi and Dar es-Salaam, the emergence of a virulent global operational network, with bin Laden presiding, had become clear to every major element of the U.S. national security apparatus. The FBI sent nine hundred Special Agents to investigate the embassy bombings, exercising its extraterritorial jurisdiction more robustly than ever before.[33] These developments, along with revelations about the extent of Iraq's biological and chemical arsenals and the Soviet Union's Cold War biological weapons program and its experiments with smallpox, had made Clinton himself keenly concerned about the prospect of mass-casualty terrorism, and his National Security Council staff conducted an ominous "tabletop" bioterrorism exercise in late 1998 that left the participants both shuddering and galvanized.[34] In May 1998, an internal FBI memorandum to the Oklahoma City field office noted that a special agent had "observed large numbers of Middle Eastern males receiving flight training at Oklahoma airports in recent months," and that this was a "recent phenomenon and may be related to planned terrorist activity." The activity contemplated, however, was the airborne dispensing of chemical or biological toxins.[35] At about the same time, President Clinton signed PDD-62, which established the Office of the National Coordinator for Security, Infrastructure Protection and Counter-Terrorism to supervise and integrate homeland security programs aimed at preventing terrorism. Meanwhile, the GAO reported that while some progress on aviation security had been made, it still wasn't up to snuff—especially as to automated passenger profiling.[36]

However large and dangerous the growing global terrorist network was, it appeared content to employ conventional terrorist methods: high explosives detonated without warning, or perhaps hijacked military weapons. To many in the wider counterterrorism community, Aum Shinrikyo still seemed an aberration, and

Jenkins's assessment a reliable orthodoxy. Most U.S. government officials seemed to acknowledge terrorism as a standing threat that could not be allowed to palsy daily life and governance. But, with hundreds of millions of dollars earmarked for "superterrorism" response in the 1999 federal budget, there was also skepticism about basing policy and spending money on worst-case scenarios. Some questioned the policy implications of "the capabilities proposition," which said that just about anyone with college-level scientific training might be capable of producing and deploying biological and chemical WMD, and "the chaos proposition," which argued that Lake's "nexus" of maligned nonstate actors was uncontrolled and undeterrable. While the first proposition was true, two corollaries of Jenkins's body-count hypothesis suggested that the second might not be. First, terrorists usually operate in groups and are therefore easier to detect than individuals. Second, if terrorists are to develop mass-casualty intent, they will do so only over time, as their political objectives are progressively frustrated, and will still state their threats publicly in an effort to wrest political concessions from target governments. These terrorist characteristics, it was thought, would yield governments ample strategic warning. This assessment was premised on a terrorist typology whereby the groups most likely to use WMD were millenarian cults like Aum Shinrikyo that bizarrely associated redemption with Armageddon; groups that have suffered mass brutalization, perhaps in the form of genocide, and blamed and sought vengeance against the world at large; and small, socially nihilistic cells that miscalculated the true effects of WMD. Hezbollah, Hamas, and Palestinian Islamic Jihad—all of which had and still have geographically circumscribed goals and exercised and still exercise operational restraint—did not belong in any of the four categories. But al-Qaeda, which by then was well known to the counterterrorism community, did.

Critics like Ehud Sprinzak, an Israeli who viewed terrorism as a fact of life, were flamboyantly cynical about the sensationalism, 1950s-vintage paranoia, and civil-defense impulses, and the breathless government activity that the superterrorism scare had produced, as well as the boondoggle that it meant to the science and technology industry. Ultimately, however, he conceded that the likelihood of unconventional terrorism had indeed increased and made several prescient recommendations—among them the enhancement of the FBI's authority to collect domestic intelligence, more searching international intelligence gathering, and more tightly co-ordinated federal consequence-management capabilities.[37] But his concluding tone now seems too sanguine: "Although the threat of chemical and biological terrorism should be taken seriously, the public must know that the risk of a major catastrophe is extremely minimal."[38] Robert Osgood had defined a limited war as one in which "the belligerents restrict the purpose for which they fight to concrete, well-defined objectives that do not demand the utmost military effort of which the belligerents are capable and that can be accommodated in a negotiated settlement."[39] Terrorist and insurgency groups had broadly adhered to that concept of limited war—until al-Qaeda came along.

The millennial advent came and went without the apocalyptic domestic terrorist attack that many had anticipated—not so much from Islamic groups as from mainly U.S.-based right-wing extremist Christian cults or "new world order" conspiracy theorists attaching unique doctrinal significance to 2000 as the year of reckoning.[40] There was, of course, a "Millennium Plot" of sorts. Ahmed Ressam, an Algerian Muslim who had fraudulently won asylum in Canada and become part of a largely Algerian network in North America, planned to detonate a bomb at Los Angeles

International Airport around New Year's Day, but U.S. Customs agents arrested him on December 14, 1999, after he had ferried from British Columbia to Washington state with explosives concealed in his car's spare-tire well. An Algerian/Jordanian cell allied with al-Qaeda also plotted large-scale attacks on the SAS Radisson Hotel in downtown Amman, border crossings from Jordan into Israel, two Christian holy sites, a local airport in Jordan, and other religious and cultural sites on New Year's Eve. Jordanian security forces handily quashed the operation.

While the Millennium Plot raised some consternation over its revelation that jihadists were more widely distributed and ambitious than expected, the stronger reaction was one of reassurance owing to the fact that the plot was so easily foiled. Though linked to al-Qaeda by virtue of having trained in Afghanistan in 1998–99, Ressam appeared so hapless and inept—he tipped off the Customs agents with his nervous behavior and guaranteed his arrest by trying to flee—as to bolster rather than weaken confidence in the security of the American homeland. Throughout the region, the detection of the Jordanian plot inspired fervid activity among security forces, which rolled up cells and disrupted operations in over a dozen countries. From the perspective of U.S. homeland security, forward security, in areas from which anti-American Muslim terrorists originated, thus also appeared under control. Even within the U.S. security community, at least outside the executive branch, many remained disinclined to worry. Several allies and partners—especially in Europe—were also skeptical about the magnitude of the threat.[41]

Overall, the terrorism scare seemed as hyped as the morbidly anticipated Y2K implosion of information technology that never happened. But in early spring 2000, Steven Simon and Daniel Benjamin—former senior director and director, respectively, for transnational threats on the NSC staff under

Clinton—published an article in the IISS quarterly *Survival* that challenged the prevailing calm. While chronicling Iran's singular activity as a state sponsor of terrorism, the authors emphasized that state-sponsored terrorism—though perhaps a strategic instrument—was still bounded by the states' natural interest in preserving a measure of legitimacy and a range of political options and in avoiding crippling major-power retaliation.[42] But they also argued that the rising influence of radical religious beliefs on terrorist groups was changing the rules of the game. Noting the jihadists' maximalist desire to reprise the seventh- and eighth-century caliphate, they backed up the argument with the forceful observation that had the 1993 World Trade Center bombing been fully successful and had Operation Bojinka been executed, jihadists' casualties would have numbered in the tens of thousands. Simon and Benjamin quoted bin Laden's February 1998 fatwa, which established the duty of all Muslims "to kill the Americans and their allies."[43] Then the authors—who had been present at the realization of the jihadist threat in the highest level of U.S. government—noted that "spectacular goals require spectacular means." That meant that al-Qaeda and its affiliates were seeking WMD and had the apocalyptic disposition to use them. Finally, they concluded that attacks on U.S. soil were likely, and that the United States "should increase its efforts to address its vulnerabilities since emerging threats may be of a nature and provenance that cannot be anticipated, pre-empted or prevented." These efforts should include improved homeland security (including civil defense) as well as domestic and intergovernmental law enforcement and intelligence coordination.[44]

To most experts, however, it was the new terrorists' operational conservatism and lack of imagination that shined though. Until 9/11, most reputable counterterrorism analysts blanched at characterizing terrorism as a strategic threat.[45] In the published debate that followed Simon and Benjamin's proffer of strategic warning, Bruce Hoffman, then RAND's leading terrorism expert, portrayed them as alarmist. Soporifically he suggested that "the gun and the bomb continue to be the terrorists' main weapons of choice" and held that they would "adhere to the same familiar and narrow tactical repertoire that past terrorists have mastered."[46] Simon and Benjamin archly confessed to being "intrigued by Hoffman's heavy reliance on arguments based on historical inference at a time of dramatic change in the ideology of important terrorist groups and rapid technological advances. To be sure, history should be consulted, but it is by no means a foolproof indicator."[47] They had a point.* In 1976, even as perspicacious an observer as Roberta Wohlstetter considered the IRA to be "indiscriminate."[48] Perhaps it was in comparison to its predecessors, but in the present context the IRA is rightly judged the epitome of a constrained, politically sensitive, and realistic "old" terrorist group. In 2004, Jenkins, with a whiff of sheepishness, wrote:

> At one time I would have argued that there was a firebreak between weapons proliferation at the national level and the potential terrorist use of weapons of mass destruction. Historically, terrorists seldom sought mass casualties. Morality and self-image plus practical concerns about group cohesion, alienating perceived constituents, or provoking popular crackdowns constrained their violence. . . . As we have seen, however, these self-imposed constraints, which were never universal or immutable, eroded significantly in the last decade of the 20th century,

---

*When Simon and Benjamin signed the publishing contract for their seminal book on al-Qaeda in early 2001, the book's working title was *The Coming Age of Sacred Terror.* By the time the book was ready for release, in 2002, that first adjective had to be dropped.

especially among those inspired by religious ideologies, which, in their view, provided God's mandate.[49]

Still Behind the Curve

Only in the late 1990s, after the United States' overwhelming conventional military superiority had unequivocally showed itself in the first Gulf War, did U.S. military planners begin to understand that most adversaries would not choose to fight the United States on its own terms, and would resort to unconventional asymmetrical threats. Even on 9/11, Air Force procedures contemplated an attack by a foreign aircraft originating from outside the continental United States—the same threat, in its operational contours, that it anticipated during the Cold War. It may be that the success of Cold War deterrence and the failure of terrorists for fifty years to acquire or use WMD entrenched complacency about nuclear weapons and other WMD. Yet, as John McPhee observes, "in the lamination of time, 50 years is nothing. The gloomy thing to me is that I can't see how you can really stop it."[50] On the other hand, in the late 1980s, Schelling wrote that terrorism had accomplished very little. While he conceded that in Northern Ireland it had kept alive the interests of the IRA by demonstrating that it was not extinct, even there it had yielded no political dividends. Were it not for its expressive value, terrorism could simply be dismissed as a strategic factor. Compared to nuclear war, said Schelling, "terrorism just wasn't worth worrying about."[51] To Schelling, the main reason for its futility was that, in relative terms, the damage terrorism had caused was minuscule.

Admittedly, terrorists have blown up far fewer people than a nuclear bomb would. But if the goal of terrorism is to terrorize, the current generation of Islamist terrorists has been wildly successful. It makes sense to ask what else they want, for surely there is something else. "A lot of people think you can judge the motivations by the word 'terror': what they're trying to do is create terror. Well, I think that fatalistic notion doesn't get you very far. I think the Twin Towers attack made the question of objectives overdetermined," Schelling comments.[52] The enormous body count of that single event tempts the breezy conclusion that Islamist terrorists simply want to kill as many infidels as possible—whether in a blind rage, or, more purposefully, to inspire a mass mobilization of Muslims envisioned as ultimately restoring Islam's stature as a civilization.

In addition to murdering roughly three thousand people on 9/11, however, al-Qaeda made terrorism a global media spectacle and gained the respect—and in some cases, the adulation—of hundreds of millions of people around the world. It also demonstrated that the United States could be caught off guard and, frankly, humiliated. Surely bin Laden, Zawahiri, and their successors aim to build on those impressive dividends adaptively, to attain something more concrete and fortifying than another large body count or one more opportunity to threaten the United States and its partners with an obscure reversal of fortune. Yet neither the U.S. government nor the network of analysts and professors from which it seeks advice has tried, dispassionately and in earnest, to ascertain what they really want.

The intellectual framework of deterrence is still highly relevant, but the quandary of isolating terrorists' true objectives from what is often vague and inflammatory rhetoric makes deterrence doubly problematic. In Quester's words, "you gotta be imaginative and ask how can you deter people who can't be deterred in the classical coinage. If you can't hit their cities or kill their women and children, how else do we ever deter? You can snatch things out of old arguments that the Soviets can't be deterred that way, either, we also have to be able to defeat them on the battlefield. You can deter by looking hard at what they really care about, and you can certainly deter by making their attacks look fruitless."[53] The latter is what Snyder dubbed deterrence by denial. "If all they do by trying to knock over another tall building is lose twenty of their best operatives because you've got very good defenses—defense is a very good deterrent—that would work. But it's a much harder problem when the other side doesn't have cities in which it has a vested interest. It's not as if it's a new problem, but this one is different enough so that it's much harder."[54]

As misguided as it has turned out to be, the 2003 Iraq war can be viewed as an attempt—perhaps, in part, even a sincere one—to reestablish deterrence as a primarily military function by threatening a state posited to be essential to the power of nonstate groups to harm the United States and its friends. But that position was factually wrong. Al-Qaeda was not dependent on, or even operationally linked to, Saddam's regime, and thus for the most part lacked the leveling factors to defend—a state, society, and industrial infrastructure—that provided a reasonable basis for the assumption of a degree of shared rationality or prudence between adversaries. The defensive jihad cut states out of the deterrence calculus by personalizing what is essentially an intergenerational, civilizational grievance harbored by Muslims against the West.

Deterrence therefore cannot easily be remilitarized. But thinking on the uses of soft power—for example, diplomacy, information, and economic inducement—to establish deterrence, against the exaggeratedly hopeless but tenacious post-9/11 assumption that those willing to commit suicide in their cause are irreconcilable, has emerged slowly. A consensus seems to be building that, in spite of the religiously absolute imperatives laid down by al-Qaeda's leadership, the highly dispersed and pragmatic character of the transnational Islamic terrorist network means that terrorists' religious and political intensity and tactical mind-sets are highly variable. Like more manageable "old" terrorist groups, al-Qaeda, too, encompasses professional terrorists and wavering "fellow travelers" as well as maniacal true believers. Thus, it would be a mistake to cast all transnational Islamist terrorists and even most of their more peripheral supporters as impervious to political and tactical influence.[55] Furthermore, respected analysts have noted that suicide attacks in any case are not acts of desperate martyrdom but highly efficient and calculated measures of asymmetrical warfare: suicide attacks make tactical sense because a human being constitutes a cheap and accurate terminal-guidance system whose death will deny the adversary operational intelligence, and strategic sense because "looking a little crazy" raises the cost of resistance to the adversary and encourages accommodation.[56]

So Lawrence Freedman, for one, is not ready to give up on deterrence—especially deterrence by denial of an adversary's objectives. He would concede that the shared ignorance on which Schelling premises his imputation of a "minimax" solution to rational adversaries is even more extreme between states and terrorists than it was between the United States and the Soviet Union. If diplomacy can shrink the gap, it may lessen antagonism between Western states and at least some of the terrorists. That direct diplomacy will tame even most jihadists, of course, is a very shaky bet. In that light, Freedman realizes that a deterrence strategy based on the enforcement of norms rather than the imposition of threats makes the most analytic sense. It would be established through persuading not the jihadists but the rest of the international community, including especially Muslims, to accept principles and relationships that comprehensively reject terrorism. He declares that "all political groups, however apparently fanatical in their ideology, adjust to shifting power relationships and act with some thought to the consequences."[57] If Western policies are explicitly designed to politically isolate terrorists by establishing an accommodation with their potential recruits, terrorist violence will not have the desired effect and should diminish. As Freedman explains, "The argument that deterrence does not work with terrorism can be challenged, not because for every terrorist challenge a sure-fire form of deterrence can be devised, but because over time it becomes apparent that this is a threat for which the community has made adequate provision to the point where, even if some attacks succeed, little of political consequence will follow."[58] What's needed is "an international order in which there are formidable restraints on the use of force, and where the main legitimate role of force is to enforce these restraints."[59]

In so premising deterrence on norms rather than interests, Freedman poses the not insubstantial challenge of expanding the consensus on the boundaries of acceptable behavior by both state and nonstate actors. He also appears too dismissive of the intrinsic satisfaction that politically frustrated people may gain from purely expressive violence: even if they recognize that a terrorist act will not lead to a broader tactical advantage, political mobilization, or a change in their station in this world, they may still regard a violent statement of that very futility as meaningful consolation or as a guarantee of religious salvation. The upshot is that neutralizing transnational terrorism as a strategic threat will not involve mass surrenders, altered legal boundaries, enforceable cease-fires, or even the extinction of mass-casualty attacks. Its main quality will be, simply yet obscurely, much less terrorism and terrorist activity. It will involve, albeit distastefully, siding with and lending at least qualified support to illiberal leaders like Egyptian president Hosni Mubarak and, indeed, Syrian president Bashir al-Assad, who have been effective in controlling Islamists. Deterrence, from this perspective, amounts to a kind of political encirclement and attrition, informed by realpolitik, and is more a function of soft power than hard. Yet, at the end of the day, the same could be said of nuclear deterrence during the Cold War.[60]

6

Selective Nostalgia

During the Cold War the United States enjoyed the luxury of having a single enemy. In that enemy, political and physical catastrophe—ideological defeat and military devastation—merged. The sharp focus afforded by the overarching aim of deterring one unprecedentedly dangerous enemy helped bestow on Cold War thinking the virtue of intellectual fearlessness: brains with attitude. Containment and deterrence were comfortable boxes that nobody really wanted to escape, and even the most adventurous of strategists were insufficiently pragmatic to think outside them. In 1992, Sir Michael Howard hit at the fundamentally ahistorical, unempirical, and sterile nature of Cold War strategic thought, acidly musing that in the Cold War era "the subject under discussion was not how to fight wars, the traditional concern of strategists, but how to prevent them. Most of the contributors had never heard a shot fired, or even a bomb dropped, in anger, which gave their writing a curiously arid quality; but then, their concern was not how to do it, but how to ensure that it was never done. Now their work is beginning to seem as remote as that of sixteenth-century theologians, their jargon as abstruse and irrelevant as the vocabulary of transubstantiation and consubstantiation."[1] Nuclear bipolarity and its blessings, he was suggesting, were aberrational.

Freedman's notion that it was all a "charade" anyhow underlines Howard's suggestion that what the great nuclear strategists concocted about deterrence may have turned out to be nugatory. And attempting to shoehorn current problems into Cold War styles of thought could prove not merely futile, but reckless. Herman Kahn liked to quip with respect to the game of Chicken that it helps to "look a little crazy."[2] Paradoxically, the United States and the Soviet Union could get away with "looking a little crazy" via large nuclear arms buildups both sides knew they weren't supposed to be used at all under the overarching logic of MAD. But it is operationally ineffective to play the maniac against suicide bombers or quixotic rogue leaders, and politically and ethically unacceptable to recklessly threaten collateral damage to peripheral supporters or innocent Muslims to effect deterrence.[3]

Yet even though the higher calculus of nuclear deterrence is now more a historical curiosity than an applied science, it would be a mistake to throw out the methodological baby with the substantive bathwater. If the essential fault of nuclear strategy lies in its rigidity, equally its essential merit resides in its rigor. The Cold War strategists set extraordinarily high standards of analytic scrutiny and thoroughness, no matter how cloistered and exclusive their intellectual environment might have been. However esoteric all of those meditations on first and second strike, on counterforce and countervalue, seem now, they engendered a way of thinking that is worth preserving. Beyond that, perhaps what remains of greatest value in the Cold War's intellectual legacy is a sense of mission wedded to national purpose. Richard Betts observed in 1997 that strategic studies, though born during the Cold War, had become all the more relevant "because it focuses on the essential Clausewitzean problem: how to make force a rational instrument of policy rather than mindless murder—how to integrate politics and war."[4] That's still the basic problem. The deficit in U.S. thinking on post–Cold War threats consisted not in the absence of an intellectual architecture, but a blinkered perception of the threats. Since 9/11, the deficit has not been blinkered threat perceptions, but an inability to see "the political forest for the military trees."[5] The virtue of making civilian think tanks the repositories of leading-edge strategic thinking was that it avoided that kind of myopia with respect to nuclear war. So there are sound reasons to indulge a certain degree of nostalgia, albeit selective, for the Cold War's intellectual dispensation.

Power vs. Truth

In eschewing close analysis for tendentious sophistry, and favoring absolutism over pragmatism, the George W. Bush administration has recapitulated the shortcomings of Cold War thinking rather than marshaling its strengths. When he took office in January 2001, President Bush bestrode a world that was essentially unipolar. Next to the looming Armageddon of 1945–91, the new strategic exigencies—ethnic wars, humanitarian intervention, peacekeeping, poverty eradication—seemed prosaic, grubby, and unglamorous. In fact, the Bush administration was expressly disinclined to engage in the "foreign policy as social work" that the Clinton administration seemed to consider necessary to deal with them.[6] The Bush team spurned conflict resolution and most other forms of foreign policy that involved cultivating deeper sensitivities to alien cultures. Yet the gravest and most immediate strategic concerns were no longer Russia and the Warsaw Pact, but rogue states and nonstate extremist groups. Their deterrability was concededly less certain than that of the Soviet Union. The United States could not take the "hyper-rationality" of its adversaries for granted, which meant that understanding their cultural peculiarities was essential to determining how they could be dissuaded from imperiling U.S. interests and minimizing the threats they posed.

The Bush team, however, took on the new challenge with a combination of abrasive and parochial idealism and puerile faith in military technology. Cultural and ideological learning did not figure into its calculations. It is well known that Bush's top foreign-policy advisers were initially dismissive of the transnational Islamist terrorist threat, and unwilling to embrace an inclusive, bipartisan approach to the terrorism problem. Neoconservatives like Richard Perle and Paul Wolfowitz—often simplistically described as Wohlstetter's disciples and as "Straussians"—became prohibitively influential in the Bush administration. They cavalierly discounted negative Arab and Muslim perceptions of the United States' Middle East policies and how those perceptions might inform decisions and actions. The result was a pre-9/11 policy that largely derogated Arab and Muslim concerns. Despite urgent admonitions starting in January 2001 from one of the most knowledgeable counterterrorism experts in Washington—NSC Coordinator for Security and Counter-terrorism Richard A. Clarke, who had sounded the alarm over the transnational expansion of Islamist terrorists during the Clinton years—no meeting of the NSC Principals Committee about that threat was held until a week before the 9/11 attacks.[7]

The attacks themselves raised the administration's perception of the threat, but did not prompt any greater appreciation for the need for national security officials to educate themselves about the Islamic world. President Bush himself openly, almost proudly, displayed an anti-intellectual proclivity for submerging history and cultural scholarship as ingredients of strategy-building, and to promote simplistically framed "big ideas" like "freedom" and "democracy" with a naive grandiosity.[8] By his own admission, Bush didn't "do nuance," fancied himself a "gut player," and wasn't "a big reader." Making good on those representations, he discomfited Muslims with the declaration that they were "either with us or against us," and then unsettled U.S. allies and partners by attempting to install American-style democracy in Iraq and Afghanistan on the basis of little more than a faith-based conviction that almost everyone in his heart preferred and would embrace the American way of life. In this aspect, the Iraq intervention seemed a crowningly vulgar caricature of the thesis that the triumph of the West in the Cold War had enshrined the ascendance of economics over history and softer forms of social science as the most relevant discipline.[9] The elevation of Adam Smith above John Maynard Keynes, the endorsement of profit-maximizing behavior as the fulfillment of one's social duty, the "greed is good" ethos of the 1980s—all of these tropes emerged in Bush's language and deeds. There is a sustainable argument for the proposition that the administration's faith that the self-interest of American companies and the Iraqi people and the availability of Iraqi oil would happily coalesce to the advantage of all obscured the obvious dangers of the U.S. intervention, such as Sunni insurgency, jihadist suspicion and opportunism, and wider regional discord. In the event, the demolition of the Twin Towers and the scarring of the Pentagon had delivered bin Laden's message, and the movement was now able to sustain itself and indeed expand on the basis of that stunning historic keynote and additional attacks on targets of opportunity. Moreover, after Afghanistan, terrorists, having dispersed and become less amenable to military power, had become too complex a strategic problem to subsume under any strategy premised on state-to-state relationships and confrontations and large-force military power.

Wohlstetter had often warned of the fallacy of lesser included cases—that is, the tendency to assume that a strong deterrent, by virtue of meeting a formidable military challenge, would perforce deter less formidable contingencies. Because power was a nonscalar, discontinuous phenomenon, he said, many if not most lesser cases turned out to be *excluded*. The threat of massive nuclear retaliation in the 1950s was not an effective deterrent of Third World insurgencies. Nor was the United States' nuclear retaliatory capacity sufficient to prevent regional wars in the Persian Gulf in the 1970s and 1980s.[10] Well into the 1990s, however, U.S. military planners were content to believe that lower-intensity "military operations other than war," such as peacekeeping, humanitarian intervention, and counterterrorism, could be handled by a Cold War–era major-war force structure.[11]

Eventually, American officials and analysts came to understand that a security architecture left over from the Cold War, centered on robust nuclear and conventional military capabilities for thwarting well-equipped states, was not suitable for combating the asymmetrical warfare practiced by terrorist groups. Asymmetrical warfare, that is, was a lesser excluded case. In statutory and budgetary terms, greater emphasis was duly placed on homeland security, law enforcement and intelligence, and rendering the U.S. force structure better able to handle asymmetrical threats. To protect the United States against rogue-state ballistic missile attacks on the United States or its allies, a technically dubious American missile defense shield was deployed. Nuclear earth-penetrating "bunker buster" bombs were developed to enable the United States to hit deeply buried WMD caches. Secretary of Defense Rumsfeld accelerated the technological transformation of the U.S. military—supposedly from a cumbersome Cold War relic into a nimble and versatile machine capable of myriad forms of warfare—in an attempt to complete the vaunted "revolution in military affairs."

But just as nuclear deterrence did not automatically translate into conventional deterrence, making military capabilities more flexible and potential targets (theoretically) less vulnerable to certain high-end terrorist attacks did not necessarily address cruder and less predictable operations. A ballistic missile defense would not repel cruise-missile attacks or hijacked commercial airliners steered into buildings by suicidal terrorists. While precision-guided munitions and speedier, lighter, more maneuverable units enabled the U.S. military to take down Iraq's government quickly and with relatively few ground troops, they added little value in countering insurgency and terrorism. For these labor-intensive endeavors, immense offensive military power was no substitute for enhanced intelligence and constabulary capabilities, or for manpower. More fundamentally, the programmatic strategic solution to the international terrorism problem—operationally defeating the global terrorist network and physically protecting populations—neglected the fact that the terrorist network's mere survival against an overwhelmingly superior foe amounted to a provisional political victory, and kept recruits in train.*

There remained an unpaid premium on the U.S. government's need to know its adversaries far better than it did. It translated into a reactive post-9/11 policy that amplified the costs of ignorance—particularly via U.S.-led intervention in Iraq, in

---

*The same basic mistake was made in Vietnam. The Tet offensive was a tactical failure in the sense that it cost Hanoi and the Vietcong far more fighters than it did the Americans and the South Vietnamese, but a strategic victory in the sense that it demonstrated the resolve and competence needed to keep up enlistment. The results are now well known.

which officials with little or no Middle East expertise were accorded key roles. Lip service, to be sure, was paid to "winning hearts and minds," as it was in Vietnam, and to the importance of public diplomacy and the perverse effects of American hegemony. And many serious thinkers stressed the need to reincorporate realism into U.S. policy, and went a step further in urging policy makers to reconsider the "American exceptionalism" that ascribed superior moral authority to the United States.[12] But these entreaties did not penetrate actual policy. Instead, Bush's emphasis on victory rather than reconciliation tended to draw emotional, reactive responses. Thus, policy forked toward two extreme positions, one morally and politically unpalatable and the other risky and destructive.

The first, premised on the belief that it is too late to fine-tune the policies that have alienated Muslims, involves the substantial capitulation of the United States to the implicit demands of bin Ladenism, whereby the United States would abandon Israel, jettison its strategic relationships with Saudi Arabia and Egypt, and forsake much of its leverage and standing in the Arab world.[13] Some would argue that this is simple realism. But if so, it is realism taken to the extreme of strictly relegating long-standing ethical principles of U.S. foreign policy, such as durable support for allies, to the preservation of merely prudential American interests, such as access to oil. The second stance on Middle East policy reflects the basic reaction of George W. Bush—who, ironically, campaigned in 2000 as a realist in his father's mold—to September 11.[14] It envisages a full-scale Western mobilization against transnational Islamist terrorism—a *total* war on terror. This is neoconservatism on steroids, a revolutionary idealism—not in the Wilsonian sense of elevating enlightened American political standards to the level of universal law through international consensus and agency, but in the unprecedented sense of imposing those ideals for the most part unilaterally on the pretext of America's presumptive singular destiny to enlighten the world. Under this scenario, the West's intelligence, law enforcement, and military assets would be brought to bear against any actual or potential terrorist strongholds or supporters as Muslim governments "bandwagoned" behind a hegemonic America.[15] This vision of the world simply did not materialize.

The choice, crudely, seemed to be between negotiating with terrorists, perhaps yielding them victory, or furnishing bin Laden, at prohibitively high risk, with precisely the violent "clash of civilizations" that he wanted to power the apocalypse. From these vantage points, no sensible middle ground was visible: Muslims had to be either appeased or dominated. This sort of reductive dichotomizing is entirely consistent with, and was probably conditioned by, the Cold War strategic mindset, which had two very distinctive features. One was the assumption of the zero-sum bipolar strategic confrontation of the Cold War. The other was the preference for studying technological and analytic progress as the means of controlling behavior, rather than culture as a key to anticipating and understanding such behavior. The fate of humankind was linked inextricably to the science of nuclear weapons, and it was suspected that a deep understanding of Soviet culture would only reinforce the absolute necessity of a decisive ideological victory for the West.*

The new threats, of course, don't fit into the Cold War grid. Back then, for instance, both sides came to appreciate arms control—

---

*Other matters, such as regional stability and local conflict, were viewed as subordinate to that victory. In fact, the United States or the Soviet Union would actually encourage local or regional tensions or disputes if the alternative was to concede a tactical advantage or a political triumph to the other side. Thus did the Arab jihadists who fought the Soviets in Afghanistan become empowered.

which called for the control of military technology—because it restrained spending while preserving mutual deterrence via nuclear parity, minimized the likelihood of a preemptive surprise attack, and fostered a reciprocal understanding of how a crisis would be handled. Now, the other side—al-Qaeda and its affiliates—is not interested in that sort of strategic stability or predictability. Since it cannot hope for military parity, it must safeguard its capacity to surprise with asymmetrical means. As a consequence, those seeking to counter jihadist terrorism cannot rely on the partial or tacit cooperation of their adversary in controlling dangerous technology. Logically, the priority should therefore be on comprehending Muslim grievances and trying to ameliorate them.

A "third way" is needed through which the United States can both honor its commitments and strike an accommodation with Islam sufficient to marginalize bin Laden and his followers. That is the core strategic challenge of counterterrorism. The challenge is so hard to meet because it requires a new way of thinking about American power and place. The intelligence trawl of postintervention Afghanistan—in the notorious videotapes depicting dogs painfully dying in experiments as well as less lurid documentation—unambiguously revealed al-Qaeda's keen interest in developing chemical and biological weapons and radiological "dirty bombs" as well as an ultimate desire for a full-fledged nuclear capability. But even if Islamist terrorists managed to get hold of a nuclear weapon or some nasty biological agents, the level of human and material damage of which they were capable would be orders of magnitude lower than what the Soviet Union and the United States could have inflicted during the Cold War (and Russia and the United States still could inflict). The notion that is so difficult for American strategists to get their heads around is not that Islamists are so militarily powerful, but rather that U.S. military and economic might is now of more limited political utility than was hoped at the end of the Cold War.

Al-Qaeda's hard-core members and followers—that is, those, like bin Laden himself, who are driven by what they see as the West's historical and cultural humiliation of Islam—are willing to martyr themselves and unwilling to bargain explicitly. While there is undoubtedly some daylight between their lurid rhetoric and what they would accept, the latter is opaque. It is fair to assume that they would like to precipitate an apocalypse in its truest theological sense, which involves a dramatic reversal of fortune that will rescue an entire people or civilization through spiritual force, and that they believe that such force is most assuredly expressed through massive physical destruction and human carnage. Perhaps the most vexing strategic prospect now is not thermonuclear war, but the possibility that victory in the Cold War, in its liberation of pent-up historical and geopolitical grievances and resentments, may in fact have meant the mitigation of America's power to the extent that it cannot easily quell the likes of al-Qaeda. Relenting on the jihadists' stated terms—shattered economic (mainly, oil) relationships, the destruction of geostrategic stability, fundamental change in the legal bases for international relations by virtue of violent religious uprising—*would* be unthinkable. But a nonviolent reversal of fortune for Islam as a whole—which has undeniably been economically and politically beleaguered—is not only thinkable but in fact the programmatic solution to the problem.

Reviving Pragmatism

Arranging such a strategic epiphany requires the rejection of the chauvinistic—at times, nakedly jingoistic—idealism espoused by the Bush administration. And it involves more than the painstaking linkage of technological capability to political and military calculations that was the centerpiece of nuclear deterrence. During the Cold War, the strong suits that the United States presented to the rest of the world—especially the Soviet Union—were a vision of the future, a corresponding push to progress, and technological and economic superiority. In a sense, these attributes won the Cold War—or at least the Soviets' dearth of them lost it. Yet the forces of radical Islam are to a significant degree both retrogressive impulses against secularization and secularism and visionary thrusts toward an unprecedented universal community.[16] While bin Laden and his followers manifest a drive to transcend the modern Westphalian system of states and forge a new age of religious nations and peoples, their stated goals—a transnational caliphate and the purgation of Islam of Western influences—are more deeply premised on the past humiliation of Muslims at the hands of the West and inspired by Islam's medieval glory. The challenge that radical Islam has issued, then, calls for ways of thinking that diverge from the pristine rationalism of the nuclear age. More affirmative, it calls for an expansive brand of wisdom that Reinhold Niebuhr—one of the twentieth century's most discerning realists—said emerged from "the triumph of experience over dogma."[17]

The most promising mode of philosophical discourse for arriving at wisdom so defined is pragmatism. As Menand has noted, pragmatism was a casualty of the Cold War, with which a more positivistic approach featuring the precise application of scientific method to achieve a definite result was far more compatible. Although that era's most vital intellects nurtured pragmatic thinking, they did so only in subtle and incomplete ways. Wohlstetter extolled, and was heavily influenced by, Peirce, perhaps the most enterprising of the early pragmatists, and may have been the only one among the great nuclear strategists to explicitly embrace the philosophy of pragmatism. Schelling's eclectic approach to strategy demonstrated an instrumental conception of ideas and an appreciation of their expansive utility that reflect pragmatic impulses. But the existential preoccupation with preventing nuclear war kept them from being terribly searching in the broader realm of strategy. They were pragmatists only within the confines of the U.S.-Soviet nuclear confrontation.* In the larger context, rationalism, insofar as it enshrined absolute truth, prevailed over pragmatism, which as such rusticated. The great nuclear strategists took the confrontation and Soviet implacability as givens, and did not flex their pragmatic sensibility so as to question the world order as a whole. Doing so may have seemed a pointless exercise at that stage of history. It is crucial now.

Pragmatism's central tenet—that even cherished and seemingly immutable principles are just educated bets on the future— will not sit well with those Americans, of which there are many, who see the American way as the culmination of civilization, to which all should aspire. It's true that victory in the Cold War, among other things, may have certified American-style capitalist democracy as a pretty good bet on the future. But it's just as true that 9/11 was a bare-knuckled challenge to the American way. Protecting it may involve rigidity in some areas, but it will require flexibility in others: hedging the bet. The lone superpower has to be, as the pragmatists were, respectful of "other ways of being in the world."[18] Like America after the Civil War, the present world order needs careful repair and reconciliation far

---

*Both men did try to extend their methods to areas beyond nuclear deterrence. Wohlstetter applied an intellectual acuity honed on geopolitics and nuclear strategy to racial unrest in America, while Schelling moved on to a remarkable array of inventive applications to subjects ranging from law enforcement to self-discipline. Albert and Roberta Wohlstetter, "Metaphors and Models: Inequalities and Disorder at Home and Abroad, RAND D–17664–RC/ISA (Santa Monica, CA: RAND Corporation, 1968); and Thomas C. Schelling, *Choice and Consequence* (Cambridge, MA: Harvard University Press, 1985). But these efforts occurred conspicuously outside the domain of strategy.

more than it does bald triumph and subjugation. While U.S. foreign policy must rest on clear principles, they have to be applied, the way Holmes as a judge applied the common law, with *tolerance*—informed by experience and circumstance, and not the sterile black letter of doctrine—as the quintessential guide.* Even the more iconoclastic contemporary pragmatists like Cornel West acknowledge "the inescapable and inexpungible character of tradition, the burden and buoyancy of that which is transmitted from the past to the present."[19]

Of course Holmes, on account of his indelibly sobering experience as a young soldier in the Civil War—throughout his life he kept two of his bloodied army uniforms in his bedroom closet—was a deep skeptic about beliefs in general. He would not have called himself a pragmatist. But the other pragmatists were not so cynical. Peirce, for example, thought people could have beliefs as long as they used pragmatic methods to arrive at them. His form of pragmatism simply acknowledges that the validity of beliefs is not necessarily permanent.[20] This is consistent with a broadly American ideology, and not vulnerable to the charge of ethical relativism sometimes leveled at pragmatists. Pragmatism, while concededly at

---

* It was Holmes who penned arguably the most famous sentence in American jurisprudence: "The life of the law has not been logic; it has been experience." Oliver Wendell Holmes Jr., *The Common Law* (Boston: Little, Brown, 1881), p. 1. This notion is distinctly pragmatic in the philosophical sense. Judge Richard Posner, probably Holmes's closest living intellectual descendant and an avowed pragmatist, has provided a fine explication of his magisterial declaration: "Pragmatism in the sense that I find congenial means looking at problems concretely, experimentally, without illusions, with full awareness of the limitations of human reason, with a sense of the 'localness' of human knowledge, the difficulty of translations between cultures, the unattainability of 'truth,' the consequent importance of keeping diverse paths of inquiry open, the dependence of inquiry on culture and social institutions, and above all the insistence that social thought and action be evaluated as instruments to valued human goals rather than as ends in themselves." Richard A. Posner, "A Pragmatist Manifesto," chapter 15 in *The Problems of Jurisprudence* (Cambridge, MA: Harvard University Press, 1990), p. 465.

odds with absolutism or "foundationalism," is a form of "fallibilism"—a term coined by Peirce—rather than relativism.[21] The pragmatists' "alternative to foundationalism," political philosopher
Richard Bernstein has explained, "was to elaborate a thoroughgo-
ing fallibilism where we realize that although we must begin any
inquiry with prejudgments and can never call everything into question at once, nevertheless there is no belief or thesis—no matter
how fundamental—that is not open to further interpretation and
criticism."[22] Fallibilism, then, rejects the notion that propositions
(including beliefs) can be known for sure, and holds that they are
simply contentions to be empirically demonstrated.

In a very circumscribed context, Wohlstetter related this aspect
of pragmatism to his inquiry into SAC basing systems at RAND.
The statement "I know X" implies that X is true. A fallibilist challenge, however, would ask, "How do you know X is true?" or "On
what basis is X true?" That is, the fallibilist seeks justification for
not only the truth of the statement itself, but also for its underlying foundation.* Wohlstetter brought this sort of approach to the
specific proposition that forward basing provided for the best
American nuclear deterrent, probing the validity of the criteria

---

*Thomas Powell, a professor of management at Oxford, drives home just how
pragmatic fallibilism is: "Because the fallibilist view arises in the spirit of balancing, rather than replacing, opposite views, it does not imply or advocate the re-
placement of prevailing epistemologies. Fallibilists recognize that objectivist
assumptions inform common sense and transport the enterprise of objective science, and that subjectivism expresses a perceptually grounded antithesis that
helps researchers understand the subjective, existential nature of conscious experience. Indeed, fallibilists are not above using subjectivist arguments to refute
objectivist knowledge claims, and vice versa. Where objectivism and subjectivism have critiqued one another as thesis and antithesis, fallibilism enters the
scene as a metacritique of the objectivist-subjectivist debate, not as synthesis. Fallibilism reminds us that existing perspectives reflect epistemological decisions
that might have been made differently; that existing perspectives constrain as
well as facilitate." T. C. Powell, "Fallibilism and Organizational Research: The
Third Epistemology," *Journal of Management Research,* vol. 1, no. 4 (September–
December 2001), pp. 201–19.

used to establish that proposition. A pragmatic foreign policy would apply the approach to more general propositions, such as the policy of democracy promotion. Such an inquiry would not, for example, call for the denigration of democracy promotion writ large, for the American principle of democracy has been tested by experience and a widespread belief in its validity thus justified. But policy makers would have to craft tailored assessments of how quickly democratization can realistically proceed (if at all), and how the United States might—or might not—be able to help deliver it according to what criteria have determined its successful application in the past.[23] In this light, the watchwords of grand strategy ought to be trial and error and give-and-take—not anything as neat and peremptory as containment or rollback—with an eye to establishing a better accommodation between the West and Islam, one that bin Laden cannot credibly repudiate.*

*The work of political scientist Barry O'Neill, much influenced by Schelling, may provide valuable guidance for injecting tolerance into U.S. foreign policy. O'Neill's basic insight is that even among mature nations attuned to prudentially protecting national interests, honor plays a huge role in conflict. Honor, in turn, has extraordinary unifying power in that the members of any group extolling it expect such honor in practice to subsume a wide range of traits and modes of behavior. Furthermore, there are two concepts of honor: an individual's personal capacity and society's estimate of that capacity. In the context of the defensive global jihad that bin Laden has proclaimed, in which every Muslim in the *umma* has a personal duty to participate in the struggle, there is immense pressure on each person to meet the collective expectations of his Muslim peers. While this is no earthshaking revelation, apprehending the deeper objective of counterterrorism as a matter of comprehending and appreciating the *umma*'s definition of honor is a clear and useful starting point. O'Neill's insights about the function of apology in foreign policy may also be important. He notes, in particular, that "though apologizing can be the honorable thing to do, it means admitting that we were wrong and on that account losing face." Or, to put it more succinctly, "apologizers can lose face but gain honor." Despite the loss of face involved, it may be worth it to the United States to apologize for the occupation of Iraq, the indefinite detention of terrorist suspects at Guantánamo Bay, and the abusive American practices at Abu Ghraib prison in order to recoup its honor. Barry O'Neill, *Honor, Symbols, and War* (Ann Arbor, MI: University of Michigan Press, 2001).

Meeting the Challenge

One of the features that failed to catch light in Wohlstetter's truncated application of the philosophy of pragmatism was the conviction that knowledge is by nature social and communal, a product of the individual's interaction with the rest of the world. Closely related to this idea was Dewey's conception of democracy as a mechanism for realizing the "sovereignty of the citizen" as a member of society who "has concentrated within himself its intelligence and will."[24] It is true that the teamwork ethos and open-ended approach cultivated at RAND engendered a kind of limited marketplace of ideas, but only an intellectual elite that shared the same basic worldview—in which the United States and the Soviet Union were engaged in a titanic zero-sum struggle—were privileged to enter that marketplace. "The Cold War," Diane Stone has written, "clarified the political uses of knowledge." That is, "by recasting nuclear strategy as a technical problem, to be addressed by experts, the security intellectuals at RAND, IISS and elsewhere displaced public political discussion and dominated the security agenda."[25]

Thus, the Cold War dispensation reinforced the "privileged managerialism" espoused by Walter Lippmann and Harold Lasswell during the interwar years as the best way to make democracy work in an increasingly complex world.[26] The fact that nuclear strategy worked, of course, made courting its wider approval a less pressing matter. Although men like Schelling and Wohlstetter did become public intellectuals, they presented themselves as oracles who condescended to speak from the commanding heights, and who were not open to serious challenge from the layman or the generalist. The only strategist of the Cold War to truly engage, and seek engagement, with society at large was Herman Kahn, and his celebrity was broadly disdained by his brethren. It is no accident that in the fullness of time he has come to be taken the least seriously. Nuclear strategy was a matter for the elite. The common folk were not invited to the table, and the knowledge that emerged from RAND studies therefore could not, under true pragmatist criteria, be considered fully tested or developed.

More-particular brands of exclusivity also developed during the Cold War. RAND's relentlessly analytic and rationalistic mode of thinking disfavored history as a basis for strategy, and the Vietnam War and related social and intellectual trends helped alienate entire swathes of academia—notably, Middle East scholars—from the national security endeavor.[27] According to a 2003 American Historical Association study, "history graduate programs at all types of institutions are prone to ignore large areas of the world in their course offerings. More than half of the history graduate programs do not offer graduate-level courses in fields outside of the United States and Europe."[28] The toxic rifts that have arisen in Middle East studies over Orientalism and U.S. support for Israel have also disinclined students to take on Middle Eastern history in particular. "Why spend my career being abused?" they ask, and study, say, China. The salience of political Islam and the challenges of emerging new dynamics in the Middle East and the Persian Gulf are likely to reinvigorate the status and attractiveness of Middle Eastern studies of their own force, and to encourage young scholars to work for their country. But the process will take time. Even those who were immediately inspired by the crumbling of the Twin Towers will not be ready for action—as primed, for instance, as RAND's finest were when Kennedy was nominated in 1961—until they finish school and intellectually mature, several years down the road.

Congress could accelerate the process with more purposeful financial support for strategic thought. A major congressional-level effort may be needed to revive Middle Eastern history—as well as

Middle Eastern studies in general—as an eminent and career-enhancing discipline. While Title VI of the National Defense Education Act of 1958 has long provided federal financial support for security-related education and research, Martin Kramer has argued forcefully that funding has been directed primarily toward language and area studies, and that the public-private synergy Title VI was meant to nurture has been stunted by the post-Orientalist backlash.[29] Starting in 2003, several leading decriers of Middle East studies in the United States—in particular, Kramer and Stanley Kurtz—pushed for closer government control of Title VI funding, which came to about $100 million a year following the 26 percent increase prompted by 9/11. In essence, their argument was that while it made sense to increase government funding to build knowledge about international affairs, it would not be money well spent unless it aimed specifically to correct the biases and shortcomings in academic research that had contributed to the nation's lack of strategic warning with respect to Islamist terrorism.

The first palpable fruit of their efforts was the International Studies in Higher Education Act of 2003, known less formally as H.R. 3077. The bill, passed by the House in October 2003, would require the creation of a seven-member advisory board to review government research grant allocations under Title VI and determine how they might better meet government needs. Two members would be chosen by the Speaker of the House, two by the president pro tem of the Senate, and three by the secretary of education with the proviso that two of those so chosen represent government agencies with national security responsibilities. Though disappointed that the board would be merely advisory rather than supervisory, and its recommendations consequently nonbinding, Kramer and Kurtz understood that inevitable backlash over academic freedom made mandatory powers for the board politically unrealistic.[30] Others, like their colleague Daniel

Pipes, preferred completely eliminating the post-9/11 windfall from Title VI coffers and diverting the money to a network of research centers devoted to terrorism studies.[31] A family of research centers covering a diverse range of subjects and outlooks is a specific goal of the board activities contemplated by H.R. 3077, but those concentrating on terrorism are not singled out. In any case, the bill was not passed by the Senate, and was reintroduced in February 2005 as H.R. 509, only to stall again in the Senate after clearing the House.*

Much of H.R. 3077's problem lay with the turbulent history of Middle East studies. Because H.R. 3077 was structured merely as an adjustment to Title VI, and Title VI had bankrolled controversial activities, the bill could hardly avoid becoming a new battleground for the old fight between putative neoconservatives who impugned the academy for its alleged lack of patriotism, and anti-Orientalists who disdained what they perceived as the neoconservatives' intellectual fascism. Miriam Cooke of Duke University derisively characterized H.R. 3077 as "the brainchild of Campus Watch"—the watchdog group launched by Kramer and other neoconservatives.[32] Professor Rashid Khalidi, a Palestinian appointed in late 2003 to the new Edward Said Chair of Middle East Studies at Columbia University and characterized along with other Columbia professors in a *New York Post* op-ed by Daniel Pipes and Jonathan Calt Harris as having "venomous feelings

* In March 2007, the National Research Council of the National Academies issued a report recommending legislative changes to increase Title VI accountability. While the report did not cover bias and boycott issues, it did propose the creation of a presidentially appointed and Senate-confirmed coordinator of all international education and foreign language programs, housed in the Department of Education and charged with ensuring that federal subsidies to university language and area studies programs can fill national needs—including those of defense and intelligence agencies. Stanley Kurtz, "Title Bout," *National Review Online*, April 2, 2007. http://article.nationalreview.com/?q-NTlkYmJINTk5MDYy ZDdkYmU2YWM4YWI2NTR1YjM1OWE=.

for the United States," contended that the legislation created "a highly partisan ideological litmus test for academics" that could limit freedom of expression.[33] More generally, the fraught background of H.R. 3077 raised the fear that it would skew rather than broaden the array of thinkers who would ultimately be admitted to the strategic community. That eventuality would cut against the pragmatic imperative of drawing on the full range of society's resources, and reprise the one major flaw of Cold War thinking: its exclusivity.

One possible way to keep this political morass from impeding a fresh intellectual mobilization would be to create an entirely new statutory research institution with an independent source of government funding. This new institution would become a repository of a wide range of scholars and policy intellectuals motivated by 9/11 and the subsequent deterioration of U.S. foreign and security policy to fashion a more stable and hopeful strategic enviroment. It's easy to see the potential pitfalls of crash programs designed to meet emergent needs: the CIA's post-9/11 drive to recruit operations officers for collecting human intelligence, for instance, produced several classes of callow (albeit zealous) "millennials" who are not proving up to the job.[34] A government-designated think tank could perhaps be seen as an inordinate delegation of intellectual authority, which Dewey feared could deprive society of "a unified and articulate will" even in a democracy.[35] And of course, the vituperative debate within academia over Middle East studies and its public funding would continue to roil. But with appropriately neutral oversight, a congressionally backed effort to nurture a new generation of leading-edge strategists would be well structured to cast its net widely and without political bias while also imposing high academic and professional qualifications.

In drawing in the most capable and enthusiastic people from a large, deep pool, such a campaign would reincorporate, for example, historians and Middle East experts as key players in the formulation of American strategy. The work of RAND and the civilian strategists during the Cold War did not silence pacifists or abolitionists, or preclude serious protestations like Philip Green's *Deadly Logic* or wry ones like *Report from Iron Mountain,* and it certainly did not seduce or include the fiercest doubters of U.S. nuclear strategy. But that work did build and consolidate a conventional wisdom about nuclear deterrence that won a very broad societal consensus. Thus, provided the new institution produced objective, well-defended studies, its work might become a mechanism for at least calming the storm in Middle East studies and paving the way for greater harmony. Furthermore, provided its mandate explicitly incorporated a degree of inclusion that RAND's charter admittedly never did, the talent pool that the new institution created would scarcely constitute the Platonic aristocracy—the "blasphemy against personality"—that Dewey regarded as dangerously retrograde.[36] Rather, it might qualify as the vehicle through which the public, by way of its elected representatives, could at least roughly frame policies that remained subject to democratic debate and approval.[37]

A new government-chartered think tank would make bureaucratic as well as political sense. In his prescient 1977 government study of the challenges posed by terrorism, Robert Kupperman asked: "Without seeking a 'shadow-government' solution, how can a viable counterterrorism program be developed in an environment controlled by the problems of the moment?"[38] The answer is that it probably cannot. A new organizational structure is required through which intellectual capital can be channeled into shaping policy. Government agencies have their hands full just keeping terrorists at bay. In the rush of operations, they are not empowered or practically able to take a fully balanced strategic view or, in most cases, to look far into the future. Back in 1962, Herman Kahn, with typically aggressive candor, noted that "most people do not appreciate just how ill-equipped our government is to perform long-range planning. The most able officials are constantly involved in the meeting of day-to-day crises, congressional investigations, budgetary problems, and administrative detail, with little time to devote to the long-range problems in which the civilian non-government research corporation specializes. Rarely, if ever, can a government agency allow one man to be free from what Professor Samuel Sharp calls 'the tyranny of the in-and-out box' for more than just a few months."[39]

The integrity of State Department policy planning—which was formidable under George Kennan and Paul Nitze during the Cold War and later under Dennis Ross in anticipating early post–Cold War challenges—has proven extremely difficult to maintain against the relentless day-to-day demands of foreign relations and crisis management, which became even more varied and complicated in the 1990s. The Defense Department has an important policy-planning role in determining the size and makeup of military forces, as well as their roles and missions, but this does not extend to subtler inquiries about terrorist threats, motivations, and ideology. The National Security Council is charged primarily with coordinating rather than formulating policy. During the Clinton administration, its "strategic planning" unit was essentially a speechwriting office. During the George W. Bush administration, that unit transmogrified into what amounted to a propaganda cell, in which NSC staffers, in the face of declining support for the Iraq war, concocted a cynical thirty-five-page document titled "Our Strategy for Victory in Iraq," released to the public in November 2005, on the basis of an analysis not of substantive military strategy at all but rather polling data that indicated that the American public would tolerate a war with

mounting casualties if they ultimately believed it would succeed.*
The CIA's remit, as well as that of the new national intelligence
directorate, is to factually inform rather than devise policy.

All government agencies are constrained, to a greater or lesser
degree, by organizational mind-sets and biases.[40] The tendency of
the organizations composing government to operate according to
familiar rules, patterns, and priorities made the shift from Cold
War to asymmetrical threats difficult to achieve. Intelligence agencies were especially prone to mistaking the unfamiliar for the improbable as a result of grandfathering basic analyses from one
generation to the next.[†] Furthermore, agencies in charge of running the government are to a large extent bound by policies
devised by, or at least subject to, the final approval of elected officials, and thus limited by external political realities. For example,
the new interagency National Counterterrorism Center (NCTC),
though mandated to render objective and nonpartisan appraisals
of the terrorist threat, is also obligated to help implement the Bush
administration's counterterrorism strategy. While the NCTC is de-

---

*The intellectual force behind the paper was Duke University political scientist
Peter D. Feaver, who had been appointed special adviser to the president for strategic planning and institutional reform on the NSC staff. Peter Baker and Dan
Balz, "Bush Words Reflect Public Opinion Strategy," *Washington Post*, June 30,
2005, p. Al; Scott Shane, "Bush's Speech on Iraq War Echoes Voice of an Analyst,"
New York Times, December 4, 2005, p. Al. Feaver's findings were published in a
peer-reviewed scholarly journal. See Peter D. Feaver, Christopher F. Gelpi, and Ja-
son Reifler, "Success Matters: Casualty Sensitivity and the War in Iraq," *International Security*, vol. 30, no. 3 (Winter 2005/06), pp. 7–46.

†The most frequently cited articulation of this conflation is Schelling's, with reference to the Japanese surprise attack on Pearl Harbor: "Rarely has a government
been more expectant. We just expected wrong. And it was not our warning that
was most at fault, but our strategic analysis. . . . There is a tendency in our planning to confuse the unfamiliar with the improbable. The contingency we have
not considered seriously looks strange; what looks strange is thought improbable; what is improbable need not be considered seriously." Thomas C. Schelling,
Foreword to Roberta Wohlstetter, *Pearl Harbor: Warning and Decision* (Stanford, CA:
Stanford University Press, 1962), p. vii.

veloping a mechanism for strategic assessment—that is, for diagnosing the effectiveness of that strategy and prompting changes if necessary—the feedback loop through which its findings must go to affect policy is long, convoluted, and politically treacherous.

These limitations on government agencies' capacity to foresee threats and formulate strategy, of course, do not necessarily mean that outside analysts and think tanks would do any better. But there is precedent. In the 1950s, with RAND's basing study, and early 1960s, with Wohlstetter's "delicate balance" and Schelling's "strategy of conflict," they were ahead of the government's curve. Government took control of nuclear strategy when McNamara became secretary of defense and consolidated that control through Kissinger's tenure as secretary of state. As Israel and the Arab states became more salient in strategic affairs, government's grip on strategy got even tighter by default, in part due to the discord in Middle Eastern studies. This assumed burden inevitably led to mistakes in that government became responsible for more than it could handle: in addition to running U.S. foreign policy on a day-to-day basis, it was tasked to see threats years and decades out. Mechanisms like CIA's Office of National Estimates up to 1973 and the National Intelligence Council thereafter, while useful, were not sufficiently funded or staffed to fulfill this latter duty. They may have forecast problems authoritatively, but they have never offered remedies. Those insiders who did see the rising strategic threat of transnational Islamist terrorism found themselves in the uncomfortable position of lobbying their own organizations for shifts in priorities that they themselves had helped set.

Under the burden of these evolved practices, it is unlikely that any existing federally funded research and development center (FFRDC) would be able to insulate its operations from its sponsors' preoccupations with contemporary circumstances to allow "new stream thinkers" to flourish. To be sure, in 2002, RAND did produce a monograph tightly focusing on the deterrability of transnational Islamist terrorists and their amenability to political suasion.[41] Though relatively short and theoretical, it might have served as a source of deeper and more-particular questions about the motivations of terrorists. But it went largely untapped. In 2004, at the behest of the Air Force, RAND produced an anodyne, if competent, primer on terrorism that was curiously unfocused on Islamist groups.[42] Into early 2005, a careful RAND study still viewed counterproliferation as the principal means of thwarting unconventional mass-casualty Islamist terrorism, ominously finding that terrorists had the will but consolingly concluding that they lacked the way and leaving it at that.[43] Other RAND studies have dealt with matters like modes of Islamist terrorist recruiting and military requirements to deal with transregional threats. They were conducted, respectively, at the behest of the intelligence community and the Army. These have probably helped RAND's government taskmasters pursue and interdict terrorists, but they have only glancingly addressed terrorists' more profound motivations and more dire objectives.[44] No cadre of researchers has yet looked at the risk systematically—as a problem requiring integrated consideration of apocalyptic mind-sets, criminal networks, dual-use technologies, infrastructure security, "feral cities," failed states, and pandemic detection—because no single organization brings together all of the different skill sets required.*

---

*Non-FFRDC organizations and analysts have taken up some of the slack, stressing the need for more searching study and occasionally undertaking it. But the basic discussion still has not advanced much past a standoff between those who think terrorists are a long way from getting WMD, and those who think they are getting close. In either case, the main remedy is physical security with respect to "loose nukes" in conjunction with a preemptive declaratory policy whereby even enrichment of nuclear material subjects a state to attack; more motivationally aimed dissuasion strategies don't generally come into play. A default position, based on the post-9/11 consensus behind comprehensive "capabilities-based" in contrast to "threat-based" security planning, is that

At the apex of the FFRDCs' influence and policy entrepreneurship, in the fifties and sixties, an outfit like RAND might have been able to sit Air Force officers or Pentagon officials down and tell them that a government-commissioned study, involving full access to classified information, needed to be executed forthwith in order to allow the administration to formulate the best possible policy for—to take just one possible requirement—procuring strategic bombers, ICBMs, and SLBMs. Now it is not that easy. Perhaps that is the way it ought to be. The Cold War was exceptional in that nobody—the generals and admirals included—had ever fought a nuclear war. The current campaign against terrorism, though, is not so rarefied. Those on the front line of policy execution may not have faced such dark and implacable terrorists, but they have dealt with plenty of lesser and still formidable varieties. They are likely to know better than informed observers just what they need. But they are also apt to frame the problem according to their own political predispositions, and to call on think tanks that cater to their biases. In staffing the Coalition Provisional Authority that ineptly ran Iraq for the first year following the Iraq invasion, for example, the Bush administration recruited a crew of wet-behind-the-ears Republican ideologues— almost none of whom had Middle East experience or expertise— mainly through the Heritage Foundation, an overtly ideological think tank.[45] It remains lamentable that FFRDCs' capacity for in-depth research that could at least stimulate new directions and enrich policy implementation has atrophied. It is also fixable.

RAND's original location in Santa Monica, far from Washington, symbolized operating "on the edge" in the best way. RAND traditionalists have always feared that its Washington office—which,

---

the risk might as well be deemed high because the consequences of a WMD terrorist attack would be so dire.

though still considerably smaller than the Santa Monica headquarters, now employs over one hundred analysts—placed researchers too close to their government customers, making them slaves to their in-box mentalities rather than practitioners of the investigator-initiated research that put RAND on the map. The point is not that a think tank separated from both quotidian Washington and the roiling academic world would produce clinical, objective assessments that would always be superior.* Only two leading RANDites—Charles Wolf, an economist, and Harry Rowen—scrutinized the costs of Soviet expansion and military spending during the 1980s and rated them not only unsustainable but deleterious to Soviet power over the long haul.[46] Nevertheless, a new-look think tank, linked loosely to government, would be able to step back from the maelstrom of the daily business of national security and investigate operational and policy options with a reasonable degree of freshness and at least relative objectivity—to function, in Kahn's formulation, as "a sort of loyal opposition which is privy to most of an agency's 'secrets,' and yet can be disowned by the agency."[47]

A new FFRDC, rather than a wholly independent think tank, would work best. FFRDC status would allow its employees some level of government clearance and access to classified information as well as to government officials. This intimate working relationship would ensure that the think tank was clued to policy makers' needs and concerns. Unless the think tanks were endowed with such special status, it's doubtful that officials would regard it as a sufficiently authoritative source of guidance to make its creation worthwhile.† Wohlstetter's original basing

---

*The philosopher Thomas Nagel has demonstrated that there is no such thing as true objectivity—that there can exist no "view from nowhere." Thomas Nagel, *The View from Nowhere* (New York: Oxford University Press, 1986).

†Many of the ranking experts on Islamic history and culture gravitate toward purely academic institutions. Gilles Kepel and Olivier Roy, leading French scholars of Islam, have put forth intensive and learned assessments of radical Islamic mo-

study had such a profound influence on government policy precisely because of RAND's access to classified data. Before the
study was undertaken, the U.S. government presumed the Strategic Air Command's bomber force to be invulnerable because the
National Security Council's Net Evaluation Committee posited
only Soviet attacks so large and requiring such perceptible prep-
aration that the SAC could not help but have sufficiently early
warning to rally to invulnerable positions. Because this assessment was highly classified, outside analysts had no basis for dis-
puting the presumption. Wohlstetter & Company, though, had
high-level clearances, and saw new possibilities in challenging
the Net Evaluation Committee's worst-case assumption. Once
they hypothesized more modest Soviet strikes requiring less conspicuous planning—for example, an attack designed simply to
destroy the SAC on the ground—any convictions of invulnerability crumbled.[48]

In the few circumstances in which independent, politically
driven think tanks have had direct influence over policy
implementation—as, for instance, the Heritage Foundation exercised over the staffing of the Coalition Provisional Authority that

---

tivations. Olivier Roy, *Globalised Islam: The Search for the New Ummah* (New
York: Columbia University Press, 2004); Gilles Kepel, *The War for Muslim Minds:
Islam and the West* (Cambridge, MA: Belknap Press, 2006). Public intellectuals like
Fareed Zakaria have asked, "Why do they hate us?" Fareed Zakaria, "The Politics of
Rage: Why Do They Hate Us?" *Newsweek*, October 15, 2001, pp. 22–40. But the
influence of these voices on government is highly attenuated. More often than
not, officials responsible for implementing policy apprehend their arguments as
soft hurdles that already-planned government courses of action need to finesse or
sidestep rather than sharp prompts to actually change policy. Alternatively, they
might simply regard deeper inquiry as interesting, but of insufficient immediacy
to affect government operations. "Occasionally an outsider may provide perspective," Henry Kissinger has noted dismissively. "Almost never does he have enough
knowledge to advise soundly on tactical moves." Henry A. Kissinger, *The White
House Years* (New York: Simon & Schuster, 1979), p. 39. Indeed, when Herman
Kahn—then no longer at RAND—sought to segue from policy guru to hands-on
adviser with respect to the Vietnam War, he was largely ignored.

oversaw Iraq during the first year of the American occupation—
ideology has trumped professionalism, and the results have been
distinctly inauspicious. In contrast, in the 1950s and 1960s,
RAND, owing to its special quasi-governmental status and access to high-echelon policy makers, was optimally qualified to
attract the cream of the crop of subject-matter experts, who were
also those least likely to substitute ideology for analysis. RAND
drew and nurtured a core of innovative intellectual leaders
around whom younger talent coalesced. Wohlstetter, Kahn, and
Marshall were not faultless, but they did view themselves as professional analysts, quite self-consciously placed themselves above
partisan politics, and managed to stay true to that conceit for
most of their respective careers. Early in the Cold War, RAND
thus became the ranking de facto center of excellence for strategic affairs, the primary channel of leading-edge strategic thinking, and the research institution of first resort for those in
government seeking strategic guidance uninflected by ideological bias. Properly conceived and structured, a new FFRDC could
perform a comparable function in the age of terror.

Congress, then, ought to consider chartering a new think tank
along existing FFRDC lines. Ties between the think tank and the
federal government would facilitate timely communication and
a degree of healthy synergy, but they would not be so cozy as to
inhibit "outside the box" thinking. That capacity would be pre-
served by an expansive mandate and the kind of flexible bud-
geting that prevailed at RAND in the early days of Project Air
Force, but have long since eroded. The Defense Advanced Research Projects Agency (DARPA)—which really did invent the
Internet—is an example of a quasi-independent government
institution that, given sufficiently broad operating parameters,
has proven that it can both think outside the box and serve the
practical needs of its "customers." The vast majority of DARPA's

work, of course, is in the relatively arcane arena of engineering.[49] In contrast, a new think tank would be charged with refining precisely the sorts of concepts that generate media interest, public attention, and congressional scrutiny. On the rare occasions when DARPA has ventured into such conspicuous and politically sensitive territory, its inventive take on policy has not fared well. Two potent recent examples in the counterterrorism area are the Total Information Awareness data-mining program and the terrorism betting exchange designed to collect and sift information about terrorist risks. Although these ideas contained some promising elements, because they respectively impinged dangerously on individual liberties and were rolled out in a remarkably naive and tone-deaf manner, both met with public consternation and were suspended by Congress.[50] The new FFRDC would need a dedicated external relations department to vet new ideas and articulate them clearly for public consumption. Unduly acute sensitization to public opinion, of course, would defeat the purpose of the new arrangement. But any new institution should also aspire to Dewey's vision of technocratic accountability.

Thinking Inside the Tank

During the Cold War, the more classical strategists like Brodie and Howard who saw strategic affairs in the round were marginalized because they couldn't master the technical material relating to nuclear weapons as people like Wohlstetter could. The ascent of arms control, which involved considerations of encryption and telemetry, only elevated the centrality of technical expertise to strategic thinking. Intellectual claustrophobia, notes Freedman, made the technocrats "unable to stand back and ask, does this really matter as much as we think it does?"[51] Now things are different. Understanding and thwarting radical Islamist terrorism carries no technical premium.* Thus, the new institution should not seek to replicate all of the attributes of the old RAND. In particular, the rational-choice theory developed in the 1950s by economist Kenneth Arrow, a RAND consultant and Harvard economist, formed an important basis of RAND'S methodology but also deemphasized history as a basis for policy. The Pentagon Papers were intended to invoke history to illuminate American missteps in Vietnam, but they were buried, quite literally, at RAND until Ellsberg liberated them. For many, probably most, of the Americans who read them, they confirmed the evolved preconception that Vietnam was a grand and tragic mistake. But some also read them more critically as self-consciously apologist screeds that employed the theory of bureaucratic politics from the realm of political science, rather than candid, professional historical analysis, to absolve individuals of blame.[52] Still others deciphered in the documents the vindication of a political system designed to generate a long-term domestic consensus on strategic matters and carry it through, even if it did produce a perversely bad result: Vietnam, despite its cost, was consistent with the grand strategy of containment and largely reflected the government's successful sale of that strategy to the electorate.[53] In any case, the strictures of containment and deterrence and the cold insularity of political science left little room for

---

*There have been some highly questionable calls from military officers for predominantly technical solutions to twenty-first-century security challenges. In April 2005, for example, General Lance T. Lord, commander of the Air Force's Space Command, exhorted a National Defense University Foundation audience to create a new generation of "wizards of Armageddon" to determine new uses for the five hundred Cold War–era Minuteman III ICBMs that remained on alert, and for exploiting the United States' "asymmetrical advantage in space." Walter Pincus, "Commander Seeks Alternate Uses for ICBMs," *Washington Post*, April 21, 2005, p. A24.

cultural scrutiny, which had been studiously avoided in the case of Vietnam.

At the same time, although the Cold War strategists' body of work offers no direct or set-piece prescriptions for new-stream strategic thinking, vintage RAND did make some methodological contributions that are quite well suited to dealing fluidly with the complexity, atomization, and maximalism of the transnational Islamist terrorist threat. In its best Cold War iterations—especially in Schelling's work—deterrence did not assume perfect rationality, at least not at the operational and tactical levels. The concept of "net assessment"—most closely associated with Andrew Marshall, but also applied by Wohlstetter, at RAND—describes an approach whereby the human and environmental uncertainties, historical niceties, and peculiarities of bureaucratic behavior elided by opposed systems design and systems analysis are taken into account to arrive at an overall picture that, while less neat than a rigid scenario, is a more realistic and fully contextualized form of policy guidance. Properly executed, net assessment places intelligence data and operational military analysis into the larger context of society's mobilization for a military campaign, and yields results based on a wide range of relevant situational, cultural, historical, and psychological considerations.[54]

Net assessment seeks to optimize U.S. strategy by correlating it directly to its adversary's strategy. Just as important, it looks well beyond both the short horizon of the news cycle and the longer—but still artificially short—span of the next political administration, so as to illuminate "the tyranny of small decisions" that a series of incremental bureaucratic steps might, if unchecked, impose on national security decision-making.[55] The byword of net assessment is *model simple and think complex*.[56] Near the end of the Cold War, wondering about a world in which the United States' most vicious enemies were not nuclear-armed states but minimally armed terrorists didn't occur to anyone because the problems that drew the most media and popular attention and demanded the most sophisticated scientific applications still consisted of Soviet ballistic missiles aimed at American cities. Had the challenge of sustaining nuclear deterrence and thwarting the Soviets in Afghanistan been a little less consuming, a little more talent and imagination might have been released to anticipate, through net assessment, the strategic threats latent in the empowerment of the Arab mujahideen in Afghanistan that culminated in the September 11 attacks. From a more operational perspective, there seems little doubt that a merely competent net assessment would have forecast that a Sunni insurgency would grip Iraq after the end of "major military operations" absent a larger American troop deployment and more selective de-Baathification.

Herbert Simon, the Nobel Prize–winning economist and pioneer of the theory of organizational behavior, noted that "short-term thinking drives out long-term strategy, every time." Net assessment calls for projecting history in order to formulate strategy. With few exceptions, those in government have no choice but to think essentially ahistorically, in the short term, because they have to act quickly on their thoughts. The purposeful detachment of elite thinkers from the churn of everyday governance would enable them to stand back, with no rigid obligation to take an immediate position, and arrive at a view that is demonstrably more considered than the plausible alternatives. Net assessment is more tightly bound by conventions and assumptions than pragmatism writ large. But in their endeavor to understand other points of view, practitioners of net assessment could generate unexpected and sometimes revelatory scenarios and forecasts that could militate in favor of changing those conventions and assumptions, and thus tilt toward a more pragmatic strategic approach.*

Without doubt, strategy for the new age calls on thoroughly catholic sensibilities. The ethnic, national, and ideological diversity of Islamist terrorists introduces a multiplicity of motivations that the essentially monolithic Soviet threat did not raise. Further, today's threat from a flat network of nonstate actors is far more heterogeneous than the highly centralized, state-controlled Soviet threat. And, whereas the compulsion of preserving the state stabilized U.S.-Soviet relations and made nuclear weapons unlikely war-fighting tools, al-Qaeda's core leadership appears to view them as prime instruments of religious deliverance.[57] At the same time, the prospect of a long campaign suggests that the United States and its allies must take greater pains to measure accurately the gap between rhetorical strategic intentions and actual ones. During the Cold War, the Soviets and the Americans had an interest in taking the other's grandiose pronouncements of resolve at face value: doing so justified arming themselves to the teeth.† They could get away with it because as long as deterrence worked, rhetoric would not be tested by reality; each side was free to assume the implacable truth of its strategic position. In a drawn-out conflict with terrorists, actual intentions will be far more sensitive to political and operational developments even if the rhetoric stays the same.

Terrorists will be deterrable, albeit in ways that are harder to decipher. So the logic and criteria of deterrence developed during the Cold War remains of practical value. They can help

---

*Net assessment, of course, is practiced at the Pentagon and other U.S. agencies, but on a highly compartmentalized basis.

†In his somewhat cheeky essay on Kahn's intellectual legacy, Louis Menand illuminates the reciprocal nature of the American and Soviet positions: "If the United States assigned the Soviets the role of mechanized Enemy Other, the Soviets did their best to play it." Louis Menand, "Fat Man," *The New Yorker,* June 27, 2005, p. 98.

clarify to what extent terrorist groups are deterrable and how they might be deterred. "Obviously you can't deter people who are going to blow themselves up by threats of punishment," notes Freedman, "but you can deter them by denial and you can deter organizations by threats of punishment. Deterrence isn't irrelevant, but it's much more difficult."[58] However bloodthirsty terrorist rhetoric may be, however prone to martyrdom terrorists appear, and whatever their investment in religious faith and divine guidance, they would not perpetrate attacks were it not in furtherance of real-world political objectives. In the case of the most maximal jihadists, the broad objective is to purge Islam of Western (especially American) influence, and mass-casualty suicide attacks seem to discourage Westerners from staying in and going to Muslim countries. Proving to terrorists that their goals are more likely to be frustrated if they persist than if they desist will give many, if not most, of them pause.

Assigning an aggressive mentality to religiously motivated terrorists is sensible but so is ascribing a constraining mentality to them. Bin Laden's insistence on a global caliphate won by large-scale violence against the West, Israel, and "apostate" Arab regimes may evolve—or have evolved—into something less radical owing to the atomization of the global jihad and, therefore, of the motivations of its soldiers. One means of stimulating and advancing such a trend might be to encourage the political legitimacy of Islamism and its constitution in statelike forms that are inherently more subject to deterrence and, therefore, restraint. This measure seems, at first blush, counterintuitive to say the least. Why would the United States want to promote a religious ideology that has heretofore counseled the destruction of its own state structure, political system, and culture? The answer is to furnish its leaders with something tangible to value—and, therefore, potential adversaries with something to threaten. Paradoxical as this formulation may sound, it is no more so than deterrence itself, which aims to maintain peace by promising destruction. The slow—and as yet incomplete—evolution of the militant Shiite group Hezbollah from an unregenerate anti-Israeli terrorist group into a powerful and substantially legitimate political player in Lebanon is a case in point. Hezbollah admittedly does not have strong incentives for disarming, and may be content with accepting the patronage of its partners in exchange for their endorsement of its armed status. At the same time, its freedom to return to large-scale violence is limited because doing so would mean forsaking a large measure of its hard-won political clout. The general formula for establishing similar foundations for deterrence elsewhere is the United States' exercise of political tolerance on a global scale to an extent that has been unthinkable in American government circles since 9/11. Yet it may prove especially expeditious if, as it appears, the Muslim world is becoming more, not less, religious, which makes any putative policy of secularization or even religious moderation all the more dubious.

The reigning factual assumption has been that liberal democracies discourage religious extremism and political violence, and that their creation would simply diminish the threat of terrorism rather than make it more deterrable. Spurred by the frustrated efforts of the United States to build a liberal pluralistic state in Iraq, the U.S. government has belatedly acknowledged that this dynamic will not take hold in many, perhaps most, Muslim countries, and reluctantly recognized that the exportation of democracy must proceed more slowly, gently, and selectively than originally hoped in 2003. But illiberal regimes, the thinking runs, must

remain secure in places like Egypt lest Islamists gain decisive political power and reject U.S. and broader Western influence. Actively organizing the dismantling of such
governments would indeed be imprudent, in that it could
undermine crucial bilateral American relationships or produce traumatic shocks that might touch off wider violence
and instability. Allowing Islamists to nonviolently gain political legitimacy at the national level, however, might yield
them a concrete stake in an existing polity that they would
be loath to jeopardize through transnational jihadist violence. Partially fulfilled Islamists like Hezbollah and Hamas
might well be easier to influence, co-opt, and deter.

The fact remains, unfortunately, that nobody knows what
will happen if Islamists gain power through normal, orderly
political processes, for there is no real precedent squarely on
point. Khomeini's rise to power in Iran in 1979 was not evolutionary but revolutionary, and characteristically distorted by an
excrescence of nationalism directed at the United States. Hamas's successful participation in free and fair elections in 2006
vaulted it into the Palestinian Authority's government, but
unique circumstances make any analogy dubious: Hamas's
legitimacy was immediately challenged by Israel, the United
States, and Europe as well as its secular Palestinian rivals,
prompting Ismail Haniya to establish a separate unrecognized
government in Gaza. Hezbollah, though part of Lebanon's government, contentiously shares legitimate authority with Sunni,
Druze, and Christian factions. In Jordan, the Muslim Brotherhood participates cooperatively in governance, but the situation
is aberrational in that the state is ruled by a virtually absolute
Hashemite monarchy with muscular superpower backing; it is
difficult, if not impossible, to tell how the Brotherhood would

behave if in power, in the absence of these presumptively inhibiting factors. Hassan al-Turabi's ascension to political dominance in Sudan is arguably indicative of how strong Islamist elements can insinuate themselves into national government and use it as a platform for further Islamization, but much of his progress occurred by virtue of coercion—in particular, the 1989 coup staged by Omar al-Bashir—rather than nonviolent politics, and Turabi's power was severely checked by his political rivalry with Bashir.

Thus, ignorance of what Islamist rule truly arrived at through legitimate political processes would look like is one of the most serious epistemological gaps facing current strategists. Even in an unfathomable political and strategic context, they are compelled to use what limited tools and knowledge they do have, and therefore can't avoid a degree of analytic rigidity. There is little choice but to apply the criterion of deterrability to these starkly imperfect examples to support broader strategic arguments. Appropriate doses of pragmatism can minimize mistakes. Nevertheless, the logic of deterrence—in essence, hostage-taking—is still least likely to apply to religiously motivated parties who sometimes regard expressive, self-sacrificial violence as an end in itself, who expect to be attacked, and who gain validation from being victimized.

From this perspective, it goes almost without saying that terrorists probably will not be self-deterred to the extent that scholars of the Cold War like Freedman argue that the superpowers were. For that reason, it's worth highlighting one of Freedman's less sardonic points about nuclear strategy. He comments that "what was really important was the effect of nuclear policy on the [Western] alliance in terms of grand strategy: how nations related to one another."[59] That is, the reality of two opposing superpowers with immense nuclear arsenals forced nations to form partnerships and alliances and open dialogues (for instance, on surprise attack and arms control) that made them safer, and nuclear strategy strengthened the glue among those nations through innovations like collective security, extended deterrence, and arms control. Al-Qaeda and its followers lack the brute military strength of the Axis powers, but their potential political appeal is far wider, extending to an entire world religion. At least in terms of the mobilization required of the United States and its partners, they may be at something resembling war. Characterizations like "the long war," however, seem intended in part to absolve the governments that use them from responsibility for ending the conflict and gathering all of the resources at their disposal to do so. Relationships and tools comparable to those developed and employed during the Cold War are all the more urgently required to battle a less deterrable (if also less lethal) foe than the Soviet Union. Forging them will be harder because a wider range of cultures, peoples, nations, and religious sects is involved, and one of the largest and most important embodiments of such groupings—Islam—has become embattled by its own radicalism and sectarianism and challenged by broad Western suspicions.

Perhaps the most important mission of new strategic thinkers will be to determine future threats—which fire next time—and how to deal with them. Provided they proceed with historical, sociological, and anthropological nuance and sound methodologies, their work could expand the West's array of strategic options. Analysts could develop different scenarios and combinations of scenarios involving, for instance, a U.S. withdrawal from Iraq, its strategic distancing of Saudi Arabia, an American shift to a more neutral position on the Israeli-Palestinian conflict, Iran's realization of a nuclear capability, the military prevention of an Iranian nuclear capability, a more aggressive U.S. pursuit of al-Qaeda's core leadership in the tribal areas on border of Pakistan and Afghanistan, or a robust and committed U.S. civil defense program.* Beyond these relatively narrow and immediate security matters, broader ones could be explored. Do the evident rise in Muslim radicalism and terrorism in Europe and Muslims' increasing proportion of Europe's population portend anti-Americanism in Europe with sufficient political traction to fracture NATO and dampen transatlantic counterterrorism cooperation? Should the moderation and quiescence of American Muslims be taken for granted, or are they also susceptible to the pervasive influences of radical Islam? And if they are, what policies are required to alleviate their restiveness? Is the "democratic peace" vaunted by the Bush administration a plausible vision for the Muslim world or a wishful artifact of Western history?

The great Cold War strategists, though they failed to conceptualize a plausible strategic alternative to containment or to master the subtleties of counterinsurgency, still thought outside the box

---

*Mass casualties are one aim of Islamist terrorists. Civil defense—the obsession that demonized Kahn in the minds of many—may have been futile in the face of multimegaton Soviet hydrogen bombs. Thus, during the Cold War, nuclear deterrence, not civil defense, came to be seen as the principal mechanism of homeland security against an attack of extremely high consequence but very low probability. Islamist terrorists threaten attacks with low-yield nukes, dirty bombs, or crude biological weapons of unknown probability. Such attacks, to be sure, would have relatively high consequences, but they would still be considerably more manageable than those of a thermonuclear strike. Accordingly, civil defense could be an effective tool of deterrence by denial. Indeed, PDD-62, signed by President Clinton in May 1998, is titled "Protection Against Unconventional Threats to the Homeland and Americans Overseas," and specifically distinguishes earlier civil defense efforts in creating Office of the National Coordinator for Security, Infrastructure Protection, and Counter-Terrorism within the Executive Office of the President to coordinate counterterrorism policy, preparedness, and consequence management. PDD-62, in bureaucratic effect, revived civil defense in the post–Cold War security context.

in which the U.S. government was forced to operate early in the Cold War with respect to nuclear weapons. That is why nuclear deterrence acquired a palpable degree of stability, and why the old RAND remains a worthy model of intellectual fertility. Beyond demonstrating the virtues of bureaucratic independence and focused imagination, the great strategists' signal achievement was the avoidance of nuclear war over the course of a forty-year confrontation. That success was the product of an evolving vision of American foreign policy that tied short-term actions to long-term results—that is, tactics to strategy. The substance of those strategists' solutions was very different from what is needed now. But the demand for policy-level linkage of tactics to strategy remains, and it's impossible to meet unless the strategy is formulated first.

The Vietnam War did not fundamentally change American attitudes or U.S. policy because it was perceived—rightly or wrongly—as a merely tactical error in the pursuit of a sound containment strategy. The Civil War, on the other hand, represented the near-fatal demise of the entire American project, the ultimate strategic failure. And it cast doubt upon a belief in America in which its citizens had previously developed an abiding faith. During the twentieth century, that belief was fitfully rebuilt, and by the time World War II had drawn to a close, durable confidence in the idea of the United States had again taken firm root. The Iraq War, while it does not menace the integrity of the American nation, may on an international scale be more like the Civil War than the Vietnam War. Certainly the invasion and occupation of Iraq and the string of unfortunate post-9/11 decisions on alliances, prisoners, and international law surrounding them embody an invidious revolution in American foreign policy that has led other peoples and states, and indeed some Americans, to question America's authority if not its power. As a matter of grand strategy, the U.S. government—and the American people—are now compelled to remedy this state of affairs or live with diminished legitimacy and standing. Collective brainpower, purposefully channeled, is obligatory. Herman Kahn's most indispensable tagline—it is etched on his gravestone at Fair Ridge Cemetery in Chappaqua, New York—was: "barring bad luck and bad management." Nothing can preclude bad luck. But some of the best minds of their generation once did, for the most part, minimize bad management. If ever such a national capability were required, it is required now.

Acknowledgments

Lawrence Freedman, Dennis Gormley, and Steven Simon, my invaluable friends and colleagues, read and incisively commented on earlier drafts of this book, for which they have my heartfelt thanks. I am also indebted to Louis Menand, who kindly perused the portions of the narrative dealing with the philosophy of pragmatism and furnished extremely focused and constructive feedback. My editor Wendy Wolf's painstaking and insightful analyses of the manuscript through various incarnations, both structurally and line by line, added inestimable value to the final product; I am grateful for her guidance and also for her unvarying good cheer. I'm thankful to Flip Brophy, my agent, for wisely pairing me with Wendy and convincing her I could deliver. My appreciation, too, to the Special Collections staff at the library of National Defense University, Fort McNair, Washington, D.C., who were extraordinarily accommodating and helpful in providing me access to the Hudson Institute Papers. I am similarly grateful to the staff of the National Security Archive at The George Washington University, also in Washington, D.C.

On the ergonomic level, I thank my stepdaughter, Lena Butler Curland, for affording me needed quiet—and occasionally comic relief—while I worked at home. Finally, my wife, Sharon L.

Butler, not only gave me her unstinting love, support, and patience throughout the process of my writing the book, but also critically read the entire manuscript and enabled me to shape and refine it according to the demands of the intelligent general reader—the most important member of any writer's constituency. I only hope I can repay her the favor. Any errors or indiscretions, of course, are mine alone.

Notes

1 | Harnessing Doom

1. Margaret Macmillan, *Paris 1919: Six Months That Changed the World* (New York: Random House, 2002), p. 28.
2. The description is drawn from John Cornwall, *Hitler's Scientists: Science, War and the Devil's Pact* (New York: Viking, 2003), p. 6.
3. Paul Fussell, *The Great War and Modern Memory* (Oxford: Oxford University Press, 1975), p. 74.
4. Quoted in Ron Rosenbaum, *Explaining Hitler: The Search for the Origins of His Evil* (New York: Harper Perennial, 1999), p. 173.
5. Richard Rhodes, *The Making of the Atomic Bomb* (New York: Random House, 1986), p. 676.
6. J. Robert Oppenheimer, *The Atomic Bomb and College Education*, quoted in *Bartlett's Familiar Quotations*, 16th ed. (Boston: Little, Brown, 1992), p. 714.
7. Sun Tzu, *The Art of War* (London: Hodder & Stoughton, 1995), p. 23.
8. Carl von Clausewitz, *On War*, eds. and trans. Michael Howard and Peter Paret (London: Everyman's Library, 1993), p. 702.
9. Ibid., p. 713.
10. Jennet Conant, *109 East Palace: Robert Oppenheimer and the Secret City of Los Alamos* (New York: Simon & Schuster, 2005), pp. 54–55.
11. Ibid., pp. 298–312.
12. Author interview with Deborah Kahn, Chappaqua, New York, November 24, 2003.
13. Author interview with Freeman Dyson, Princeton, New Jersey, March 12, 2004.
14. Author interview with Thomas C. Schelling, Bethesda, Maryland, December 1, 2003.
15. James Digby and Joan Goldhamer, "The Development of Strategic Thinking at RAND, 1948–63: A Mathematical Logician's View—An Interview with Albert Wohlstetter," July 5, 1985, p. 32 [transcript copyrighted by the RAND Corporation, 1997].
16. Schelling interview, December 1, 2003.

17. Lawrence Freedman, *The Evolution of Nuclear Strategy*, 3rd ed. (Basingstoke, UK: Palgrave Macmillan, 2003), pp. 30–31.
18. Vannevar Bush, *Modern Arms and Free Men* (London: Heinemann, 1950), p. 100.
19. James Digby, *Strategic Thought at RAND, 1948–1963: The Ideas, Their Origins, Their Fates,* N-3096-RC (Santa Monica, CA: RAND Corporation, 1990), p. 1.
20. Freedman, *The Evolution of Nuclear Strategy,* p. 42.
21. Freedman, *Evolution,* p. 46.
22. See Defense Threat Reduction Agency, *Defense's Nuclear Agency, 1947–1997* (Washington, DC: Department of Defense, 2002), pp. 47–94.
23. Freedman, *Evolution,* p. 53.
24. Author interview with Michael Wheeler, McLean, Virginia, March 11, 2004.
25. Wheeler interview, March 11, 2004.
26. Author interview with Henry S. Rowen, London, November 23, 2003.
27. Author interview with Sir Lawrence Freedman, London, June 1, 2004.
28. Freedman, *Evolution,* p. 64.
29. John Foster Dulles, "The Strategy of Massive Retaliation," Speech before the Council on Foreign Relations, January 12, 1954.
30. Fred Kaplan, *The Wizards of Armageddon* (New York: Simon & Schuster, 1983), p. 179.
31. John Foster Dulles, "Thoughts on Soviet Foreign Policy," *Life,* May 3, 1946, p. 118. On the spiritual roots of Dulles's foreign policy, see generally Townsend Hoopes, *The Devil and John Foster Dulles* (New York: Little, Brown, 1973), pp. 63–66.
32. Dulles, "Thoughts on Soviet Foreign Policy," p. 118.
33. John Foster Dulles, "A Policy of Boldness," *Life,* May 19, 1952, p. 154.
34. Freedman interview, June 1, 2004.
35. John Foster Dulles, "Policy for Security and Peace," *Foreign Affairs,* vol. 32, no. 3 (April 1954), p. 356.
36. Freedman interview, June 1, 2004.
37. William Kaufmann, ed., *Military Policy and National Security* (Princeton, NJ: Princeton University Press, 1956), introduction, pp. 21, 24–25.
38. Henry Kissinger, *Nuclear Weapons and Foreign Policy* (New York: Harper & Row, 1957), pp. 145–46.
39. Glenn Snyder, *Deterrence by Denial and Punishment,* Research Monograph No. 1, Center of International Studies, Princeton University, January 2, 1959. He later produced a book embodying the same ideas, *Deterrence and Defense* (Princeton, NJ: Princeton University Press, 1961).
40. Henry Rowen, *National Security and the National Economy in the 1960's,* Study Paper No. 18, Joint Economic Committee, 86th Congress, 2nd Session, Government Printing Office, January 30, 1960, p. 36.
41. Freedman, *Evolution,* p. 122.

2 | American Ways of Thinking

1. Carl von Clausewitz, *On War,* ed. and trans. Michael Howard and Peter Paret (London: Everyman's Library, 1993), pp. 717–18.
2. Bruce L. R. Smith, *The RAND Corporation: Case Study of a Nonprofit Advisory Corporation* (Cambridge, MA: Harvard University Press, 1966).

3. Author interview with Thomas C. Schelling, Bethesda, Maryland, December 1, 2003.
4. Glen Segell and James Edward King, *Nuclear Strategy: The Jim King Manuscripts* (self-published by Glen Segell, 2006), pp. 48–49; Michael Rubin, "Cole Is Poor Choice for Mideast Position," *Yale Daily News,* April 18, 2006.
5. Author interview with Andrew Marshall, The Pentagon, Arlington, VA, March 11, 2004.
6. Ibid.
7. Kaplan, *The Wizards of Armageddon,* p. 254, note 6.
8. Recounted in Paul Bracken, "Net Assessment: A Practical Guide," *Parameters,* vol. 36, no. 1 (Spring 2006), p. 95.
9. Priscilla J. McMillan, *The Ruin of J. Robert Oppenheimer and the Birth of the Modern Arms Race* (New York: Viking, 2005), pp. 127–35.
10. Kaplan, *The Wizards of Armageddon,* p. 122.
11. Author interview with Joan Wohlstetter Hall, New York, New York, March 15, 2004.
12. Ibid.
13. James Digby and Joan Goldhamer, "The Development of Strategic Thinking at RAND, 1948–63: "A Mathematical Logician's View—An Interview with Albert Wohlstetter," July 5, 1985, p. 4 [transcript copyrighted by the RAND Corporation, 1997].
14. Ibid., pp. 8–16.
15. Ibid., p. 17.
16. Ibid., p. 23.
17. Ibid.
18. Ibid., p. 35.
19. A. J. Wohlstetter, F. S. Hoffman, R. J. Lutz, and H. S. Rowen, *Selection and Use of Strategic Air Bases,* RAND R–266, April 1, 1954 (declassified 1962).
20. Author interview with George Quester, College Park, Maryland, March 8, 2004.
21. Ibid.
22. Albert Wohlstetter, "The Delicate Balance of Terror," *Foreign Affairs,* vol. 37, no. 2 (January 1959), pp. 211–33.
23. Digby and Goldhamer interview with Wohlstetter, 1985, pp. 36–37.
24. Ibid., p. 19.
25. Ibid., p. 61.
26. Quoted in Louis Menand, *The Metaphysical Club: A Story of Ideas in America* (New York: Farrar, Straus and Giroux, 2001), p. 367.
27. Digby and Goldhamer interview with Wohlstetter, 1985, p. 92.
28. The key players were Hempel at Princeton and Ernest Nagel at Columbia. See Carl Hempel, *Aspects of Scientific Explanation and Other Essays in the Philosophy of Science* (New York: The Free Press, 1965); Ernest Nagel, *The Structure of Science: Problems in the Logic of Scientific Explanation* (New York: Harcourt, Brace & World, 1961).
29. Charles Hitch and Roland N. McKean, *The Economics of Defense in the Nuclear Age* (Cambridge, MA: Harvard University Press, 1960).
30. Albert Wohlstetter, "Analysis and Design of Conflict Systems," in Edward S. Quade, ed., *Analysis for Military Decisions: The RAND Lectures on Systems Analysis* (New York: Rand McNally, 1967), p. 122.

31. Marshall interview, March 11, 2004. See Nathan Constantin Leites, *The Operational Code of the Politburo* (New York: McGraw-Hill, 1951).

32. Quester interview, March 8, 2004.

33. Author interview with Sir Michael Howard, London, February 26, 2004.

34. Author interview with Thomas C. Schelling, Bethesda, Maryland, March 9, 2004.

35. Ibid.

36. Ibid.

37. Author interview with Sir Michael Howard, London, May 14, 2004.

38. Ibid.

39. Howard interview, February 26, 2004.

40. Clausewitz, *On War,* Michael Howard and Peter Paret, eds. and trans., pp. 86, 88 (emphasis in original).

41. Ibid., p. 88 (emphasis in original).

42. Digby and Goldhamer interview with Wohlstetter, 1985, pp. 58–60.

43. Ibid.

44. Howard interview, February 26, 2004.

45. Schelling interview, March 9, 2004.

46. Lawrence Freedman, *The Evolution of Nuclear Strategy,* 3rd ed. (Basingstoke, UK: Palgrave Macmillan, 2003), p. 208.

47. Robert Ayson, *Thomas Schelling and the Nuclear Age: Strategy as Social Science* (London and New York: Frank Cass, 2004), p. 154.

48. Schelling interview, March 9, 2004.

49. Thomas C. Schelling, *The Strategy of Conflict* (Cambridge, MA: Harvard University Press, 1960), p. 4.

50. Schelling interview, December 1, 2003.

51. Ibid.

52. Letter to Michael Howard from Albert Wohlstetter, November 6, 1968, p. 30; provided to the author by Sir Michael Howard.

53. Freedman, *Evolution,* p. 196.

54. Schelling, *The Strategy of Conflict,* p. 91.

55. Thomas C. Schelling, *Arms and Influence* (New Haven, CT: Yale University Press, 1966), p. 134.

56. Schelling, *The Strategy of Conflict,* p. 188.

57. Schelling, *Arms and Influence,* pp. 43–49.

58. Ibid., p. 124.

59. Author interview with Sir Lawrence Freedman, London, June 1, 2004.

60. Quoted in Fred Kaplan, *The Wizards of Armageddon* (New York: Simon & Schuster, 1983), p. 297.

61. Transcript, Smithsonian Videohistory Program, *The RAND Corporation, Session Four, Research and Culture: Collection Division Two,* January 27, 1989, pp. 35, 57.

62. Marshall interview, March 11, 2004.

63. Author interview with Henry S. Rowen, London, November 23, 2003.

64. Daniel Guttman and Barry Willner, *The Shadow Government* (New York: Pantheon Books, 1976), pp. 128–29.

65. Herman Kahn, *Thinking About the Unthinkable* (New York: Avon Books, 1962), pp. 96–97.

66. Ibid., p. 35.

67. Herman Kahn, *On Thermonuclear War* (Princeton, NJ: Princeton University Press, 1960), p. 32.
68. Kahn, *Thinking About the Unthinkable,* pp. 38–40.
69. Schelling interview, March 9, 2004.
70. Letter to Herman Kahn from Robert Keedick, December 3, 1962; letter to Keedick from Kahn, December 11, 1962; from the Hudson Institute Papers, National Defense University Special Collections, Fort McNair, Washington, DC.
71. Wohlstetter Hall interview, March 15, 2004.
72. Digby and Goldhamer interview with Wohlstetter, 1985, p. 63.
73. Letter to Carl E. Rosenfeld from Herman Kahn, April 26, 1965; from the Hudson Institute Papers, National Defense University Special Collections, Fort McNair, Washington, DC.
74. Rowen interview, November 23, 2003.
75. Schelling interview, December 1, 2001.
76. Letter to Herman Kahn from Mrs. William H. Short, November 19, 1961; from the Hudson Institute Papers, National Defense University Special Collections, Fort McNair, Washington, DC.
77. Letter to Joseph Romm, Assistant Director of Civil Defense (Policy and Programs), Department of Defense, from Herman Kahn, June 9, 1965; from the Hudson Institute Papers, National Defense University Special Collections, Fort McNair, Washington, DC (emphasis in original).
78. Herman Kahn, *On Escalation: Metaphors and Scenarios* (New York: Praeger, 1965), p. 290.
79. Kahn, *On Thermonuclear War,* pp. 145–47.
80. James R. Newman, "Two Discussions of Thermonuclear War," *Scientific American,* vol. 204, no. 3 (March 1961), pp. 197–98, 200.
81. Author interview with Deborah Kahn, Chappaqua, New York, November 24, 2003.
82. Letter to Max Singer, Acting President, Hudson Institute, from Dean Acheson, December 18, 1961; letter to D. G. Brennan from John J. McCloy, January 17, 1962; from the Hudson Institute Papers, National Defense University Special Collections, Fort McNair, Washington, DC.
83. Fred Kaplan, "Truth Stranger than 'Strangelove,'" *New York Times,* October 10, 2004.
84. "The Prototype for Dr. Strangelove," *Sunday Times,* February 9, 1964.
85. Deborah Kahn, personal note to the author, December 10, 2003.
86. Letter to Bruce D. Evans, Esq., Debevoise, Plimpton, Lyons & Gates, from Herman Kahn, December 1, 1964; letter to H. M. Dickie, Esq., Freshfields, from Oscar M. Ruebhausen, Esq., Debevoise, Plimpton, Lyons & Gates, January 29, 1965; letter from Dickie to Ruebhausen, February 9, 1965; from the Hudson Institute Papers, National Defense University Special Collections, Fort McNair, Washington, DC.
87. Maurice Richardson, "Soul-Shakers from the States," *Daily Telegraph* (London), January 1, 1965.
88. Philip Green, *Deadly Logic: The Theory of Nuclear Deterrence* (Columbus, OH: Ohio State University Press, 1966), p. 92.
89. Freedman interview, June 1, 2004.
90. Schelling interview, March 9, 2004.

91. Schelling interview, December 1, 2003.
92. Letter from Dennis Flanagan to Herman Kahn, March 15, 1961; from the Hudson Institute Papers, National Defense University Special Collections, Fort McNair, Washington, DC.

3 | Sidelining the Unthinkable

1. Louis Menand, "Fat Man," *The New Yorker,* June 27, 2005, pp. 96–97.
2. Letter to Herman Kahn from Louis J. Henrich, August 25, 1961; from the Hudson Institute Papers, National Defense University Special Collections, Fort McNair, Washington, DC.
3. For details, see Sharon Ghamari-Tabrizi, *The Worlds of Herman Kahn: The Intuitive Science of Thermonuclear War* (Cambridge, MA: Harvard University Press, 2005), pp. 74–75.
4. Letter to W. H. McGlothlin from William M. Brown, August 1, 1962; letter to Sydney [*sic*] Cohen from Herman Kahn, October 8, 1962; letter to Herman Kahn from William H. McGlothlin, October 9, 1962; letter to William McGlothlin from Herman Kahn, with enclosures, October 15, 1962; letter to Herman Kahn from Sidney Cohen, October 11, 1962; from the Hudson Institute Papers, National Defense University Special Collections, Fort McNair, Washington, DC.
5. Letter to Patricia Stone from Herman Kahn, November 6, 1961; letter to Herman Kahn from Patricia Stone, October 23, 1961; from the Hudson Institute Papers, National Defense University Special Collections, Fort McNair, Washington, DC.
6. Letter to Harrison Salisbury from Donald Brennan, November 12, 1965; from the Hudson Institute Papers, National Defense University Special Collections, Fort McNair, Washington, DC.
7. Louis Menand, *The Metaphysical Club: A Story of Ideas in America* (New York: Farrar, Straus and Giroux, 2001), p. 374.
8. Cecil V. Crabb Jr., *American Diplomacy and the Pragmatic Tradition* (Baton Rouge, LA, and London: Louisiana State University Press, 1989), pp. 87–131.
9. Menand, *The Metaphysical Club,* p. 375.
10. Ibid., p. 441.
11. For vivid and incisive accounts of the most flagrant examples, such as the coups in Iran, Guatemala, and Chile, see Stephen Kinzer, *Overthrow: America's Century of Regime Change from Hawaii to Iraq* (New York: Times Books, 2006).
12. Menand, *The Metaphysical Club,* p. 439.
13. James Digby, *Strategic Thought at RAND, 1948–1963: The Ideas, Their Origins, Their Fates,* N-3096-RC (Santa Monica. CA: RAND Corporation, 1990), pp. 1–2.
14. See generally Donald E. Abelson, *Think-Tanks and Their Role in US Foreign Policy* (New York: St Martin's Press, 1996), pp. 72–79.
15. The full citation for the book is Thomas C. Schelling and Morton H. Halperin, *Strategy and Arms Control* (New York: Twentieth Century Fund, 1961).
16. Author interview with Thomas C. Schelling, Bethesda, Maryland, December 1, 2003.
17. Fred Kaplan, *The Wizards of Armageddon* (New York: Simon & Schuster, 1983), pp. 169–70.
18. James Digby and Joan Goldhamer, "The Development of Strategic Thinking at RAND, 1948–63: A Mathematical Logician's View—An Interview with Albert

Wohlstetter," July 5, 1985, pp. 78–79 [transcript copyrighted by the RAND Corporation, 1997].

19. Richard E. Neustadt, *Presidential Power: The Politics of Leadership* (New York: John Wiley, 1960).

20. Colin S. Gray, "What RAND Hath Wrought," *Foreign Policy*, no. 4 (Autumn 1971), p. 119.

21. See, for example, James Allen Smith, *The Idea Brokers: Think-tanks and the Rise of the New Policy Elite* (New York: The Free Press, 1991), pp. 134–36.

22. Schelling interview, December 1, 2003.

23. Alain Enthoven and K. Wayne Smith, *How Much Is Enough? Shaping the Defense Program 1961–1969* (New York: Harper & Row, 1971), chapter 4.

24. Bernard Brodie, "What Price Conventional Capabilities in Europe?" *The Reporter*, May 23, 1963, pp. 25–33; *Escalation and the Nuclear Option* (Princeton, NJ: Princeton University Press, 1966), chapter X.

25. Albert Wohlstetter, "Nuclear Sharing: NATO and the N+1 Country," *Foreign Affairs*, vol. 39, no. 3 (April 1961), pp. 355–87.

26. *Report from Iron Mountain: On the Possibility and Desirability of Peace*, p. ix.

27. Jon Elliston, "Highbrow Hoax Mocks National Security Speak," *Parascope*, 1996, http://www.parascope.com/articles/1296/iron.htm.

28. *Report from Iron Mountain*, p. xx (emphasis in original).

29. Ibid., p. 13.

30. Ibid., p. 29.

31. Ibid., p. 53.

32. Ibid., pp. 54–55.

33. Ibid., p. 59.

34. Ibid., pp. 100–101.

35. Author interview with Deborah Kahn, Chappaqua, New York, November 24, 2003.

36. Jerome Wiesner and Herbert York, "National Security and the Nuclear Test Ban," *Scientific American*, vol. 211, no. 10 (October 1964), pp. 27–35.

37. Robert S. McNamara, "The Dynamics of Nuclear Strategy," *Department of State Bulletin*, vol. 57, October 9, 1967.

38. See, for example, Benjamin M. Elson, "Scientists Differ on Use of ABM System," *Aviation Week & Space Technology*, January 8, 1968, p. 83.

39. McGeorge Bundy, "To Cap the Volcano," *Foreign Affairs*, vol. 48, no. 1 (October 1969), p. 10 (emphasis in original).

40. Statement by Donald G. Brennan before the Subcommittee on International Organization and Disarmament Affairs of the Committee on Foreign Relations, U.S. Senate, March 28, 1969, pp. 11–12.

41. Statement of Dr. Thomas Schelling, Professor of Economics, Harvard University, before the Subcommittee on National Security Policy and Scientific Developments of the Committee on Foreign Affairs, U.S. House of Representatives, March 18, 1969, pp. 5–6.

42. Statement of Albert Wohlstetter before the Senate Armed Services Committee, May 19, 1970, p. 24.

43. D. G. Brennan, "Ballistic Missile Defense," HI-1043-BN, Nuclear Defense Design Summer Institute, University of Wisconsin, July 10, 1968, p. 28; from the Hudson Institute Papers, National Defense University Special Collections, Fort McNair, Washington, DC.

44. Donald Brennan, "The Case for Population Defense," in Johan Holst and William Schneider, eds., *Why ABM?* (New York: Pergamon Press, 1969).

45. Schelling interview, December 1, 2003.

46. Lawrence Freedman, *The Evolution of Nuclear Strategy*, 3rd ed. (Basingstoke, UK: Palgrave Macmillan, 2003), p. 217.

47. See, for example, Gray, "What RAND Hath Wrought," pp. 118–22.

48. Diane Stone, *Capturing the Political Imagination: Think-tanks and the Policy Process* (London: Frank Cass & Co., 1996), p. 193.

49. Bruce Kuklick, *Blind Oracles: Intellectuals and War from Kennan to Kissinger* (Princeton, NJ: Princeton University Press, 2006), pp. 142–43.

50. Note to Herman Kahn from Philip Worchel, February 21, 1968; from the Hudson Institute Papers, National Defense University Special Collections, Fort McNair, Washington, DC.

51. Amrom H. Katz, "The War in Vietnam Becomes a Kahn Game," *Washington Post*, June 20, 1968, p. A23.

52. John M. Mecklin, "Attrition–Pressure–Ouch and Other Theories," *New York Times Book Review*, June 30, 1968, p. 3.

53. Letter to General Creighton Abrams from Herman Kahn, with enclosures, June 3, 1969; from the Hudson Institute Papers, National Defense University Special Collections, Fort McNair, Washington, DC.

54. Letter to Melvin R. Laird from Herman Kahn, with enclosures, June 2, 1968; from the Hudson Institute Papers, National Defense University Special Collections, Fort McNair, Washington, DC.

55. Ibid., Annex 3, pp. 2–3.

56. Draft Memorandum to Henry Kissinger from Herman Kahn re: "Vietnam," June 27, 1969; from the Hudson Institute Papers, National Defense University Special Collections, Fort McNair, Washington, DC.

57. Letter to Henry A. Kissinger from Herman Kahn, with enclosures, July 5, 1969; from the Hudson Institute Papers, National Defense University Special Collections, Fort McNair, Washington, DC.

58. Memorandum to General Earle G. Wheeler from Herman Kahn re: "Two Contexts for Vietnamization," July 23, 1969; Memo to H. Kissinger from H. Kahn re: "Suggestions," October 24, 1969; from the Hudson Institute Papers, National Defense University Special Collections, Fort McNair, Washington, DC.

59. Letter to Henry A. Kissinger from Herman Kahn, April 28, 1970; from the Hudson Institute Papers, National Defense University Special Collections, Fort McNair, Washington, DC.

60. Letter to Henry A. Kissinger from Herman Kahn, August 12, 1970, p. 3; from the Hudson Institute Papers, National Defense University Special Collections, Fort McNair, Washington, DC.

61. Katz, "The War in Vietnam Becomes a Kahn Game."

62. Author interview with Sir Lawrence Freedman, London, June 1, 2004. He alleviated this shortcoming in writing *Kennedy's Wars: Berlin, Cuba, Laos and Vietnam* (New York: Oxford University Press, 2000).

63. The argument from earlier writings and lectures is reconstituted in Thomas C. Schelling, *Arms and Influence* (New Haven, CT, and London: Yale University Press, 1966), pp. 141–51, 170–72.

64. Alexander L. George, *Some Thoughts on Graduated Escalation*, RM-4844-PR

(Santa Monica, CA: RAND Corporation, 1965). See also William E. Simons, "The Vietnam Intervention, 1964–65," in Alexander George and William E. Simons, eds., *The Limits of Coercive Diplomacy* (Boulder, CO: Westview Press, 1994).

65. Kuklick, *Blind Oracles*, pp. 145–50.
66. Daniel Ellsberg, *Secrets: A Memoir of Vietnam and the Pentagon Papers* (New York: Viking, 2002), p. 36.
67. Ibid., pp. 126–32.
68. Ibid., pp. 176–77, 181–82.
69. Ibid., p. 243.
70. Ibid., p. 232.
71. Robert Komer, *Impact of Pacification on Insurgency in South Vietnam*, RP-4443 (Santa Monica, CA: RAND Corporation, 1970).
72. Stephen T. Hosmer, *Viet Cong Repression and Its Implications for the Future* (Lexington, MA: Heath, 1970).
73. Ellsberg, *Secrets*, p. 228.
74. Henry Kissinger, *Nuclear Weapons and Foreign Policy* (New York: Harper & Row, 1957), p. 410.
75. Author interview with Sir Michael Howard, London, United Kingdom, February 26, 2004.
76. Donald G. Brennan, "Strategic Alternatives: I," *New York Times,* May 24, 1971, p. 31; and "Strategic Alternatives: II," *New York Times,* May 25, 1971, p. 39.
77. Albert Wohlstetter, "Is There a Strategic Arms Race?" *Foreign Policy,* no. 15 (Summer 1974), pp. 2–21; "Rivals But No 'Race,'" *Foreign Policy,* no. 16 (Autumn 1974), pp. 48–81; "Optimal Ways to Confuse Ourselves," *Foreign Policy,* no. 20 (Autumn 1975), pp. 170–98.
78. Fred Iklé, "Can Nuclear Deterrence Last Out the Century?" *Foreign Affairs,* vol. 51, no. 2 (January 1973), pp. 267–85.
79. Freedman, *The Evolution of Nuclear Strategy,* p. 339.
80. Ibid., p. 323.
81. Howard, "The Influence of Clausewitz" in Carl von Clausewitz, *On War,* ed. and trans. Michael Howard and Peter Paret (London: Everyman's Library, 1993), p. 49.

4 | Intellectual Dislocations of the Cold War

1. See, for example, Martin J. Collins, *Cold War Laboratory: RAND, the Air Force and the American State* (Washington, DC: Smithsonian Institution Press, 2002).
2. Author telephone interview with Frank Thomas, May 7, 2007.
3. Ibid.
4. Correspondence with Dennis M. Gormley, March 2007. Gormley was senior vice president of Pacific-Sierra Research Corporation and founded its Defense Policy Group.
5. Andrew Rich and R. Kent Weaver, "Advocates and Analysts: Think-tanks and the Politicization of Expertise," in Allan J. Cigler and Burdett A. Loomis, eds., *Interest Group Politics,* 5th ed. (Washington, DC: Congressional Quarterly Press, 1998), pp. 239–45.
6. Ibid., pp. 245–46.
7. James Allen Smith, *The Idea Brokers: Think-tanks and the Rise of the New Policy Elite* (New York: The Free Press, 1991), pp. 232–39.

8. Donald E. Abelson, "The Business of Ideas: The Think-tank Industry in the USA," in Diane Stone and Andrew Denham, eds., *Think-tank Traditions: Policy Research and the Politics of Ideas* (Manchester, UK: Manchester University Press, 2004), p. 220.

9. Author interview with Thomas C. Schelling, Bethesda, Maryland, March 9, 2004.

10. Richard Betts, "Should Strategic Studies Survive?" *World Politics,* vol. 50, no. 1 (October 1997), p. 16.

11. Donald E. Abelson, *Think-tanks and Their Role in US Foreign Policy* (New York: St Martin's Press, 1996), pp. 106.

12. Andrew Rich, *Think-tanks, Public Policy, and the Politics of Expertise* (Cambridge and New York: Cambridge University Press, 2004), p. 66.

13. Defense Threat Reduction Agency, *Defense's Nuclear Agency, 1947–1997* (Washington, DC: Department of Defense, 2002), pp. 223–24.

14. See, for example, David L. Schalk, *War and the Ivory Tower* (New York: Oxford University Press, 1991), pp. 112–26.

15. Richard Rorty, "Postmodernist Bourgeois Liberalism," reprinted in Richard Rorty, *Objectivity, Relativism, and Truth: Philosophical Papers, Volume 1* (Cambridge: Cambridge University Press, 1991), p. 201.

16. Jacques Derrida, "Force of Law: 'The Mystical Foundation of Authority,'" *Cardozo Law Review,* vol. 11, nos. 5–6 (1990), pp. 920–1045.

17. See, for example, Roberto M. Unger, *The Critical Legal Studies Movement* (Cambridge, MA: Harvard University Press, 1986).

18. Derrida, "Force of Law," p. 967.

19. Edward Said, *Orientalism: Western Conceptions of the Orient* (New York: Pantheon, 1979); and Edward Said, *Culture and Imperialism* (New York: Vintage, 1994).

20. See, for example, Fazal Rivzi and Bob Lingard, "Edward Said and the Cultural Politics of Education," *Discourse,* vol. 27, no. 3 (September 2006). For an acknowledgment of the influence of Said's thesis as well as a withering critique of that thesis, see Keith Windschuttle, "Edward Said's *Orientalism* Revisited," *The New Criterion,* vol. 17, no. 5 (January 1999), pp. 30–38.

21. Allan Bloom, *The Closing of the American Mind: How Higher Education Has Failed Democracy and Impoverished the Souls of Today's Students* (New York: Simon & Schuster, 1987). On how some dubious interpretations of Strauss have influenced neoconservatives who rose to positions of national power, see Anne Norton, *Leo Strauss and the Politics of American Empire* (New Haven, CT: Yale University Press, 2004).

22. Representative works for each side include, respectively, Martin Kramer, *Ivory Towers on Sand: The Failure of Middle Eastern Studies in America* (Washington, DC: Washington Institute for Near East Policy, 2001); and Joel Beinin, "The Israelization of American Middle East Policy Discourse," *Social Text,* vol. 21, no. 2 (Summer 2003), pp. 125–39. On the boycotting practice, see Stanley Kurtz, "Boycott Exposure," *National Review Online,* April 1, 2004. See generally Michael Dobbs, "Middle East Studies Under Scrutiny in U.S.," *Washington Post,* January 13, 2004, p. A1.

23. Kramer, *Ivory Towers on Sand,* pp. 91–98.

24. Louis Menand, *The Metaphysical Club: A Story of Ideas in America* (New York: Farrar, Straus and Giroux, 2001), p. 441.

25. Daniel Benjamin and Steven Simon, *The Age of Sacred Terror* (New York: Random House, 2002), pp. 160–61, 192–93.

26. Author interview with Henry S. Rowen, London, November 23, 2003.

27. Memorandum for [National Security Adviser] Zbigniew Brzezinski from [NSC staff member] Paul B. Henze re: The U.S. and the Islamic World, November 27, 1979; DNSA Item No. TE00612; declassified May 20, 1999.

28. Central Intelligence Agency, Directorate of Intelligence, *Terrorism Review,* February 2, 1984; DNSA Item No. TE00703; declassified.

29. Central Intelligence Agency, Directorate of Intelligence, *Terrorism Review,* March 1, 1984; DNSA Item No. TE00704; declassified.

30. Central Intelligence Agency, Directorate of Intelligence, "Iran: The Struggle to Define and Control Foreign Policy," Research Paper, May 1985; declassified August 29, 2002; CIA Freedom of Information Act (FOIA) Electronic Reading Room.

31. "Iranian Support for International Terrorism," Memorandum for the Director of Central Intelligence, November 22, 1986; declassified July 7, 1999; CIA FOIA Electronic Reading Room.

32. See Central Intelligence Agency, Directorate of Intelligence, "Soviet-Iranian Relations After Khomeini," June 23, 1989; CIA FOIA Electronic Reading Room; declassified July 30, 2001.

33. National Security Decision Directive No. 207, January 20, 1986; CIA FOIA Electronic Reading Room; declassified November 27, 1992.

34. Author interview with Michael Wheeler, McLean, Virginia, March 11, 2004.

35. These included those to the left and to the right. See, for example, Fred Halliday, *The Making of the Second Cold War* (London: Verso, 1983); Paul Johnson, *A History of the Modern World: From 1917 to the 1980s* (London: Weidenfeld & Nicolson, 1983).

36. Author interview with Sir Michael Howard, London, February 26, 2004.

37. E. P. Thompson and Dan Smith, eds., *Protest and Survive* (London: Penguin, 1980).

38. See, e.g., Frances FitzGerald, *Way Out There in the Blue: Reagan, Star Wars and the End of the Cold War* (New York: Simon & Schuster, 2000), pp. 88–89.

39. Ibid., p. 180.

40. Author interview with Freeman Dyson, Princeton, New Jersey, March 12, 2004.

41. Lawrence Freedman, *The Evolution of Nuclear Strategy,* 3rd ed. (Basingstoke, UK: Palgrave Macmillan, 2003), pp. 384.

42. Herman Kahn, *Thinking About the Unthinkable in the 1980s* (New York: Touchstone, 1985).

43. Freedman, *Evolution,* p. 395.

44. FitzGerald, *Way Out There in the Blue,* p. 264.

45. Dyson interview, March 12, 2004.

46. FitzGerald, *Way Out There in the Blue,* pp. 294–95.

47. Ibid., pp. 408–9.

48. Author interview with Thomas C. Schelling, Bethesda, Maryland, December 1, 2003.

49. Freedman interview, June 1, 2004.
50. FitzGerald, *Way Out There in the Blue,* p. 420.
51. National Intelligence Estimate No. 11-7-63, *The Clandestine Introduction of Weapons of Mass Destruction into the US,* Director of Central Intelligence, March 13, 1963; Digital National Security Archive (DNSA) Item No. TE00001; declassified April 4, 1994.
52. Author interview with George Quester, College Park, Maryland, March 8, 2004.
53. John McPhee, *The Curve of Binding Energy* (New York: Farrar, Straus and Giroux, 1980), p. 3.
54. Ibid., pp. 15, 155–56.
55. Ibid., pp. 123–24.
56. Ibid., p. 221.
57. Quoted in ibid., p. 52.
58. Quoted in ibid., p. 219.
59. Dyson interview, March 12, 2004.
60. McPhee, *The Curve of Binding Energy,* p. 202.
61. John Aristotle Phillips and David Michaelis, *Mushroom: The Story of the A-Bomb Kid* (New York: William Morrow, 1978).
62. Howard Morland, "The H-Bomb Secret: How We Got It, Why We're Telling It," *The Progressive,* vol. 43, no. 11 (November 1979), pp. 14–23.
63. Frank Bass and Randy Herschaft, "U.S. Foresaw Terror Threats in 1970s," Associated Press, January 23, 2005.
64. See, for example, Department of State Briefing Memorandum to The Secretary [of State] from Lewis Hoffacker [chairman, Cabinet Committee to Combat Terrorism] re: Major Problems in Combatting [sic] Terrorism, October 4, 1973; DNSA Item. No. TE00285; declassified January 29, 2002.
65. Letter from Robert H. Kupperman, Chief Scientist, U.S. Arms Control and Disarmament Agency, to John O. Marsh, Counsellor to the President, November 19, 1975; DNSA TE00462; declassified January 16, 1986.
66. Memorandum for Jack Marsh from Mike Duval re: Terrorism, November 28, 1975; DNSA Item No. TE00465.
67. Memorandum to Members of and Participants in the Working Group/Cabinet Committee to Combat Terrorism from Robert A. Fearey, Chairman of the Working Group/Cabinet Committee to Combat Terrorism, January 22, 1976 (with "attached draft terms of reference"); DNSA Item No. TE00488; declassified November 27, 2000.
68. Draft Action Memorandum to Secretary of State Henry A. Kissinger from Robert A. Fearey, Chairman of the Working Group/Cabinet Committee to Combat Terrorism, May 14, 1976; DNSA Item No. 00523; declassified August 18, 1994. Secretary Kissinger forwarded a finalized version of the memorandum to Members of the CCCT on June 5, 1976. Memorandum for Members of the Cabinet Committee to Combat Terrorism from Henry A. Kissinger, Chairman re: "Intermediate" Terrorism, June 5, 1976 (with enclosed Briefing Memorandum); DNSA Item No. TE00530; declassified August 18, 1994.
69. Memorandum for Dick Cheney from Mike Duval re: Terrorism, June 21, 1976; DNSA Item No. TE00536.
70. Draft National Security Decision Memorandum, November 23, 1976; DNSA Item No. TE00566; declassified August 21, 1996.

71. Letter from Leo Cherne, Chairman, President's Foreign Intelligence Advisory Board, to Robert Kupperman, Chief Scientist, U.S. Arms Control and Disarmament Agency, July 19, 1976; DNSA Item No. TE00545.

72. Thomas C. Schelling, "Who Will Have The Bomb?" *International Security*, vol. 1, no. 1 (Summer 1976), pp. 77–91.

73. Brian Jenkins, *Will Terrorists Go Nuclear?* RAND Document P-5541 (Santa Monica, CA: RAND Corporation, 1975).

74. Brian Michael Jenkins, *Terrorism and the Nuclear Safeguards Issue*, RAND Document P-5611 (Santa Monica, CA: RAND Corporation, 1976).

75. Brian Michael Jenkins, "The Future Course of International Terrorism," *The Futurist*, July–August 1987.

76. Ibid.

77. Brian Michael Jenkins, *The Impact of Nuclear Terrorism*, September 1978; DNSA Item No. TE00593.

78. Brian Michael Jenkins, "Terrorism in the 1980s," address to the 26th Annual Seminar of the American Society for Industrial Security, Miami Beach Florida, September 25, 1980.

79. Jenkins, "The Future Course of International Terrorism."

80. "Growing Terrorist Danger for Americans," Central Intelligence Agency, National Foreign Assessment Center, December 23, 1981; DNSA Item No. TE00679; declassified August 22, 2000.

81. Andreas Killen, "The First Hijackers," *New York Times Magazine*, January 16, 2005, pp. 22, 24.

82. Thomas C. Schelling, "Thinking About Nuclear Terrorism," *International Security*, vol. 6, no. 4 (Spring 1982), p. 67.

83. Ibid., p. 71.

84. Ibid., p. 73.

85. Ibid., pp. 75–76.

86. Freedman, *Evolution*, pp. 462–63.

87. Author interview with Sir Lawrence Freedman, London, June 1, 2004.

88. "Marshal Ogarkov Analysis of the 'Zapad' Exercise, May 30–June 9, 1977," National Security Archive, George Washington University, Electronic Briefing Book for Vojtech Mastny and Malcolm Byrne, eds., *A Cardboard Castle: A History of the Warsaw Pact, 1955–1991* (New York: Central European University Press, 2005), Document No. 81.

89. Defense Threat Reduction Agency, *Defense's Nuclear Agency, 1947–1997* (Washington, DC: Department of Defense, 2002), p. 259.

90. See, for example, William E. Odom, *The Collapse of the Soviet Military* (New Haven, CT: Yale University Press, 1998), pp. 70, 151–53.

91. Freedman interview, June 1, 2004.

92. Schelling interview, December 1, 2003.

93. Ibid.

94. Max Boot, *The Savage Wars of Peace: Small Wars and the Rise of American Power* (New York: Basic Books, 2002), p. 319.

95. Barry O'Neill, *Honor, Symbols, and War* (Ann Arbor, MI: University of Michigan Press, 2001), p. 215.

96. Ibid., pp. 216–17.

97. U.S. Army Test & Evaluation Command, *Psychological Impact of Mass Casualty*

Weapons (CB) With Respect to Target Vulnerability, July 1980, Chemical and Biological Warfare Collection, box 10, Threat Assessments, The National Security Archive, Washington, D.C., no. 54995, p. III–51.

98. For example, Strategic Studies Institute, U.S. Army War College, NATO CW Policy, CAN 80013, Final Report, August 3, 1981, Chemical and Biological Warfare Collection, box 10, Threat Assessments, The National Security Archive, Washington, D.C., no. 56980.

99. See Don T. Parker, Ronald D. Stricklett, William H. Rose, and Bruce S. Grim, U.S. Army Test & Evaluation Command, Studies Branch, *Biological Vulnerability Assessment: The Middle East,* February 1978, Chemical and Biological Warfare Collection, box 10, Threat Assessments, The National Security Archive, Washington, D.C., no. 59184.

100. See, for example, Ronald D. Stricklett, U.S. Army Test & Evaluation Command, Studies Branch, *Target Vulnerability Analysis: NATO Central Front,* September 1981, Chemical and Biological Warfare Collection, box 10, Threat Assessments, The National Security Archive, Washington, D.C., no. 56969.

101. U.S. Army Test & Evaluation Command, Studies Branch, *CB Vulnerability of Selected Naval Vessels,* September 1981, Chemical and Biological Warfare Collection, box 10a, Threat Assessments, The National Security Archive, Washington, D.C., no. 59187.

102. Ronald D. Stricklett, U.S. Army Test & Evaluation Command, Studies Branch, *Current Factors Affecting the Possible Use of Biological Weapons by Terrorists,* April 1986, Chemical and Biological Warfare Collection, box 10a, Threat Assessments, The National Security Archive, Washington, D.C., no. 59194, p. 2.

103. Ibid., p. 3.

104. Ibid., p. 6.

105. U.S. General Accounting Office, Report to the Chairman, Subcommittee on Environment, Energy and Natural Resources, Committee on Government Operations, House of representatives, *Hazardous Materials: DOD Should Eliminate DS2 From Its Inventory of Decontaminants,* GAO/NSIAD-90-10, April 1990, pp. 3–4, 21–22.

5 | The Halting Leap Forward

1. Lawrence Freedman, *The Evolution of Nuclear Strategy,* 3rd ed. (Basingstoke, UK: Palgrave Macmillan, 2003), p. 424.

2. Ibid., p. 418.

3. Jeffrey D. Simon, *Terrorists and the Potential Use of Biological Weapons: A Discussion of Possibilities,* RAND Document R-3771-AFMIC (Santa Monica, CA: RAND Corporation, 1989), p. 3.

4. Ibid., pp. 7, 11.

5. Defense Intelligence Agency, "Lebanese Shia in West Africa: Potential Support for Terrorism," *Defense Intelligence Brief,* January 1990; DNSA Item No. TE01003.

6. Simon, *Terrorists and the Potential Use of Biological Weapons,* p. 17.

7. Ibid., p. vii.

8. Barry Wolf, "When the Weak Attack the Strong: Failures of Deterrence," RAND Note N-3261-A (Santa Monica, CA: RAND Corporation, 1991), p. iii.

9. Ibid., pp. 7–8.

10. Ibid., pp. 13–14.

11. Ibid., p. 2.
12. Ibid., p. 17.
13. National Commission on Terrorist Attacks, *The 9/11 Commission Report: Final Report on Terrorist Attacks Upon the United States* (New York: W.W. Norton, 2004), p. 252.
14. Ibid.
15. Richard Garwin and George Charpak, *Megawatts and Megatons: A Turning Point in the Nuclear Age?* (New York: Alfred A. Knopf, 2001), pp. 322–23, 350.
16. Ibid., pp. 325–27.
17. Ibid., pp. 337–43.
18. John F. Sopko, "The Changing Proliferation Threat," *Foreign Policy,* no. 105 (Winter 1996–97), pp. 16–17.
19. David Remnick, *Lenin's Tomb: The Last Days of the Soviet Empire* (New York: Vintage, 1994), p. 482.
20. Ibid., p. 496.
21. Osama bin Laden, interview with Peter Arnett, Afghanistan, CNN, March 1993; quoted in Benjamin and Simon, *The Age of Sacred Terror,* p. 106.
22. Benjamin and Simon, *The Age of Sacred Terror,* pp. 102–9.
23. Sopko, "The Changing Proliferation Threat," p. 4. In a similar vein, see Walter Laqueur, "Postmodern Terrorism," *Foreign Affairs,* vol. 75, no. 5 (September/October 1996), pp. 24–36.
24. Sopko, "The Changing Proliferation Threat," p. 11.
25. Ibid., p. 15.
26. Ibid., p. 12.
27. Ibid., p. 19.
28. Author interview with George Quester, College Park, Maryland, March 8, 2004.
29. See generally John L. Hirsch and Robert B. Oakley, *Somalia and Operation Restore Hope: Reflections on Peacemaking and Peacekeeping* (Washington, DC: United States Institute of Peace, 1995).
30. See, for example, Federal Emergency Management Agency, "Consequence Management for Nuclear, Biological, and Chemical (NBC) Terrorism—The Federal Response Plan: A Status Report to the President," January 19, 1996; DNSA Item No. TE01111.
31. General Accounting Office, Testimony Before the Committee on Commerce, Science and Transportation, U.S. Senate, Statement of Keith O. Fultz, Assistant Comptroller General, Resources, Community and Economic Development Division, "Aviation Security: Immediate Action Needed to Improve Security," August 1, 1996, p. 2; DNSA Item No. TE01126.
32. Central Intelligence Agency, Biographical Sketch—"Usama bin Ladin: Extremist Financier," 1996; DNSA Item No. TE01108.
33. U.S. Department of Justice, Federal Bureau of Investigation, Counterterrorism Threat Assessment and Warning Unit, National Security Division, "Terrorism in the United States, 1998," pp. 2, 16.
34. Daniel Benjamin and Steven Simon, *The Age of Sacred Terror* (New York: Random House, 2002), pp. 219–55.
35. FBI Memorandum to Oklahoma City [Field Office] from Special Agent [name redacted] re: Weapons of Mass Destruction, May 19, 1998; CIA FOIA Electronic Reading Room.

36. General Accounting Office, Testimony Before the Subcommittee on Aviation, Committee on Transportation and Infrastructure, House of Representatives, Statement of Keith O. Fultz, Assistant Comptroller General, Resources, Community and Economic Development Division, "Aviation Security: Progress Being Made, but Long-Term Attention Is Needed," May 14, 1998; DNSA Item No. TE01172.

37. See, for example, Ehud Sprinzak, "The Great Superterrorism Scare," *Foreign Policy*, no. 112 (Fall 1998), pp. 116–22.

38. Ibid., pp. 122–23.

39. Robert E. Osgood, *Limited War: The Challenge to American Strategy* (Chicago: University of Chicago Press, 1965), pp. 1–2.

40. See, for example, Federal Bureau of Investigation, "Project Megiddo," November 1999; DNSA Item No. TE01220.

41. Benjamin and Simon, *The Age of Sacred Terror,* pp. 311–15.

42. Steven Simon and Daniel Benjamin, "America and the New Terrorism," *Survival,* vol. 42, no. 1 (Spring 2000), pp. 62–66.

43. Ibid., pp. 66–69.

44. Ibid., p. 73.

45. See, for example, Paul R. Pillar, *Terrorism and U.S. Foreign Policy* (Washington, DC.: Brookings Institution Press, 2001), pp. 41–72.

46. Olivier Roy, Bruce Hoffman, Reuven Paz, Steven Simon, and Daniel Benjamin, "America and the New Terrorism: An Exchange," *Survival,* vol. 42, no. 2 (Summer 2000), p. 163.

47. Ibid., p. 171.

48. Roberta Wohlstetter, "Terror on a Grand Scale," *Survival,* vol. 18, no. 3 (May/June 1976), p. 101.

49. Brian Michael Jenkins, "Redefining the Enemy: The World Has Changed, but Our Mind-set Has Not," *RAND Review,* vol. 28, no. 1 (Spring 2004), p. 20.

50. Author interview with John McPhee, Princeton, New Jersey, November 29, 2004.

51. Author interview with Thomas C. Schelling, Bethesda, Maryland, December 1, 2003.

52. Ibid.

53. Quester interview, March 8, 2004.

54. Ibid.

55. RAND analysts have made this point. See Paul K. Davis and Brian Michael Jenkins, *Deterrence and Influence in Counterterrorism: A Component in the War on al Qaeda* (Santa Monica, CA: RAND Corporation, 2002); *Symposium: Diagnosing Al Qaeda,* August 18, 2003,www.rand.org/news/newslinks/fp.html; and Paul K. Davis and Brian Michael Jenkins, "The Influence Component of Counterterrorism," *RAND Review,* vol. 27, no. 1 (Spring 2003), pp. 12–15. See also Robert F. Trager and Dessie P. Zagorcheva, "Deterring Terrorism: It Can Be Done," *International Security,* vol. 30, no. 3 (Winter 2005–6), pp. 87–123.

56. Mia Bloom, *Dying to Kill: The Allure of Suicide Terror* (New York: Columbia University Press, 2005), p. 63; Robert A. Pape, *Dying to Win: The Strategic Logic of Suicide Terrorism* (New York: Random House, 2005), p. 93.

57. Lawrence Freedman, *Deterrence* (Cambridge: Polity Press, 2004), p. 128.

58. Ibid., p. 124.

59. Ibid., p. 119.
60. For a particularly penetrating examination of this proposition, see Dana H. Allin, *Cold War Illusions: America, Europe and Soviet Power 1969–1989* (New York: St. Martin's Press, 1997).

6 | Selective Nostalgia

1. Michael Howard, "Brodie, Wohlstetter and American Nuclear Strategy," *Survival*, vol. 34, no. 2 (Summer 1992), p. 107.
2. Barry O'Neill, *Honor, Symbols, and War* (Ann Arbor, MI: University of Michigan Press, 2001), p. 223. See also Herman Kahn, *Thinking About the Unthinkable* (New York: Avon Books, 1962), pp. 47–48.
3. For an argument suggesting the contrary, see Anonymous, *Imperial Hubris: Why the West Is Losing the War on Terror* (Washington, DC.: Potomac Books, 2004). Shortly after the book's publication, the author was revealed to be former CIA analyst Michael Scheuer.
4. Richard Betts, "Should Strategic Studies Survive?" *World Politics*, vol. 50, no. 1 (October 1997), p. 8.
5. Ibid., p. 9.
6. Michael Mandelbaum, "Foreign Policy as Social Work," *Foreign Affairs*, vol. 75, no. 1 (January–February 1996), pp. 16–32.
7. Richard A. Clarke, *Against All Enemies: Inside America's War on Terror* (New York: The Free Press, 2004), pp. 227–38.
8. Stefan Halper, "Big Ideas, Big Problems," *The National Interest*, no. 88 (March–April 2007), pp. 92–96.
9. See, for example, Francis Fukuyama, *The End of History and the Last Man* (New York: The Free Press, 1992).
10. See, for example, Albert Wohlstetter, "'Lesser' Excluded Cases," *New York Times*, February 14, 1979, p. A25. See also Albert Wohlstetter, "Foreword" to K. Scott McMahon and Dennis M. Gormley, *Controlling the Spread of Land-Attack Cruise Missiles* (Marina del Ray, CA: American Institute for Strategic Cooperation, 1995), p. v.
11. Jennifer M. Taw and Alan Vick, "From Sideshow to Center Stage: The Role of the Army and Air Force in Military Operations Other Than War," in Zalmay M. Khalilzad and David A. Ochmanek, eds., *Strategic Appraisal 1997: Strategy and Defense Planning for the 21st Century*, RAND/MR-826-AF (Santa Monica, CA: RAND Corporation, 1997).
12. See, for example, Anatol Lieven, "The Two Fukuyamas," *The National Interest*, no. 84 (Summer 2006), pp. 123–30.
13. See, for example, John J. Mearsheimer and Stephen M. Walt, "The Israel Lobby," *London Review of Books*, vol. 28, no. 6, March 23, 2006, pp. 3–12; Patrick Seale, "A Costly Friendship," *The Nation*, July 21, 2003.
14. Nicholas Lemann, "The Next World Order," *The New Yorker*, April 1, 2002, pp. 42–48.
15. See, for example, Robert F. Ellsworth, "From Awakening to War," *The National Interest*, no. 84 (Summer 2006), pp. 138–44; Danielle Pletka, "Arabs on the Verge of Democracy," *New York Times*, August 9, 2004, p. A15; Amir Taheri, "What Do Muslims Think?" *The American Interest*, vol. 2, no. 5 (May–June 2007), pp. 6–18.

16. See Oliver Roy, *Secularism Confronts Islam* (New York: Columbia University Press, 2007). See also John Gray, " Faith in Reason: Secular Fantasies of a Godless Age," *Harper's,* January 2008, pp. 85–89.

17. Reinhold Niebuhr, *The Irony of American History* (New York: Scribner, 1985), chapter 5. For more on Niebuhr's complex relevance to contemporary affairs, see Paul Elie, "A Man for All Reasons," *The Atlantic,* vol. 300, no. 4 (November 2007), pp. 83–96.

18. Louis Menand, *The Metaphysical Club: A Story of Ideas in America* (New York: Farrar, Straus and Giroux, 2001), p. 440.

19. Cornel West, *The American Evasion of Philosophy* (Madison, WI: University of Wisconsin Press, 1989), p. 213.

20. Menand, *The Metaphysical Club,* p. 441.

21. C. S. Peirce, "The Scientific Attitude and Fallibilism" (1896) in Justus Buchler, ed., *The Philosophical Writings of C. S. Peirce* (New York: Dover, 1955), pp. 42–59.

22. Richard Bernstein, "Pragmatism, Pluralism, and the Healing of Wounds" (1988), reprinted in Louis Menand, ed., *Pragmatism: A Reader* (New York: Vintage Books, 1997), p. 387.

23. See, for example, Lincoln A. Mitchell, "Beyond Bombs and Ballots: Dispelling Myths About Democracy Assistance," *The National Interest,* no. 88 (March–April 2007), pp. 32–36; Paul J. Saunders, "Learning to Appreciate France," *The National Interest,* no. 88 (March–April 2007), pp. 4–8.

24. John Dewey, *The Ethics of Democracy* (1988), reprinted in Louis Menand, ed., *Pragmatism: A Reader* (New York: Vintage Books, 1997), p. 190.

25. Diane Stone, *Capturing the Political Imagination: Think-tanks and the Policy Process* (London: Frank Cass & Co., 1996), p. 213.

26. Bruce Kuklick, *Blind Oracles: Intellectuals and War from Kennan to Kissinger* (Princeton, NJ: Princeton University Press, 2006), p. 9.

27. Most of the themes developed in the remainder of this chapter were initially raised in Steven Simon and Jonathan Stevenson, "Thinking Outside the Tank," *The National Interest,* no. 78 (Winter 2004–5), pp. 90–98.

28. Robert B. Townsend, "History Majors and Enrollments Rose Sharply Between 1998 and 2001," *Perspectives* (February 2003), http://www.historians.org/Perspectives/issues/2003/0302/0302new2.cfm.

29. Martin Kramer, *Ivory Towers on Sand: The Failure of Middle Eastern Studies in America* (Washington, DC: Washington Institute for Near East Policy, 2001), pp. 84–99, 121–29.

30. For two examples of this attitude, see Joel Beinin, "Thought Control for Middle East Studies," CommonDreams.org, March 31, 2004; and Steven Heydermann, "Warping Middle East Judgments," *Chicago Tribune,* March 14, 2004.

31. Daniel Pipes, "Defund Middle East Studies," *New York Sun,* February 24, 2004, p. 7.

32. See, for example, Miriam Cooke, "Contesting Campus Watch: Middle East Studies Under Fire, the Academy and Democracy at Risk," *Journal of Al Azhar University-Gaza,* vol. 7, no. 1 (2004) pp. 21–40.

33. Daniel Pipes and Jonathan Calt Harris, "Columbia vs. America," *New York Post,* April 1, 2003, http://www.campus-watch.org/article/id/619; Laurie King-Irani, "We Aren't the World," *In These Times,* December 11, 2003, p. 12.

34. Shane Harris, "The Spy Gap," *Government Executive,* May 1, 2007, pp. 28–36.

35. Dewey, *The Ethics of Democracy,* p. 194.

36. Ibid., p. 201.

37. John Dewey, *The Public and Its Problems* (New York: Henry Holt, 1927), pp. 116–17, 123–25, 196–97, 202–9; and Kuklick, *Blind Oracles,* p. 9.

38. Robert H. Kupperman, *Facing Tomorrow's Terrorist Incident Today,* U.S. Department of Justice, Law Enforcement Assistance Administration, Washington, DC, October 1977, p. 24.

39. Kahn, *Thinking About the Unthinkable,* p. 35. See also Harvey Sicherman, "Cheap Hawks, Cheap Doves, and the Pursuit of Strategy," *Orbis,* vol. 49, no. 4 (Fall 2005), pp. 613–29.

40. Graham Allison and Philip Zelikow, *Essence of Decision: Explaining the Cuban Missile Crisis,* 2nd ed. (New York: Longman, 1999).

41. Paul K. Davis and Brian Michael Jenkins, *Deterrence and Influence in Counterterrorism: A Component in the War on al Qaeda* (Santa Monica, CA: RAND Corporation, 2002).

42. Kim Cragin and Sara A. Daly, *The Dynamic Terrorist Threat: An Assessment of Group Motivations and Capabilities in a Changing World* (Santa Monica, CA: RAND Corporation, 2004).

43. Sara Daly, John Parachini, and William Rosenau, *Aum Shinrikyo, Al Qaeda, and the Kinshasa Reactor,* RAND Documented Briefing (Santa Monica, CA: RAND Corporation, 2005). See also Robin Frost, *Nuclear Terrorism After 9/11,* Adelphi Paper 378 (Abingdon, UK: Routledge for the IISS, 2005).

44. Among those who have vigorously taken opposing positions on the WMD issue are Graham Allison, *Nuclear Terrorism: The Ultimate Preventable Catastrophe* (New York: Times Books, 2004); and Anna M. Pluta and Peter D. Zimmerman, "Nuclear Terrorism: A Disheartening Dissent," *Survival,* vol. 48, no. 2 (Summer 2006), pp. 55–70.

45. See, for example, Ariana Eunjung Cha, "In Iraq, the Job Opportunity of a Lifetime," *Washington Post,* May 23, 2004, p. A1; Ken Silverstein, "Undoing Bush: (3) Civil Service," *Harper's,* June 2007, pp. 47–48.

46. Charles Wolf Jr. et al., *The Costs of the Soviet Empire* (Santa Monica, CA: RAND Corporation, 1984).

47. Kahn, *Thinking About the Unthinkable,* p. 36.

48. James Digby and Joan Goldhamer, "The Development of Strategic Thinking at RAND, 1948–63: A Mathematical Logician's View—An Interview with Albert Wohlstetter," July 5, 1985, pp. 47–50 [transcript copyrighted by the RAND Corporation, 1997].

49. Barnaby J. Feder, "New Economy: A Military Agency Spends Billions on Seemingly Fantastic Projects to Ensure U.S. Battlefield Supremacy," *New York Times,* September 18, 2000, p. C4.

50. Christopher Marquis, "The Right and Wrong Stuff of Thinking Outside a Box," *New York Times,* July 31, 2003, p. A17.

51. Author interview with Sir Lawrence Freedman, London, June 1, 2004.

52. Bruce Kuklick, *Blind Oracles: Intellectuals and War from Kennan to Kissinger* (Princeton, NJ: Princeton University Press, 2006), pp. 171–480.

53. Richard Betts and Leslie Gelb, *The Irony of Vietnam: The System Worked* (Washington, DC: Brookings Institution Press, 1979).

54. Kuklick, *Blind Oracles,* pp. 150–51.

55. Paul Bracken, "Net Assessment: A Practical Guide," *Parameters,* vol. 36, no. 1 (Spring 2006), pp. 93–96.
56. Ibid., p. 100.
57. Steven Simon, "The New Terrorism: Securing the Nation Against a Messianic Foe," *The Brookings Review,* vol. 21, no. 1 (Winter 2003), pp. 18–20.
58. Freedman interview, June 1, 2004.
59. Ibid.

Index

location of, 250–51
as model for terrorism studies,
248–51, 265
Vietnam War and, 123–25, 130–31,
133–35, 147–49, 151–52, 241
"RAND letter," 148
rational-choice theory, 255
rationalism, 235, 236
Reagan, Ronald, 23, 157*n*, 161, 169
"Evil Empire" characterization of
Soviet Union by, 165, 167
nuclear abolitionism of, 165–68,
170–71, 172
Star Wars vision of, 121
Reagan administration, 152, 164, 167,
190
realism, 51*n*
Rebel Without A Cause (film), 65*n*
"Report from Iron Mountain,"
113–16, 117, 245
Republicans, 22, 150, 250
Research and Development Associ-
ates (RDA), 148
Ressam, Ahmed, 214–15
Reykjavik summit of 1986, 169
Richardson, Elliott, 128
Rockefeller Foundation, 150
Rolling Thunder bombing campaign,
130
Romm, Joseph, 85
Roosevelt, Eleanor, 94
Rorty, Richard, 154
Rosenfeld, Carl E., 83
Ross, Dennis, 246
Rostow, Walt W., 103, 104
Rowen, Harry, 19, 30, 78, 84, 105,
133, 147–48, 159, 251
Roy, Olivier, 251*n*–252*n*
Rumsfeld, Donald, 229–30
Russell, Richard, 100*n*
Russia, 172, 194, 226, 233
CTR and, 202–3

Safeguard ABM system, 120, 168–69
Sagan, Carl, 165

Said, Edward, 156
Salisbury, Harrison, 95–96
SALT (Strategic Arms Limitations
Talks) I, 137–40
SALT II, 166
Saudi Arabia, 159, 161, 179, 189, 211,
231, 263
U.S. troops in, 207–8
Schapiro, Meyer, 41
Schell, Jonathan, 164–65
Schelling, Thomas C., 10, 26, 27*n*,
34–35, 37, 54, 57, 60, 62–75,
81–82, 87, 89*n*, 90, 91, 102–3,
104, 105, 106*n*, 110, 122, 130,
131, 138, 151, 169, 181, 186,
196–97, 218–19, 239*n*, 240, 247*n*,
248, 256
analytic method of, 63–64
background of, 62–63
counterforce strategy of, 69–70
game theory and, 63–64, 66, 67–69
minimal solution and, 65, 221
on nuclear weapons as terrorism,
184–86
pragmatism of, 235–36
saving face issue and, 73–74
Schlesinger, Arthur, Jr., 104
Schlesinger, James, 176–77
Scientific American, 88, 91, 125
Scowcroft Commission, 166
self-deterrence, 18–19, 58
Sellers, Peter, 89
Senate, U.S., 122, 202, 242–43
Foreign Relations Committee of,
121
Sentinel system, 119–20, 122, 168–69
September 11, 2001, terrorist attacks,
1, 152, 175, 182, 183, 184, 202,
218, 219, 227–29, 231, 236, 241,
244, 257
al-Qaeda and, 200–201
Serber, Robert, 177
Shah of Iran (Mohammad Reza
Pahlavi), 158
Sharp, Samuel, 246
Shiites, 159–60, 198